THE KILLING OF ISHI

The Death of the Last American Stone-Age Warrior
and the Accidental Discovery of his Family Members
still in Hiding.

By James J. Callahan, Jr.

A FICTION NOVEL BASED UPON HISTORICAL FACTS

DEDICATION

To my loving wife, Suzanne,
Who gifted us with four fine Irishmen:
Casey, Christopher, Sean, and Patrick.
Thank you all for your hard work and support.

CENTRAL OREGON WOLF RECOVERY TASK FORCE OREGON DEPARTMENT OF FISH AND WILDLIFE HEADQUARTERS BEND, OREGON

EMERGENCY MEETING

Buster Higgins sat eyeing the last donut. He already had two, but he was still hungry. No breakfast, again. It was yet another early morning meeting.

Unfortunately for Buster, Mason Many Crows, a Warm Springs Indian, wanted the same donut. Buster hesitantly reached toward the plate; but Mason silently shook his head, "No." As Mason weighed nearly three-hundred pounds, all of it toned muscle on a very large frame; Buster sighed, rolled his eyes, and reluctantly pushed the donut over to Mason.

"Good call, little buddy," Mason whispered, wrapping a meaty hand around the last pastry. "Saved you from a major ass-whooping."

"But not a . . .?" asked Buster.

"Nope," said Mason. "Hate to tell you this, my friend, but you could have walked all across Indian country, way back when, completely unscathed." "How so?" asked Buster, sensing that Mason was setting him up, again.

"Embarrassment," said Mason, smiling while shrugging his massive shoulders. "You go out on a raid to fight the Englishman and come back with just a little scalp fringe for your war shirt; you would be laughed right out of the tribe."

Buster quipped, "You know that my hair loss has been a source of profound disappointment to me."

"Tough darts," said Mason, waving his long braids in Buster's direction, "should have been born an Indian, for we have beautiful hair."

Buster mentioned, again, that he was an Irishman, not an Englishman.

"Doesn't matter," said Mason. "All invading whites are Englishmen to the First Peoples. I'm pretty sure we have discussed this before."

Buster was a big game biologist for the Oregon Department of Fish and Wildlife. Mason was a tribal police officer and tracker for the Confederated Tribes of the Warm Springs Indian Reservation. Their bond of friendship went back some twenty-five years to playing football at Madras High School. Mason would mow down the opposition; Buster would run the touchdown. It was teamwork at its very best.

The Central Oregon Wolf Recovery Task Force was called to order by the acting chairman, Senior Trooper Ryan McKenna of the Oregon State Police. Tall, rangy, wearing camo fatigues, McKenna was in his eighth year with the OSP Fish and Wildlife Division. By Oregon law all game warden positions were filled by experienced troopers from the ranks of the State Police. Competition to be a warden was fierce. It was a highly coveted job, given only to the best of the best.

Ryan once told his wife, "I can't believe the State actually pays me to spend all my time out in the woods. Beautiful forests, huge trees, clean rivers. Some days I feel I should be paying them."

"Good," said Suzanne, "I'll remind you of that next time the phone rings at two in the morning about a missing elk hunter."

Warden Ryan deeply missed his wife. She had been taken from him nearly one year earlier. She made Ryan promise that he and their son, Chance, would always celebrate Christmas by decorating with her favorite tree, the Ponderosa Pine.

"I love the Ponderosas," she said. "They are the best because they smell so nice, plus you can see all our beautiful decorations. And," she added, smiling sweetly, "I'll come back to haunt you if you use anything different."

"Promise?" Ryan softly asked.

"Yes," said Suzanne, laughing. "But remember, I'll be a ghost, and there's no way you can grab a ghost. So whatever thoughts you're having, make them be gone."

Several weeks later Suzanne was gone. Near the end of her illness, Suzanne told Ryan, "I've been thinking about this dying stuff. I've come to accept it, but it's not all that great. It's like wading through a pile of cow slurry. It's just something we all have to do but, to be honest," she said, "I would much rather be taking Bailey on a morning run through the forest." She paused, "I know there are horses in heaven; and I know they are all good, but I just hope I can get one as good as Bailey."

Bailey was a mustang rescue from the Burns Wild Horse Center. A large, good-natured paint gelding, he was Suzanne's favorite horse.

"He always has such a big smile on his face, and he's so willing. I think that's what I like the best about him," said Suzanne.

Suzanne paused and then added, "Forget the slurry stuff. That's not exactly what I mean. I feel now that dying is not the end but more likely a new beginning. The one thing this sickness has convinced me of is the importance of a belief in new beginnings and especially the importance of being able to face fear. Someone once told me, 'Face your fear; watch it disappear'. That, a dose of courage and some dark chocolate can get you through most anything."

A small tear rolled down one cheek as Suzanne, genuinely smiling, turned to Ryan and said, "You've stood by me through this whole illness, and I so appreciate that. You know, you are the one that has given me the courage to fight. Without your support, I probably would have just tossed in the towel."

Ryan started to object. One of the many gifts about Suzanne—she absolutely was not a quitter.

Holding up a palm to Ryan, Suzanne added, "You say I have courage, but it is you who have given me that courage. I've noticed down through the years that your courage is not just the absence of fear; it is taking action in spite of the fear. How is that for being profound? Courage is what makes you not only a great game warden but also a great husband."

Kissing him lightly, Suzanne walked to the family room and yelled, "And father. You're a great father and that's the most important thing of all!"

Thanksgiving had just passed, and both Ryan and Chance were planning on carrying out the family tradition. This would be their first Christmas without Suzanne. Warden Ryan felt that a thermos of hot chocolate and some thick Panini sandwiches would be the first step in search of the perfect tree. Keeping with family tradition, they would go up to Paulina Mountain, part of the vast Ochoco wilderness. Probably in two weeks—weather permitting. Suzanne's favorite Ponderosas were near the summit, and Ryan felt a father and son snowmobile trip would help boost their spirits. Plus, in light of recent developments, it was absolutely essential that Ryan spend more time up on Paulina, even on his days off. One thing about being a game warden, it seemed you were always on duty.

The Governor had phoned Ryan just the day before telling him that, somehow, contact would have to be made. As Ryan had never talked to the Governor before, the call made a huge impact, especially after the Governor expressed his condolences about the loss of Suzanne. It was that personal touch, that sincere connection to the people that helped sweep the Governor into office.

"ODFW couriered the tape to my office stamped, 'Eyes Only.'" I watched the tape, then gathered a few advisors and watched the tape again. At this point, senior staff and I are convinced the tape is real and not something staged for any type of political mischief. It has a tone of authenticity to it that is quite convincing. So now the question is, what do we do?"

Answering his own question, the Governor continued, "We have to get this resolved somehow. Whether we screw up or not, the national media and probably even the international media will be all over this once the news breaks. I think the people of Oregon would want us to be pro-active and not, metaphorically speaking, running after the bus once it has left the terminal."

Pausing for a moment, the Governor added, "We have a lot at stake here. For starters, our Economic Development Department has spent a lot of taxpayer money recruiting businesses to Central Oregon, like the Oregon Project. We now have a potential of fifteen hundred family wage jobs at risk. We don't want this thing going south on us, so this is what I want the task force to consider."

The Governor spent the next few minutes detailing his plan while Ryan took copious notes. Before hanging up, the Governor gave Ryan his personal cell number, joking with him about not posting it on Facebook but telling him to call as soon as he had some news.

The core part of the Governor's plan was to have Ryan spending as much time as possible patrolling the Ochocos, looking for a way to make contact. That sat well with Ryan, fully intending to carry out the assignment to the best of his abilities. Little did he know. . . .

PLACES TO HIDE

Paulina Lake and Paulina Mountain are part of the western Ochoco Mountain Range, named after the Northern Paiute war chief, Paulina. Millions of acres of pristine Ponderosa forest include and surround the Ochocos. It is one of the most beautiful, yet remote wilderness areas left in the continental United States, with waves of different mountain ranges stretching from Central Oregon to the Idaho border. Paulina Lake sits eighteen miles in from the nearest main road and is surrounded by jagged snow covered peaks and old growth forests for the next three hundred miles east to Idaho.

Small beads of meadowland are dotted throughout the forest, providing abundant browse for vast herds of deer and elk.

Scanning the meeting agenda, Warden Ryan asked Buster Higgins to first give an overview of the State's successful wolf re-introduction program to Central Oregon, specifically, the Ochocos. Then following Buster would be Mason Many Crows for the Native American analysis of what ODFW accidentally picked up on their camera traps.

Though a press release would be sent to all media outlets after the meeting, the only item mentioned would be the wolves.

Buster walked to the podium, carefully sipping his steaming coffee. A small, high energy man with tremendous stamina, very little hair and, surprisingly, great strength, Buster began multitasking. Holding his coffee in one hand, he quickly spread out his paperwork before him and in the process, managed to spill the coffee on top of his papers—to the immense delight of Mason Many Crows.

Mason stage-whispered to Special Agent Sammi Phillips of the U.S. Fish and Wildlife Service, "Buster's just like a fart in a frying pan—he's all over the place."

At the Governor's request, five Special Agents from the various federal departments having jurisdiction over federal lands or the nearby reservation were in attendance. One agent was from the U.S. Forest Service, the second from the Bureau of Land Management, the third from the U.S. Fish and Wildlife Service, the fourth from the Bureau of Indian

Affairs, and the fifth from the National Park Service. Mason and BIA Agent Walton represented the Native Americans, while Warden Ryan McKenna and Biologist Buster Higgins represented the State. Rounding out the task force was the newest and youngest member, Deputy Johansen, from the Deschutes County Sheriff's Department. Johansen, a large, ex-marine with two tours in Afghanistan under his belt, was not shy or bashful and would prove no slouch when it came to holding his own.

The Task Force usually met on a quarterly basis to share information, mainly about the ongoing wolf recovery program but also about forest fires, timber theft, big game poaching, and artifact hunting. After today's meeting, new issues would trump all other concerns.

Quickly sopping up the coffee, Buster gave a slight nod to Warden Ryan, who went over and locked the door to the ODFW conference room, which also doubled as the employee break room. Buster held the remote and started a DVD. Instantly, on an over-sized, wall-mounted TV screen, a long line of timber wolves could be seen running directly toward the camera. Buster froze the footage with a dramatic close-up of a massive black wolf leading the pack.

"Visual confirmation," Buster said. "The timber wolf has returned to Oregon."

Everyone clapped enthusiastically.

Bowing to the group, Buster continued, "I wish I could take credit for this, but I can't. Thank our abundant food supply. Better yet, thank Idaho, because that's where all these wolves are coming from."

Deputy Johansen shifted his eyes from the TV to the locked door, then back to the TV and asked, "What's with the locked doors? Why the secrecy? *The Oregonian* has been running pictures of returning wolves for years now. They're all over the place."

"Not quite," said Buster, "and thankfully not yet, because we have a little hiccup with this particular pack. It appears they are not behaving the way wolves normally behave. They seem to be very aggressive and have greatly expanded their habitat, among other things. Several times they have been sighted running through backyards in both Bend and

Tumalo—even as far away as Redmond. Wolves and urban areas do not mix well at all."

Buster paused to emphasize his point. "For sure, our recovery program would suffer a public relations nightmare if some elderly taxpayer in Bend lets little Muffy out for a nighttime pee just as this pack decides to swing by."

Warming to his subject, Buster gave a short summary of the wolf comeback in Oregon. "Our last wild wolf was killed not too far from here in the late 1940s. It was part of a government program to protect livestock. All kinds of predators were hitting stockmen pretty hard but especially the wolves. The wolf is an apex predator, and it was widely feared by farmers and ranchers that they would quickly decimate Oregon livestock. As you know, wolves normally feed on deer and elk. That's their favorite take-out food. However, they are also opportunistic feeders. If a fat calf should present itself to a hunting wolf pack, well, in the wolf world, that's just a bonus package of kibbles on the hoof."

"Or a Muffy quarter-pounder," shouted Johansen, bringing a burst of joy to Mason Many Crows while leaving a surprised Buster momentarily speechless.

"Semper Fi, I knew you would fit in," said Mason to the beaming Johansen. "Welcome aboard."

Quickly regaining his composure, Buster continued: "So bounties were put on the wolves, and the program worked. Thousands of wolves were wiped out. Oregon was without any wolves at all, literally, for decades. As such, our big game herds rebounded with a vengeance. Our herd populations today are about the same levels as when Lewis and Clark took their little camping trip here. That's the good news."

Pausing for a moment, Buster added, "The bad news is, with so many animals now feeding off the same limited resource, the large animals are starting to outstrip their food supply. By killing off all the wolves, the natural system of checks and balances went completely topsy-turvy. By removing the wolf from the ecosystem, we allowed deer and elk to exceed the carrying capacity of the land. That was an unintended program glitch we did not foresee. We put all kinds of hurt on the wolves to remove them from their natural environment and, as a result, decades later; some of the big game herds are now in danger of starvation. That was definitely not part of the plan. By having wolves return to their former habitat, we are now seeing a much better balance of nature. The number of sick or weak animals is being greatly reduced, mainly by the wolves. It's not perfect, and I don't know if it ever is, but it is a whole lot better today than it was just a few years ago."

Deputy Johansen asked, "How many wolves in Oregon now?"

Buster answered, "For sure, several hundred at least. Nine alone in this pack, and we assume they are denning somewhere with pups."

"Cubs," yelled Mason.

"Pups, cubs—whatever—they're all little wolves-in-training. We've tagged and documented dozens of adult wolves throughout the state, so we're estimating the true number to be around two hundred or so, mostly in Eastern and Central Oregon. Plus, there are probably a lot more out there that we don't even know about. We have over ten million acres of wilderness just in Central Oregon alone—most of it without any roads or even as much as a rabbit trail. We do flyovers but, with so much forest canopy, we miss a lot of what's below."

Buster paused then added, "According to our field reports, our biggest pack is in the Imnahas with eleven wolves. Now we have established packs in the Ochocos plus new packs forming in the Cascades. We've even darted and collared wolves crossing the Cascades heading west to the Willamette Valley. Our computer model forecast is we will have wolves running on the Oregon beaches by the end of the decade."

As an aside, Buster added, "Remember that, Mason, next time you are sunbathing at the Coast."

Mason responded, "Sunbathing at the Oregon Coast? There is no sun at the Oregon Coast. Beautiful as it is, the wolves are welcome to it. Besides," he added, "why sunbathe when all Indian people have a beautiful, natural tan anyway?"

Deputy Johansen dryly asked, "If a wolf bites Mason, will Mason bite it back?"

Mason calmly answered, "Wolves are very intelligent animals. They know better than to bite Mason."

"Okay, Mason aside," Johansen continued, "what about other predators?"

"We're starting to see some impact on bears and cougars already," said Buster, regaining control of the meeting. "Some of it is downright nasty. For the most part, bears and cougars leave each other alone. Not so with wolves. Wolves will attack other predators. Whereas bears and cougars tend to hunt alone, wolves hunt in packs. If they find a bear with a fresh deer kill, they first surround the bear, and then they rush in, snarling and biting. Their goal is to drive the bear off and to not get hurt. Pretty soon the bear gets dizzy from constantly turning around, trying to swat at the biting wolves. After a few minutes, the bear just gives up and runs away. One-on-one the bear will always win, but not against an entire pack of attacking wolves."

Looking over at his friend, Buster added, "Even Mason would struggle with a wolf bite. Wolves can crunch down with some fifteen hundred pounds of force. A bite like that would really hurt. By way of comparison, that's about four times the biting power of a Great White Shark."

Breaking script, Buster said, "As a sidebar here, our bear and cougar numbers are also way up because our prey numbers are way up. We're talking over twenty-eight thousand black bears and seven thousand cougars, just in Oregon alone. Figure similar numbers for Washington, plus both Washington and Idaho now have growing populations of grizzly bears—and some of those occasionally like to swing by Oregon for a little visit."

Buster continued, "There will definitely be some interaction between these predator groups. We see that all the time because of the ecology of fear, which is a change in behavior due to attacks by predators."

Pointing onscreen to the heavily scarred, black alpha male of the Paulina pack, Buster observed, "This guy, for example, should give new meaning to the ecology of fear. He is also one for the record books. Most male wolves in the wild weigh about one fifteen- to one hundred-thirty pounds. They are much bigger than, say, a German Shepard. I'm guessing this guy will easily top two hundred fifty. He's in the prime of his life, he's huge—probably one of the biggest ever, and he rules that pack with an iron paw. He's also exhibiting some strange behavior patterns that really concern me. See, a wolf will always kill a coyote. That's a given, but usually it is a chance encounter. We think wolves kill coyotes to reduce the competition for food. Hard cheese for the coyote, but that's just the way it is. Not so with this alpha wolf. He's way beyond chance encounters. He is actively sniffing out coyote dens, and then going in there and systematically killing the denning parents and all the pups. It is the type of behavior we might expect to see during a food shortage, but right now we are in a prey surplus."

Johansen asked, "Do they eat the coyotes?"

Buster replied, "No. They kill them, shred them, but they do not eat them. They might if they were starving but, normally, no."

Johansen followed up with, "What about people?"

Buster answered, "Most wolves are generally very shy animals and *always* run off when encountering people. Not these guys. Their pack behavior is that they hold their ground. They don't give an inch. Another unusual form of their behavior is that wolves rarely run in a straight line. Usually a wolf pack is all jumbled together. They are all heading in the same direction, just not in a straight line. This guy so dominants his pack that they all run behind him. They never run next to him or ahead of him. It seems the other wolves are terrified of him and, given his size, rightly so."

Buster paused, and then added, "Plus now he has a new hobby—menacing the taxpayer."

A surprised Sammi Phillips asked, "Have there been any reports of this pack attacking anyone?"

Everyone around the table shook their head no, except for Buster who said, "Actually, yes. Stalking and maybe even trying for a kill. We're talking people, right, not livestock? I ask because these guys have also been snacking on some livestock. They recently killed a llama in Tumalo, which is a good forty miles outside their normal range, which means they had to travel through some housing developments to get there."

Buster continued with, "I am preparing an application for the Feds to allow ODFW to capture and euthanize this black wolf. He is an absolute danger to the public. I recently took a report from a couple of mountain bikers. They accidentally crossed paths with this pack. Technically speaking, normal wolf behavior is for the pack to run off because wolves have an inborn fear of man. Instead of running off, this pack just stands there, watching not the bikers but the alpha leader, as if waiting to take their cue from him. Meanwhile, the black wolf is staring at the two bikers, lips curled completely over his fangs, not making a sound. That's what was so scary to the bikers. No snarling, no charging, no lunging—but definitely menacing. Luckily for the bikers, they knew enough not to turn and run. That would have triggered an immediate attack response. That knowledge probably saved their lives."

Mason raised his hand. Buster, knowing that Mason was about to do him again, simply said, "Mason?"

"*Technically* speaking," said Mason, "under this expensive wolf recovery plan, wouldn't the correct taxonomic classification for wilderness bikers be, 'meals on wheels'?"

Though all had heard the comment before, they still enjoyed it, especially at Buster's expense. Warden McKenna gave Mason an enthusiastic two thumbs up, and then quietly said, "Folks, this is serious."

"Anyway," said Buster, quickly regaining his stride, "These guys were very lucky. They slowly backed up until they were out of sight of the wolves and then climbed a tree. They waited about an hour or so until they felt it were safe enough to ride back to their truck. According to the bikers, they estimated the truck was about two miles from their encounter. Just as they got to the truck, one biker turned around and saw the entire pack running up behind them—not more than twenty or thirty yards away. Therein lies part of the hiccup. This is not what wolves are supposed to do.

"The bikers were only a few feet from the truck. The driver hit his fob key and both doors unlocked. They dove in, slamming the doors behind them. At that very moment, the alpha male crashed into the passenger side window, completely fracturing it. He hit the ground, spun around and leaped again. One more lunge against that window, and he would have been in the truck cab. Sharing a truck cab with an angry, oversized wolf would probably have caused the bikers some high anxiety. As it was, the driver started the truck, slammed it into gear and sped off. The wolves regrouped and just stood there, staring at the truck. What was so scary for the bikers is that they never once saw the wolves on their trail. They were constantly looking back but never saw them. Then they suddenly appeared—almost out of nowhere."

Warden McKenna supported Buster's statement by adding, "As we know, car windows can withstand a tremendous force. When I was back in patrol, I once had to use a heavy steel rod to remove a side window because the driver refused to get out of his car. First whack shattered it; then it took another two to remove it. It's pretty scary when a wolf on steroids can shatter a window with only a couple of blows."

Buster nodded and continued with, "The bikers waited until the next day to retrieve their bikes. When they picked them up, the bikes reeked of urine. It seems as if the wolves wanted to either annoy the bikers or were marking the bikes as their own private property."

Buster summarized his presentation with: "Also, the State is not supporting this as a formal wolf recovery program. That's not what is happening here. This is not an expensive, funded program. We can't spend taxpayer money to bring wolves back after the Department spent tons of taxpayer money to get rid of them. That wouldn't make sense. Especially when the wolves took it upon themselves to return to Oregon, free of charge. They cross the Snake River, and here they are. I can live with that. I actually think it's a good thing. What bothers me is this guy," he said, pointing onscreen to the black wolf. "If we have wolf problems, it will be because of him. He is the alpha male. I can't account for his size, and I can't account for his behavior, but I will tell you this: I think he is a very, very dangerous animal."

Buster sat down to a smattering of applause and smiles. He looked at Mason and said, "Your turn."

"Brace yourself, little buddy," said a smiling Mason. "Your pet wolf is about to be upstaged."

TWENTY SECONDS
OF FILM FOOTAGE

L umbering up to the podium, Mason carried with him a bag labeled, "Phoebe Apperson Hearst Museum." While Mason was unzipping the bag, Warden McKenna took a moment to remind the group that, for what they were about to see, they were under an executive gag order on a need-to-know basis only.

"The Governor's main concern is for the public safety of all parties. He does not want to see a group of immature, armed vigilantes running through the woods, playing out their childhood fantasies."

Referring to Deputy Johansen, McKenna added, "You asked earlier about the secrecy? This is not just about Buster's wolf. It's about the last twenty seconds of film and what Buster accidentally picked up on his camera traps. That's the purpose of this meeting, and it is what the Governor is concerned about. For starters, he does not want to see any task force members being interviewed on the nightly news about this DVD. He and his staff are reviewing all options and, because they consider this explosive news, they definitely want to keep this under the radar."

Warden McKenna now had their undivided attention.

While Mason was removing two long arrows from the museum bag, Buster pushed his chair back to again address the group. "I can't tell you how many times I've set out my cameras to film wildlife for herd counts. I have a state-of-the-art system using only high-resolution gear and no whirling noises like the old Super 8 cameras. The same cameras can do both stills and video, much like your cell phones. Motion detectors activate my cameras and there is no flash and absolutely no sound. They are all perfectly camouflaged. Simply put, the animals do not know the cameras are there. I have done this hundreds of times in my career, and it's a perfect way to do a herd count because there are no people around to scare off the critters.

"You know what I typically get on my film? I usually get mule deer, some elk, raccoons, bear and the occasional cougar. Sometimes I don't get anything. Eight hours of film potential, and I'm not even picking up so much as a field mouse."

Continuing, Buster added, "This tape, however, makes up for all the times we struck out. This is the grand slam of wildlife filming. We put the cameras out there to catch the wolves. We got that. That alone makes this a keeper. Then we accidentally picked up a little something extra just before the film was to run out. This is something we never, ever expected to see. Creoles would call this the 'lagniappe'—the icing on the cake. We had absolutely no inkling this was even out there. And to get this on the same film as the wolves makes this one an academy award winner."

Warden McKenna jumped in with, "The Governor called me yesterday after watching the film. First time I've ever talked to the Governor. He didn't go through the chain of command or anything. Just called me to say he wants our recommendations, but he is leaning toward making contact. Might not change anything, but he would feel better if an attempt was made. Because we're all out there patrolling the wilderness, he felt we would be the ones to most logically make that initial contact. He thought we were probably being watched anyway and, as such, that familiarity might help establish some type of relationship."

"Contact . . .?" Deputy Johansen asked, putting his pen down. "Are we talking aliens here? Bigfoot . . .? Did you guys find a flying saucer out there? What are we talking about? Who are we supposed to be making contact with?"

"This will help put things in perspective," Mason said, smiling, "I know you have that Police Science degree from Monmouth, but I would bet my last feather that what you are about to see was never covered in any of your classes."

With that, Mason pointed the remote. The wolves disappeared off screen. Several deer then appeared; running through the brush, and in the lower right-hand corner, the film counter had advanced to where only twenty seconds of tape were now remaining. The motion detectors picked up movement, and then a large male Indian was filmed walking into camera range, closely followed by three other Native Americans. Like the wolves, they were in single file. The first two were middle-aged men, followed by an older teen-aged boy and then a slightly younger teen-aged girl. Each of the males was carrying a thick bow with a quiver of arrows slung over his shoulder. Each held two arrows in his bow hand and had another two under his bow arm. Though a late fall day with the Aspen leaves turning the forest a bright yellow, the males wore little except for buckskin breeches and ankle-high moccasins. The young woman bringing up the rear was also carrying a bow. She had a quiver of arrows strapped around her waist. She wore a buckskin shirt, breeches and moccasins. A long, obsidian knife with a bone handle could be seen next to her quiver. While the men had their hair tied off in braids, her long black hair freely cascaded down her back.

The three men had deerskin and bone ornaments attached to their ears.

The young male also had a wooden plug through his septum.

Each of the four carried a large pack board.

The last few seconds of film had the four walking off camera, with the young woman shifting her pack board around her shoulder. With two seconds remaining, she turned her head to the right, staring directly into the hidden camera lens and momentarily stopped. Then the film went to black.

ORIGINS

Mason held aloft two arrows from the museum bag. "Our tribal elders have whispered for years about a Stone-Age tribe hiding out in the Ochoco wilderness. The rumors were kept alive because occasionally, a tribal member would say that he or she saw them but that the Hiders always ran off before contact could be made. Most of the sightings were wishful thinking or mistaken identity, but a handful appeared to be the real thing. We believe them to be a very small group—probably the smallest tribe in the entire United States. They are real and they are here. 'The Hiders' want to live in complete isolation and not have any type of contact with outsiders—not even other Indians. We respect that and have never bothered them.

"Personally," he added, "I've never seen them and have only been told of one confirmed sighting in my lifetime, many years ago."

Mason passed the two arrows around to the group. One arrow had what Mason identified as turkey feathers for fletching. The other had "camp robber" or blue jay feathers for fletching. One arrowhead was made from obsidian. The other was made from a discarded brown beer bottle, knapped to perfection. Both arrows were painted with simple red and blue four circle rings, followed by a two-inch snake and then another four red and blue ring design.

"Think of an artist signing his paintings. It is the same with arrows. The design painted on arrows is often a signature for identifying the tribe. Look at the similarities between these arrows and the arrows on the tape."

After again watching the film, the group agreed that all the arrows appeared identical.

"Good call," said Mason, "except the arrows you are holding are more than a hundred years old."

Then, bringing one of the four onscreen bows in for a close-up, Mason continued, "Juniper wood, readily available at the lower elevations in Central Oregon. Mountain Juniper has been used since time immemorial for bows."

Pointing to the thickness of the bows, Mason added, "I'm just guessing but these bows look to have a fifty- to sixty-pound pull to them. It takes an awful lot of strength to pull back such a bow and to hold fast to a moving target. Also, take a look at their quivers. River otter," he said, pointing to the animal face, legs and long tail, which made up the whole of the quiver. "Waterproof fur in case you run into snow or rain, which helps prevent warping of the arrows."

The three Indian men had their braids tied off with a two-inch wrap of fur. Holding up one of his braids, Mason said, "Mine are tied off with cotton cloth. These guys have their braids in the ancient way. Animal fur—probably mink or marten."

Special Agent Walton from the Bureau of Indian Affairs asked Mason for a close-up of the leader's shoulders. "No vaccination marks on either arm," said Walton. "This guy has never been inoculated."

"Very true," said Mason. "It appears none of them have, from what we can see. And having grown up on the Rez, I can tell you it was mandatory for all Indian children to be vaccinated. Vaccinations leave dime-sized scars. No scars . . . no vaccinations."

Deputy Johansen added, "Also, when that big guy smiled, I didn't see any evidence of dental work. No fillings. He's got good teeth but, not seeing any lead in there, it looks to me like he's never been to a dentist."

"Exactly," said Mason. "No inoculations and no signs of any dental work. I don't think he's ever had any processed sugar—sugar of course being the leading cause of cavities. Reading the sign, I would say that these four have also never lived day one on any reservation. Plus these first two guys look to be about my age, and they are pretty lean and spare. I would love to have the washboard abs of this third guy. To my eye, all four appear to be in excellent shape."

Adjusting the close-ups, Mason continued, "If you look at the young girl's obsidian knife, you can see it is held in place by a beaded belt. Obsidian is volcanic rock sharper than surgical steel, and I bet the blade on that knife is over twelve inches long. Then there is her belt. I'm not an expert on beads, but those look to be old-fashioned trade beads—probably older than these arrows. She must also be very strong because her bow is identical to the others."

Deputy Johansen, fidgeting with his pen, asked, "Are you guys serious about this? This isn't some type of prank initiation for the boot? Are you telling me that there really is a tribe of wild Indians hiding out in the Ochocos and that no one has ever seen them? This seems a bit incredulous to me."

"I didn't say *no one* has ever seen them," said Mason. "I said *I've* never seen them. Fannie Sahala and her sister once saw them, years ago. Fannie was one of our oldest living tribal members until she passed away at a hundred and three. Her sister died some years before her. Fannie always told the story of when she and her sister went horseback riding up Paulina Mountain for some huckleberrying. This is like forty years ago. It was a late summer day and very hot. They could have driven their truck up there, but they wanted to do things in the traditional way. They tethered their horses to a tree and began walking uphill over some logjams to a favorite huckleberry patch. Both sisters carried holstered .357-caliber pistols, as bears like huckleberries as much as people. They soon came to a small, shady meadow deep in the forest surrounded by huckleberry bushes. In front of the huckleberry patch was a crystal-clear stream."

Mason slowly looked around at the task force. He had their attention. "It's what the sisters saw before them that surprised them. Three Indian women, having filled several baskets of huckleberries, were resting by the stream. All three were wearing native buckskin dress and moccasins. All three had oversized reed hats on, decorated with eagle feathers. All three were carrying long obsidian knives with bone handles. One was drinking from the stream. They had not seen Fannie and her sister. Fannie whispered, 'Who are they?' because she did not know them, which was unusual because Fannie knew nearly all the local natives. Her sister shrugged her shoulders for she did not know them either. The woman drinking suddenly looked up and saw Fannie and her sister. The two sisters waved to the women and started to walk over to them.

"The sisters were in for a surprise," Mason continued. "Because the three women suddenly jumped up and ran off into the woods, leaving all their huckleberries behind."

Looking directly at Johansen, Mason added, "Now this was very puzzling. Fannie and her sister did not know what to make of this, for this had never happened before. Indian women *always* visit whenever they are out gathering native foods. It is a cultural thing since time immemorial. Centuries ago, even women from warring tribes would sometimes set aside their differences and work together."

Mason paused, waiting for questions and then continued, "Somewhat perplexed, the sisters sat by the stream and waited awhile, but the other women never came back. Fannie then put their huckleberry baskets high on a stone ledge and protected the berries from the sun with her old cowboy hat."

Looking around the room at the assembled task force, Mason added, "The two sisters worked for the next several hours gathering their own berries. Both sisters felt they were being watched the whole time. Several times Fannie would spin around, hoping to catch a glimpse of whoever was watching them, but no one was there. Fannie heard a slight rustle in a nearby bush, and she went over to investigate. She drew her gun and held it in her hand just in case it was a bear. All she could find, though, were several branches that had been pulled aside but not broken, as if someone were peeking out at them. No one was there, and there were no visible tracks on the ground."

Buster blurted out, "Tell them about the hat."

Mason sighed and said, "A little later, tired and hot, Fannie and her sister gathered up their berries and made ready to ride home. Fannie went over to retrieve her hat, but now the hat was gone. The missing hat aroused her suspicions because it was a hot, still day without any wind. After searching for a few moments, Fannie and her sister left. It was an old, faded hat—more yellow than white and of no consequence. If Fannie lost or misplaced it, then she would have the perfect excuse to buy a new hat."

Summarizing, Mason said, "Out of curiosity, the sisters came back a few days later. The huckleberry baskets were gone, and Fannie's hat was never found. In their place were two small, beaded worry bags—an apparent gift for Fannie and her sister.

"To her dying day, Fannie maintained that she and her sister had accidentally stumbled upon some of the Hiders."

Closely examining the two arrows Mason was passing around, BIA Agent Walton asked, "Were these found up in the Ochocos?"

"No," said Mason. "They have been on loan to us for some time from the Hearst Museum at U.C. Berkeley."

"What tribe of people made these," asked Walton?

"Those two arrows were both made by the very last of the Yahi warriors, a man named 'Ishi.'   Interestingly enough, our tribal anthropologist identified the worry bags left for Fannie and her sister to be the same as those historically made by the Yahi or Mill Creeks as they were sometimes called. Same with the arrows."

Walton put on his best poker face. He knew about the Yahi. Some pieces were now starting to fall into place. In his office was an extensive file on the Yahi, but it was a very old file mostly filled with rumors and supposed Yahi sightings even well into the early and mid-part of the Twentieth Century. However, all the sightings were in Northern California—none in Oregon.

Top BIA Management viewed some of the file contents, such as the effects of the Indian Relocation Act, as an embarrassment to the Bureau and kept them hidden away from the general public. Easy to do because it was all ancient history.

Walton knew from his file readings that the Yahi were excellent guerilla fighters. The Yahi and some pioneer whites, known as the 'Guardsmen' or 'Guards,' fought each other from 1850 to 1871, and then the surviving Indians mysteriously disappeared.

The few remnants left of the Yahi tribe managed to hide away from the whites for almost the next forty years in Northern California. It was not until 1908 that they were rediscovered.

"I wonder," mused Walton, "if there is any link between our missing elk hunter and this lost tribe of Indians?"

Several years earlier, a number of Federal, State and local agencies were out searching for a hunter missing from elk camp. Even the FBI became involved because of rumors of a possible murder on Federal land. The hunter seemingly disappeared off the face of the earth. Very few clues were ever found. His body was never found nor his hunting rifle. He walked out of elk camp with two hunting partners and was never again seen.

The men he was hunting with were both considered as "persons of interest."

In spite of extensive searches and investigation by law enforcement, very little was ever turned up, and the missing hunter's disappearance was eventually moved to the cold-case file.

An unsolved case bothered Walton. It more than bothered him; anything unsolved downright annoyed him. Even when the workday was over he was always wondering what part of the case he was missing and what did he need to find to solve it. He had worked twelve homicides in his BIA career, and all twelve resulted in convictions.

Before he retired, Walton wanted to go out with a perfect record of solving the mystery of the missing elk hunter.

Special Agent Walton could feel the investigative juices flowing. Some new potential had arisen. It was a hunch, nothing more, but hunches created threads, which created leads.

SA Walton could hardly wait to get back to his office.

"Most nonnative people have never heard of the Yahi," said Mason, continuing, "but most Indian people know that historically they were the most widely feared guerilla fighters in the nation. They fought and never surrendered. They fought long after the Sioux and Apache sued for peace. When the Yahi were almost all massacred, the few survivors left went into hiding. They could have surrendered and gone to a reservation, but that would have meant giving up their freedom. They did not want to live if they had to give up their traditional way of life. The more honorable way was either death in combat or surviving by hiding.

As a young boy, Ishi survived several brutal massacres by frontier Guardsmen and lived well into the first part of the early Twentieth

Century. He actually spent forty of his first fifty-seven years of life in complete hiding before being captured in Oroville, California. During all the long years of hiding, his everyday fear was being captured and killed by pursuing whites. For the past hundred years, we thought he was the only Stone-Age warrior to have actually survived into the 20th century. We are now thinking otherwise."

THE YAHI

Ishi was born into one of the most warlike of the Yahi bands; the Yahi being a separate tribe of the Yana Nation. He was one of only four or five Yahi known to have actually lived into the Twentieth Century. The Yahi had lived in Northern California for thousands of years. They lived, like all Indian people, entirely off the land. You could have taken Ishi or any Yahi from the Nineteenth Century and sent him back in time for thousands of years, and he would have been entirely at home. Their way of life was as it always had been. There were simply no changes. They were semi-nomadic hunter-gathers who used a bow or lance for deer, elk, bear and salmon. Their women gathered seasonal acorns, roots, tubers and greens to add to the cooking pot. They were considered a primitive, Stone-Age tribe because, since the very dawn of time, their weapons and tools were fashioned mostly from stone.

The Yahi or Mill Creeks, as the whites called them, wore hardly any clothing during the hot summer months, and their long hair was always adorned with dangling shell and bone fragments. They burned their hair and scarred their bodies when in mourning. Many of the warriors wore a piece of wood or a septum plug through their nose, giving them a fierce appearance especially when going into combat. The core of their very lives revolved around family, tribe, spirituality, and, strangely enough for such a deeply religious people, war.

The Yahi lived to fight. From the moment they awakened until they fell asleep at night, they offered up prayers of thanksgiving for each meal, for the health and safety of loved ones, and especially for success in battle. Perhaps a bit of a contradiction to today's belief system, but it is how they lived their lives. Every Yahi man, woman and child was fully prepared to lay down his or her life either for a family or tribal member but especially for the sake of the Yahi religion.

They were the Spartans of all Indian tribes. The Yahi were fanatical in living their daily lives according to the beliefs and practices of their ancient religion, which consisted almost exclusively of worshipping, "Grandfather," the Creator. Their ferocious fighting skills, usually against insurmountable odds, were what made them so fearless. They were ruthless in their attacks upon all whites and all Indians from other tribes, save one—their "cousins," the Modoc.

Neighboring tribes lived in constant fear of attack by the Yahi, describing them to frontier whites as, "wild Indians."

Conversely, the children of these "wild Indians" were deeply loved and cared for by their parents. Yahi mothers would spend countless hours every day cooking for their children, bathing them and then brushing mats from their tangled hair at bedtime. The mothers and fathers would often swing a young one when out walking, sing to them at bedtime, and dote on them when they were ill.

Yahi mothers loved singing to their children. Putting the children to bed often revolved around singing. When the parents were finished singing, the children would often respond with their own songs. Any child orphaned by war or accident was immediately taken in and nurtured by other family members or even nonfamily members. Simply put, to bring a tribal member in need—child or adult—to a loving, warm lodge was the Yahi way.

Cremation of the dead was a religious obligation carried out by all members of the tribe. It was a belief paramount among all other Yahi beliefs. To not cremate the dead was an open invitation to the deceased to haunt living tribal members and make them suffer terribly for not freeing the souls of the dead to the spirit world where they would forever live in peace.

The Yahi would risk everything to cremate their dead because it was *always* the right thing to do, regardless of the risk involved.

Like most tribes, the Yahi were governed by consensus whereby tribal elders, the Chief, and the tribal council would arrive at major decisions, such as whether to go to war or sue for peace. The Yahi also followed the Hidatsa tradition of binding obligations down to the seventh generation, which was the Indian way of saying, "Forever." If the consensus of the tribe was to do something of value or importance for the tribe, then that decision would then be binding down to the seventh generation.

One binding decision the Yahi made was to kill all the whites that were doing their best at killing all the Yahi. Northern California frontier whites banded together into small groups known as the "Guardsmen" to defend against Indian attacks. Like the Yahi, the Guardsmen or "Guards" excelled at guerilla warfare and would often surround and massacre entire bands of Yahi, usually before breakfast. The rest of the Guardsmen's day would be spent looting and scalping the bodies. Any young women found still alive would be repeatedly raped and then passed on to the next Guardsman until it was time to go home. Then one of them would casually shoot her, usually by pressing his pistol against the back of her head, forcing her to her knees and pulling the trigger. Then she would be scalped for the five dollar bounty, ultimately paid for by the state of California thanks to Governor Peter Burnett.

The Yahi were often as brutal as the Guardsmen, exacting terrible vengeance for every attack by the whites, even to the point of brutally murdering innocent pioneer children.

The timing of important tribal decisions would be left to the Chief and his advisors. Decisions arrived at under Hidatsa tradition were sometimes years or decades in the making but, when they were finally decided, it was with all the solemnity and ferocity of today's Mideast *fatwas*. Once decided, action would be taken; the only question was in the timing and manner, which would ultimately be decided by both tribal consensus and respected leaders and elders.

THE YANA AND THE YAHI

The Yana was an Indian nation of some four thousand people made up of four different tribes; the Northern, Central and Southern Yana, and then the Yahi. The Yahi was the southernmost and the smallest tribe of the Yana nation, numbering only about four hundred or so. During the hot summer months, the Yahi lived high in the Sierra Nevada Mountains—especially in the cool pine forests of Mt. Lassen. During wintertime, they lived in deep canyons east of Sacramento. They lived mostly in small, brush-covered huts, easily disguised from lurking enemies. The wooden huts were shaped somewhat like teepees and could accommodate four or five people.

All other Yana, for the most part, lived in rolling, brushy hill country, also east of Sacramento. The Yana were considered "valley Indians" while the Yahi were regarded and feared as "mountain Indians."

Though the Yahi were part of the Yana Nation, they almost always kept to themselves. Even though the groups shared some Yana cultural similarities, the tribal languages were so different that they were almost unintelligible to one another.

This worked well for the Yahi because they wanted nothing more than to be left alone.

If Indians from other tribes hunted or trespassed onto Yahi land, the Yahi would hunt them down and kill them, even if the trespassers were from the Yana Nation. They did this because they had always done this and at another level, they had to do this to protect the limited food resources for their families.

Conversely, they would sometimes meet Indians from tribes that they warred against at designated neutral meadows high up on Mt. Lassen. Both sides understood that this was an opportunity for trade. After the trading was over, and all parties had returned to their traditional homeland, then the fighting would resume if so inclined, and usually the Yahi were.

The Yahi had a very strong sense of right versus wrong. When differences with other tribes arose, the Yahi believed that they were right and the others were wrong. It was that simple. To that end, they were almost *always* at war with other tribes over perceived wrongs.

Suddenly, after the discovery of gold in 1848 at Sutter's Mill, the Yahi had new enemies to fight—the pioneer whites, who were arriving by the thousands. Unfortunately for the Yahi, they were vastly outnumbered. Plus, it was considered a badge of honor for the new arrivals to displace all Indians by killing them, mainly because the Indians were considered to be so different and primitive.

By 1849 over three hundred thousand "prospectors" had flooded the goldfields of Northern California. Fighting them were barely four hundred Yahi total; maybe an average of one hundred Yahi warriors in all.

To stretch their limited food resources, the Yahi lived in small bands, usually family groups, along two creeks. The bands numbered anywhere from fifteen to forty. Mostly they lived in what early settlers called "Pineries" —large clumps of pine forests scattered along the banks of both Mill Creek and Deer Creek. The ice-cold, fast-flowing creeks, which in fact were bigger than most rivers, provided clean water for cooking and bathing, plus abundant salmon runs during the spring and fall of each year. The Pineries provided year-round firewood, food, and some degree of protection from attack by either vengeful neighboring tribes or from early settlers wanting to rid Northern California of all Native Americans.

The "Forty-Niners," as the newly arrived whites were called, quickly culled most of the deer and elk herds, which were the main source of food for all the Indian tribes. The Yahi soon found that they were on the brink of starvation. They then did what they had always done, which was to kill the invaders who, at the same time, were doing their best to kill all the Indians.

Unlike the other Yana, who only wanted peace with the whites, the Yahi lived for the fight. From the time a boy could walk, he was taught how to make a bow and schooled in the art of war. Yahi boys, and later on, girls, were taught knife fighting, shooting an enemy with arrows, and learning how to stop an attacker by using the lance and shield. They learned how to silently stalk others, swoop in for the kill and then instantly disappear, often without leaving a trace behind.

Whenever the Yahi were fleeing from the Guardsmen, they would wait for an opportune moment and suddenly turn and attack when their pursuers least expected it.

The Yahi neither gave nor received any quarter when in battle.

Young Yahi warriors were sometimes surprised that an older warrior or Chief could actually die in his sleep as opposed to dying in battle, so rare was the occasion.

In the frontier days prior to the Civil War, all settlers and Guardsmen were armed with single-shot flintlock rifles and large-caliber, five- or six-shot pistols—all single action. At first the Yahi were armed only with bows and arrows. As the years of warfare went by, the Yahi managed to acquire both rifles and pistols, mostly from the battlefield and sometimes by trade with other tribes. They became very proficient in their use. After the Civil War, the sixteen-shot Henry repeating rifle came into use and the Yahi were again heavily outgunned. An old flintlock or bow was no match for a rapid-fire Henry or Winchester.

The U. S. Army once took to the field to force the Yahi to a reservation. Trailing them day and night for weeks on end throughout a vast wilderness area, the soldiers never saw so much as one Indian, though the Yahi always had the soldiers under careful watch. Soldiers would find Yahi camps, even camps with cooking fires blazing away, but they could never find any of the Indians.

The Army failure was a great delight and source of much merriment to the local Militia and Guardsmen who knew the land well and were constantly finding and ambushing the Yahi.

The Yahi did not know any other way of life but war. Warfare had been a constant part of their lives, literally for thousands of years. Going on the warpath gave young men the chance to make a name for themselves and to become valued protectors of the tribe. Raiding neighboring tribes brought status, wealth and prestige to the warrior. The Yahi were the scourge of nearby peaceful tribes such as the Maidu, Wintun and Big River Indians. All tribes, except for the Modoc, were considered to be enemies, sometimes even other Yana. According to warfare custom, women and children captured in battle from other tribes were either kept as slaves or married into the tribe—sometimes forcibly, sometimes willingly.

The Yahi were always pegged as fierce mountain guerilla fighters. Early settlers quickly spread the word to newcomers that the Yahi were more ferocious than the Sioux and more cunning than the Apache. The settlers often called them "Mill Creeks," as many Yahi bands lived along Mill Creek; a smaller number lived along nearby Deer Creek.

The Mill Creeks did not have horses, wagons or dogs. The rocky, mountainous terrain was nearly impassable for wagons. Horses could not survive without browse, and barking dogs could signal a hidden camp to enemies.

Instead of horses, the Yahi went everywhere on foot, often at a fast pace. Most Yahi warriors could easily run twenty-five to thirty miles per day, day in and day out. Whenever they attacked a ranch or remote homestead, they would quickly kill the horses, livestock and dogs, smoking the meat into a form of "jerky" for easy transport back to the tribe.

"Easy transport" in the Yahi world meant carrying as much as they could on their pack boards, all the while running back to camp even if they were packing close to seventy or eighty pounds.

Dogs were occasionally spared but most of the time found their way into the communal cooking pot as dog meat was considered a delicacy.

No matter what name the tribe was called, the word "surrender" was unknown to them. It was the Yahi way to fight to the death, even in the face of overwhelming force. Warriors, elderly men, even young boys barely able to draw a bow, would always rise to the defense of their women and children, no matter the cost.

In 1848 James W. Marshall discovered gold at Sutter's Mill in Northern California. By 1849 most of the paying claims had been filed, yet hundreds of thousands continued to arrive but could not find any gold or work. Their lack of work, hunger, and anger over their poverty contributed to a dark stain upon American history.

None of the Yahi had ever before seen a white man. It was only a few months after arrival for a small number of the Forty-Niners to start attacking and killing the Indians. Over the next two decades, thousands of Northern California Indians from all tribes were shot, hanged, starved and enslaved.

By a strange twist of California law, even up to the early days of the Civil War, it was legal for a white man to indenture or enslave an Indian. It was as simple as grabbing one around the neck and taking him or her home, then beating the victim into submission.

The practice continued long after the law was changed.

In reality, most of the Indians taken were young women or children. Many were first taken as sex slaves and later forced into prostitution; a practice virtually unknown to most California tribes.

The enslaved Indians were given as gifts to friends, gambled away at poker, sold, traded, and often just outright killed because the owner was simply tired of them. It is estimated that from 1849 to 1871, out of the four thousand plus Indians of the Yana Nation, only a small number managed to survive until the 1871 Kingsley Cave Massacre, where thirty-three men, women and children were gunned down. All of those killed at Kingsley Cave were Yahi. With the exception of fifteen to seventeen surviving Yahi, most of the entire Yana Nation had now been either murdered or enslaved.

For those pressed into slavery, either male or female, it was usually a very short-lived experience, especially as a growing number of Northern California cities started paying five dollars for every Indian scalp collected. Thousands of Native Americans were killed for the five-dollar bounty. The drum roll for paying scalp bounties was started by local newspapermen who perhaps genuinely believed they were helping to defend the frontier community. The idea quickly spread throughout Northern California. However, when asked to join the fight against the Indians the newspapermen usually refused. They were too busy keeping the community informed.

Local politicians joined the fray, keeping only the one promise they never made: higher taxes to offset increasing costs to pay for the growing number of scalps turned in on almost a daily basis.

Small town politicians, like the newspapermen, also excused themselves from any actual fighting due to, "Pressing city business." This was kind of strange when you consider that there was actually very little city business to take care of in the 1850's. Most Northern California cities at this time consisted of a few hundred citizens, a general store, livery stable, printing press, a bar or two, a church or two, and a brothel. Sometimes the "city business' would be conducted in the brothel and sometimes at taxpayer expense. Most of the 'overworked' city fathers decided it prudent to not burden the taxpayers with that particular knowledge. The citizenry, after all, simply would not understand.

At the end of 1871, the highest count for surviving Yahi was seventeen but many of the "Guards" thought that seventeen was still too high. The Guards wanted all the Yahi exterminated and they were not willing to settle for anything less.

All Yana Indians were targets of white enmity but especially the Yahi because they were the most feared. Every single occasion, every accidental encounter, every chance meeting with the whites *always* resulted in the Yahi being killed, either by armed settlers, cowboys, miners, or by the local militia—the Guards.

Shooting was the preferred method of killing the Indians, closely followed by hanging.

The local militias were usually a strange mix of alcoholic bottom feeders, drifters, and the chronically unemployed war veterans from the 1846 War with Mexico.

During the Civil War era, the ranks of the Guardsmen were swollen by Civil War deserters from both sides and even with a few paroled Confederate soldiers known as "Galvanized Yankees." A Galvanized Yankee was a rebel prisoner of war who agreed to join the Union Army and fight, not against fellow Confederates, but against warring Indians in the Far West and Northwest. After their enlistment was up, some stayed and became volunteer Guardsmen.

Most rank and file Guardsmen barely had a third-grade education. Most were hardened by war or by POW interment. In their value system, they simply did not regard the Native Americans as people. They believed Indians to be so different that they should not be allowed to live, especially in California, forgetting who was there first. To make it easy to destroy them, they would vilify them, loudly calling them "savages" and demanding that they all be killed.

By putting the Native American down, they were trying to pull themselves up.

"Captains" or leaders of the Militias were often family men and respected community members. The uniting force between such diverse groups was a genuine fear and loathing of the Indians. As always, guns trumped arrows, and entire bands of Yahi were killed—sometimes even one or two small bands in a single day.

Newspapermen and city officials often cheered on the exploits of the local Guards.

According to several books published late in life by two surviving Guardsmen, none of the Guards, with one notable exception, ever showed the slightest bit of hesitation or remorse in taking Indian life, even the lives of innocent children.

The incessant slaughter of any and all Indians could be laid mostly at the feet of R. A. Anderson and Hiram Good, co-captains of the Guards. The two Captains believed that by killing all Indians, especially the Yahi, they were protecting the otherwise defenseless Pioneer community.

Unfortunately, their actions went far beyond self-defense. The Captains lived for the excitement of armed conflict. The term was unknown then, but they were "adrenaline junkies." They so enjoyed attacking and killing Indians that they often planned weekend trips to the mountains for what they called, ". . . a hunt."

GUARDSMEN CO-CAPTAINS:
R. A. ANDERSON AND HIRAM GOOD

In the first hour of the first weekend hunt, it was widely reported that R. A. Anderson single-handedly killed nine Yahi warriors, shooting them down one at a time even though he was under heavy fire from Yahi forces. This was no small task for Anderson as he had only an old, single-shot flintlock for a rifle.

For every shot that Anderson could get off, the Indians would typically be able to fire four or five arrows at their target. Pinned down, it was all Anderson could do to reload and fire.

One warrior, also armed with a flintlock, was shooting at Anderson who resolutely held his ground, even though the warrior's bullets were striking a small pine tree, mere inches from Anderson's head. Anderson several times had to shake his head to dislodge tiny wood fragments from his eyes. Though the warrior was constantly changing position, Anderson made an educated guess as to where he would next pop up. He steadied his flintlock against the base of the tree and when the warrior raised one eye over a rock for his next shot, Anderson snapped off a shot, hitting him in the head and killing him instantly.

Anderson had just turned nineteen when he started fighting the Mill Creeks. His fellow Guardsmen cheered him on at every kill. He quickly became a folk hero to the frontier whites.

By all accounts, Anderson personally killed well over an estimated one hundred to one hundred fifteen Indians in his lifetime, and under his leadership he was responsible for the deaths of thousands more. Researcher/author Bradley Campbell writes this about the two co-captains in *The Geometry of Genocide*: "In 1864 after the killing of two white women, Anderson and Good spent five months killing most of the Yana still remaining—about two thousand of them."

The two co-captains, sometimes with only one or two Guardsmen accompanying them, killed all Indians from all tribes without mercy. For the thousands of years that the Indians lived in Northern California, never before had they experienced such tremendous loss of life brought about by such a small handful of determined people.

An unsubstantiated rumor states that when asked late in life how many Indians he had actually killed, Anderson angrily responded, "Ducking, not counting."

It is hard to reconcile the brutal acts of Anderson with one of the few pictures of Anderson. One of his last pictures, taken late in life, shows a kindly, smiling, bespectacled grandfather. In his obituary an elderly Indian is even quoted as saying that, "Indians think very highly of him." The unnamed Indian might well have been referring to Anderson's fighting skills and courage on the battlefield. The same source most likely did not lose any family members to Anderson's many massacres; why else the compliment.

Anderson wrote in his memoirs about once shooting and killing an unsuspecting Indian because the Indian was wearing a vest that was part of a suit stolen from Anderson's brother. Just wearing the clothing was enough to convince Anderson that the Indian was a thief, regardless of the fact that Indians would often give, trade or gamble clothing away. In Anderson's mind, the mere wearing of the vest justified the shooting.

Nowhere did Anderson ever mention that he asked the Indian where he got the clothing. Instead, he hid behind a tree, ambushed him, killed him, and stripped him of the vest now made useless because of a shotgun blast through it.

Old clothing stolen today would be a minor misdemeanor and most likely would not even result in jail time.

Unfortunately, most Native Americans killed in 1864 under the leadership of Anderson and Good were from peaceful tribes such as the Yana, Big River Indians, Maidu or Wintun. Prior to 1864 the two co-captains once spent two continuous months in the saddle searching for Yahi warriors. They found and killed only one. They were so frustrated that they attacked a nearby Maidu village and, according to Anderson in his book titled, *Fighting the Mill Creeks: Being a Personal Account of Campaigns Against Indians of the Northern Sierras,* they left ". . . forty good Indians lying scattered about."

Sadly, many of Anderson's victims were unarmed women and children. They were part of his extermination policy. Killing Indians became his passion and mission in life. In his book, which Anderson wrote in 1909, he said, ". . . Hi Good and I, sometimes with Bully (Bowman) and sometimes by ourselves, made many scouting trips into the hills and managed to reduce the number of bad Indians on almost every trip. Still, the numbers remained undiminished as far as we could judge, and we became convinced that they were being constantly reinforced."

That was bad news for those who wanted to eliminate all Indians from Northern California and it was especially bad news for the Indian victims. The only ones to profit were those who collected the five-dollar scalp bounty offered by a growing number of small cities and towns.

As a reward for his prowess as an Indian fighter, Anderson was elected Sheriff of Butte County at age twenty-five, according to several contemporary reports. County records, however, indicate he was not elected Sheriff until decades later.

In the two years that he was Sheriff, he never once arrested a white for killing an Indian.

It seemed that whenever Anderson and Good could not find any Yahi to attack, they would murder and take scalps from whatever Indians they could find, even the friendly ones who worked for the whites on nearby farms and ranches. Simply put, the Indians were murdered, sometimes even in their sleep, by a small group of frontiersmen who made their own laws and were accountable to no one.

After one particular massacre of friendly Indians, both Anderson and Good could feel many members of the pioneer community starting to turn against them because they were killing non-hostile Indians.

Community feelings may have slowed them down, but it did not stop them.

The two co-captains were friends, but they also had their differences, and on several occasions nearly came to blows over policy decisions. Unlike R. A. Anderson, Hiram Good steadfastly refused to ever kill a woman or child. It was a point of contention that he and Anderson used to argue about. Good maintained that women and children were noncombatants and as such should never be harmed. Anderson disagreed. As Good stood ramrod straight at over six-feet, four inches, he was the pioneer image of a fearless Indian fighter, and whenever he spoke, his voice carried authority, especially with his fellow Guardsmen. Good was frequently described as a very muscular, courageous man who would ride all night to attack an Indian camp and then fight all day without ever getting tired.

H. H. Sauber, an admiring contemporary of Good, once accompanied him on an Indian raid and wrote that fellow Guardsmen often called Good, "The Boone of the Sierras."

In one Guardsmen raid against a sleeping Yahi camp, Good went behind a raging waterfall to fight a hiding warrior. The Indian warrior was a huge physical specimen. Each man was armed with only a knife. The two men battled it out for minutes on end. It was an exhausting fight, with both men repeatedly slashing and stabbing at the other. Both men could be heard grunting and screaming while trying for a killing stab. The two, according to contemporary reports, were very closely matched in both size and strength. The terrible blows and hand-to-hand combat seemed to stretch interminably. The noise attracted a number of Guardsmen to the falls. Hiram Good nearly met his match but, with one powerful thrust, he drove his knife all the way to the hilt in the Indian's chest. He threw the Indian out from behind the falls and then leaped into the water to scalp him, amidst the cheering and shouting of his fellow Guardsmen.

Severely wounded in several fights by Indian muskets, Good would take but a moment to tie off the bleeding wound, and then resume fighting. He quickly became a legend in the frontier community for his strength, stamina and recuperative powers.

He was widely known as a man who would always come to the rescue of neighbors whenever there was an Indian attack.

On one occasion, more out of starvation than anything else, the Yahi raided Hiram Good's cabin and made off with some of his cattle. Good, Anderson and Bully Bowman followed the Indians and attacked them. During the fighting, Good was shot in the leg. He fell to the ground, hemorrhaging from his wound. Anderson and Bowman managed to rescue

Good under a hail of gunfire. A local paper reported that the men had Good, "Throw his arms over their shoulders, bandaged his wound, and the three escaped by walking and carrying him some twenty miles back to his cabin, all the while driving the remaining cattle ahead of them."

That takes guts. Anderson, in spite of his murderous traits, was a man of raw courage who consistently risked his life to rescue or aid his fellow Guardsmen or any whites under Indian attack.

The Indians chased the three men for miles on end, shooting at them all the time. The Guardsmen were exhausted, fatigued, and Hiram Good severely wounded. At one point, the Indians were so close that, to save what few bullets they had left, they started throwing fist-sized stones at the fleeing whites. Then, for whatever reason, with success almost in hand, the Indians stopped their pursuit and simply melted away into the forest.

Perhaps they just ran out of bullets or were tired of the chase.

Settlers sometimes asked about what drove Hiram Good to such extremes, taking Indian life and constantly risking his own life in fighting the Indians. It was rumored that Good and his fiancée were crossing the Plains sometime in the late 1850s when their wagon came under attack, either by the Sioux or Snakes. Good's fiancée was killed in the attack just days away from her wedding. The loss of his bride-to-be so devastated Good that he allegedly took it upon himself, no matter the risk, to avenge her death by killing as many Indian warriors as he possibly could.

Anderson, also a brawny, muscular man, one who was *always* in the thick of the fighting at every opportunity, differed from Good in that Anderson wanted to kill all Indians. This included women and children. It was Anderson's goal to completely remove all Indians from Northern California. Anderson's favorite quote was, "Nits become lice." It was a quote he frequently used to justify his shooting of unarmed women and children.

For Good, women and children were always off limits, but any male of warrior age, either friend or foe, armed or not, was fair game.

Conversely, Anderson was for killing them all if they were Indian. He never once hesitated at shooting any Indian, including women and children.

Though Hiram Good would not kill women and children, he was absolutely relentless in the killing of warriors. He and Sandy Young, boss cowboy for the Bidwell Ranch, once spent a Sunday afternoon sneaking up to a Yahi camp and killing eight Mill Creek warriors because the Mill Creeks had earlier murdered the three Hickock children on June 19, 1862. The two men felt it was one of their better "hunts."

One of the Hickock children, a six-year-old boy, was killed in such a horrific fashion that his murder sickened and terrified even the most hardened of the Indian fighters.

It was widely believed by many in the frontier community that Anderson and Good were indirectly responsible for the murders of the Hickock children due to their relentless attacks against the Yahi.

Ironically, Hiram Good was shot and killed in 1870 by Indian Ned, a sixteen-year-old Yahi or Yana boy whose life had been spared years earlier by Good over Anderson's objections. The boy was captured hiding in the brush after the Guardsmen killed all his family and fellow tribal members. Indian Ned was originally given by Good to a nearby ranch family when Good suddenly decided one day to take Ned back and become a foster parent to him. Both Anderson and the ranch family repeatedly warned Good that he was taking a lot of risk by having Indian Ned live with him, but Good always shrugged off the danger, stating that Ned was, "A good boy." One day, however, "the good boy," Indian Ned, took it upon himself to shoot and kill Hiram Good for no other reason than ". . . to see how he will act."

Ned took a spare rifle of Good's and ambushed Good as he was returning home with some trade items from the nearby Carty Ranch. He shot Good three times, with the first shot going through the hips, the second to the legs, and the killing shot to the chest. Ned dumped Good into a ravine and covered his body under a pile of rocks. He might have gotten away with the shooting except that, for some unfathomable reason, he took to wearing Good's silver ring and riding his horse, which Ned claimed he found tied off to a tree in the wilderness.

Several of the Guardsmen believed that Ned actually killed Good to steal the four thousand dollars that Good had buried somewhere in or around his cabin from a livestock sale, a common practice in the days before banks. Four thousand dollars then would be the equivalent of well over one hundred thousand dollars today.

Two days after killing Hiram Good, Indian Ned was shot and killed by Sandy Young. Young had another man tie Indian Ned to a tree after an elderly man tricked Ned into confessing to the shooting. Indian Ned repeatedly denied shooting Good until the elderly man asked where the first shot went. Ned told him, "Through the hips," and at that point broke down and admitted to the murder. Barely minutes after confessing, Young shot the sobbing Ned, justifying it to the admiring onlookers by first having Indian Ned repeat why he shot Hiram Good. Indian Ned whispered, "To see how he will act." Sandy Young said to the assembled onlookers, ". . . Then I will see how *he* will act."

Indian Ned did not act or die well. He was shot once in the neck by Young, than slowly collapsed to the ground, quivering and shrieking with radiating waves of pain until he bled out and died.

Young refused to let anybody give the dying Ned as much as a sip of water.

His body remained tied to the tree for the next several years. He was never cremated and as such his spirit was forever doomed to haunt the earth, according to Yahi beliefs. Years after his execution, his skeletonized remains were taken to a California college for medical study.

On the day that he was shot by Indian Ned, Hiram Good had some forty Indian scalps tied to a poplar tree in the front of his cabin. Displaying the scalps was a form of bragging to the whites, saying, "This is how I protect you." It was also a message to all Indians, warning them, "You're next." Why the scalps were not turned in for the bounty is anybody's guess.

On windy days Good had to sometimes brush the scalp hair out of his face as he exited his cabin.

According to some in the pioneer community, only a handful of the scalps were taken from the warlike Mill Creeks. Good took the rest from unsuspecting Indians who were often ambushed.

Hiram Good was thirty-four years of age when killed by Indian Ned. Ned was sixteen years old when killed by Sandy Young. Young was in his early forties when shot and killed probably by Indians or possibly by a former gold mining partner. R.A. Anderson survived into the 20th century and died shortly after writing of his exploits. His obituary stated that he was a kind man renowned as an Indian fighter and as a former Sheriff of Butte County but did not give his date of death, though he was believed to be in his late seventies.

One of Good's nearby neighbors was an elderly, part-time Guardsman and full-time prospector who stitched together a bedcover out of sixty-some scalps from Indians he had killed down through the years. Every morning this serial killer would roll the scalp blanket out over his bed, and every night he would roll it up to the foot of his bed.

Like so many other frontiersmen, he was never brought to the bar of justice for all the murders he committed.

It was written in 1915 by archeologist and linguist Dr. T. T. Waterman that many of the California frontier Indian fighters, who were mostly the Guardsmen, should have been, "Hanged for their crimes against humanity."

Still, most early settlers greatly admired the Guards, especially Anderson and Good, for their willingness to spend weeks and months in the saddle pursuing attacking Indians, who were almost exclusively Yahi. The Guards were viewed as the only line of defense against the Indians. The Army was not protecting the settlers, so the settlers had to protect themselves. Time after time, the Yahi attacked the whites in retaliation for the whites killing the Indians. The Yahi had been so brutalized by the whites that they responded in kind by murdering the Hickock children— two teen-aged girls and their young brother. After the two girls were killed with numerous arrows, their little brother, literally frozen in place with fear, was captured and taken to a nearby Yahi camp. The boy was barely six years old.

When he was taken to the Yahi Camp, the crying boy asked, "Why did you hurt my sisters?"

In response, the Indians placed him in a small circle, forcibly tied him down, and then had Yahi children, many the same ages as their captive, begin to cut off his fingers and toes. The children had to sit on the little boy's arms and legs as they cut. The pain was unbearable. The frightened, hysterical boy screamed until he could cry no more. At one point, surrounded by Yahi children, he begged for them to stop. Through wretched sobs he promised to be good. Several did stop, now crying along with their victim, but most of the children, at the urging of tribal members, then began pelting the Hickock boy with stones. They ended up killing him by placing one heavy rock on top of another on his chest until he suffocated. The boy died an agonizing, painful, gruesome death that few others have ever experienced.

Two days later a search party, under the leadership of Hiram Good, found his small body amidst the pile of bloody stones. It appeared that every bone in his crushed, sunbaked body was broken. His fingers and toes were cut off. Surrounding the body were numerous small footprints. Seeing the horror and brutality of how the young boy died, many of the Guards at that moment solemnly vowed to kill every Indian in Northern California, including the friendly ones, to protect the white community. On that day the Guardsmen crossed the line from community defenders to self-appointed avengers.

Hiram Good was as deeply affected as the other Guardsmen by the hatred and brutality to the Hickock children, but he remained resolute to never deliberately kill a woman or child.

It was later published that to avenge the deaths of some twenty-five to three-hundred settlers killed over a twenty-year period—many of them women and children—some four- thousand two-hundred Yana were killed over the same period—most of them women and children.

The Yahi bore the brunt of all the reprisals. They paid dearly for the deaths of all the settlers.

Conversely, few of the Guards were ever killed by the Indians because they had the advantage of superior firepower. Guardsmen were sometimes accidentally shot by a fellow Guardsman in the "fog of war" or because their fellow Guardsmen were too drunk to shoot straight.

Many Northern California Indians were killed by "bushwhacking." A white would come across an unsuspecting Indian, shoot, kill and scalp, making sure to turn the scalp in for the five-dollar bounty. Hanging followed shooting, followed by bashing with the butt end of a rifle— usually reserved for wounded or prisoners in order to save on the cost of bullets.

Every death on either side was extremely brutal and violent.

KNOWN ATROCITIES
AND BODY COUNTS

T he attacks by whites against the Indians began in 1850 when Bill Ebben and his men attacked and killed twenty-one Yahi warriors and two women over an alleged cattle theft.

The Forty-Niners had arrived.

The warfare continued all through the 1850s and all during the Civil War years, peaking in 1865 and finally ending in 1871 with the Kingsley Cave Massacre. The few surviving Yahi then went into hiding.

In the early 1860s, forty Yahi were killed in one raid as they were innocently swimming in Mill Creek.

In 1864, in one of the worst massacres ever, three hundred peaceful Yana were killed during a morning raid as they gathered together for their annual Acorn Festival.

R. A. Anderson led or participated in the massacre, according to one un-named source, decades later. During the attack, young children fled and were quickly found hiding in bushes and tall grasses. The drunken Guardsmen grabbed the children, held them down, and shot or killed them by smashing their heads in with the butt end of a rifle.

Incredibly, hardly anyone outside of Northern California ever heard of this gruesome massacre. Yet only one decade later when Custer lost his life and the lives of some two hundred sixty-six men in his command, it was news heard around the world. Though Custer was personally spared mutilation by the intervention of two Northern Cheyenne women, most of his soldiers were not. At the Acorn Festival all three hundred Yana were savagely mutilated and scalped by their attackers. Many were raped, including the surviving children, both male and female, and after the rape were then killed by the Guardsmen.

Most of the scalps were turned in for the five-dollar bounty. A few were kept as trophies.

Hiram Good, who was not at the Acorn Festival Massacre, told a newspaper reporter that he thought *only* nine Indians had been killed. Multiple other sources that were there all reported three hundred.

Regardless of the number, Guardsmen and U.S. Army soldiers *always* drank heavily before attacking any Indian village. They drank to lower their inhibitions. Only by drinking could most murder and rape the innocent. They often spent more time drinking then fighting as some fights barely lasted twenty minutes before all the Indians were killed or escaped.

Revenge played heavily into the brutality suffered by the Indians, especially after the murders of the three Hickock children.

The whites did not suffer one single loss in either the Mill Creek or Acorn Festival attacks despite a number of them staggering around, running from tree to tree, tripping over rocks or actually falling off their horses.

The Acorn Festival massacre was one of the worst Indian massacres in nearly four hundred years of white enmity.

The *Final Solution* was in full effect, and Mill Creek literally ran red with the blood of those killed.

Shortly after the Acorn Festival Massacre, another twenty Yana, men, women and children were killed at Cottonwood Creek in an attack led by R. A. Anderson. The irony is that most of the victims, with the sole exception of the Yahi, wanted only peace with the whites.

During a five-month period in 1864, historians estimated that over two thousand Yana and Yahi were killed by various companies of Guards, exclusively under the leadership of R. A. Anderson and Hiram Good. The onslaught was savage and never ending.

By 1865 most of the Yana and Yahi were dead.

In 1865 Ishi's father was killed, quite possibly by R. A. Anderson, at the Three Knolls Massacre. Anderson consistently had the highest body count whenever fighting the Indians. Some of the other Guardsmen, by comparison, did not have any, because they were either too drunk or too stupid to figure out to not bring a broken rifle to a planned attack, as actually happened several times.

Anderson was in the thick of the fighting at Three Knolls when the child Ishi, barely nine, and his mother ran and hid in the dense brush. Ishi watched as his best friend, a boy who would always go to the creek with him to throw pebbles at schooling fish, was shot and killed. A Guardsman then punched the boy's younger sister in the back. As she struggled to get up, she was repeatedly shot by two Guardsmen now standing over her.

All around them tribal members were pushed to their knees and shot in the back of the head. During the killings, Ishi's mother wrapped her son in a blanket, and the two of them slipped into the icy water, pretending to be dead, and floated downstream with the dead bodies of family and tribal members. They were among the few survivors.

After yet another such similar massacre R. A. Anderson walked among the dead, counting them one by one and later proudly bragging to a friend that, "We left forty good Indians lying around."

In August of 1864, an eight-year-old Yana girl was helping out with chores on a local farm. The farm family loved her and treated her as family. They made a bed for her in their home and delighted in her smile at the table. Suddenly, three heavily armed Guardsmen rode to the farm, walked into the farmhouse and snatched the frightened girl from her foster family. The trembling child was forced to stand before the strutting Guardsmen. The girl was so frightened that she made no move to speak or to run away. She stood in front of the farm wife, shaking uncontrollably. In spite of the woman pleading and begging for mercy, repeatedly crying out that this was an innocent child, one of the Guardsmen pulled his pistol and abruptly shot the girl in the head, saying, "We must kill them big and little." Adding, "Nits will be lice."

The three men then rode to another farm in search of another Yana girl by the name of "Eliza." Eliza, barely fourteen, was found at a barn working with her aunt and uncle. Seeing the armed Guardsmen approaching, the three ran to the nearby farm home and sought shelter. The Guardsmen rode over to the home, and one of three yelled out, "Eliza, come out! We are going to kill you!"

Eliza began pleading for her life and the lives of her kin. She said to one of the Guardsmen, "Don't kill me. When you were here I cooked for you. I washed for you. I was kind to you. I never asked pay of you. Don't kill me now."

Eliza, her aunt and uncle, were dragged outside, stood against the barn, and were shot one by one. According to an interview later given by one of the three Guardsmen and repeated by author, Theodora Kroeber, Eliza was shot eleven times in one breast. Even after all the shooting, another of the men declared that, "I don't think that little squaw is dead yet." Taking the butt end of his rifle, he repeatedly bashed her on the head and face until she was no longer recognizable.

The three Guardsmen were never identified by name, according to historical records, though many in the pioneer community knew who they were. The term, "Nits will be lice," is usually associated with R. A. Anderson, and murdering innocent women and children certainly fit in with his personal philosophy. Also, the interview about the killings took place in the early 20th Century. One of the few Guardsmen still alive at that time was R. A. Anderson who never once shied away from his very historic public policy of killing all Indians—including women and children. According to Anderson, such shootings were fully justified as the only way to truly protect the frontier community from future Indian attacks.

In 1867 another forty-five Yahi were killed at the Campo Seco Massacre. R. A. Anderson led the Guardsmen in this massacre. Most of those killed were the women, children and the elderly.

The Mill Creek Indian War began in 1850 and ended when the surviving seventeen Yahi went into hiding after the Kingsley Cave Massacre of 1871. So good were they at hiding that almost forty years went by before any Yahi survivors were accidentally re-discovered.

Anderson was not at the Kingsley Cave Massacre, about the only one he missed, and by this time Indian Ned had already killed Hiram Good.

In the middle of this prolonged war, Ishi was born, with his estimate of his birth year being 1854. As a nine-year-old, he narrowly survived the Three Knolls Massacre. As a seventeen-year-old, he helped tribal members cremate the remains of the murdered Kingsley Cave victims.

The Three Knolls attack and the death of his father and friends traumatized Ishi for all the days of his life. At age seventeen, he went into hiding with the surviving members of his tribe for the next forty years of his life. Every day of his hiding, he feared being found and killed by the whites. It was all he had ever known.

In the very last hour of his life, death from an Englishman became his reality—but not in any way he could ever have anticipated.

THE 1865 MASSACRE
AT THREE KNOLLS

Near midnight, R. A. Anderson and Hiram Good slowly crept up to a Yahi camp along Mill Creek. Anderson and Good had been fighting the Yahi now for many years, though both were still under age thirty. It was a long, bloody struggle, but the whites were prevailing. So far, hundreds of Yana and Yahi had been killed under the leadership of the two Indian fighters.

The Massacre at Three Knolls was to avenge both the deaths of the Hickock children and the killing of three whites at the Workman Ranch in Concow Valley. On this particular trip, Guardsmen from the Concow Valley accompanied Anderson and Good, the brothers Sim and Jake Moak, and Bully Bowman, a cowboy living with Hiram Good.

The men had been tracking the Yahi for several days and finally found their hidden camp.

The two Captains were especially interested in killing the Yahi War Chief, Big-Foot Jack, a warrior widely feared for his leadership and attacks against the whites. It was believed that Big-Foot Jack was responsible for the killings at the Workman Ranch. Big-Foot Jack was so named because he had one very large foot and one very small foot. As such, his distinctive footprints always stood out whenever being tracked.

Late that night, Anderson and Good stripped off their clothing and, carrying nothing but their pistols, entered the ice-cold waters of Mill Creek. They were on a reconnaissance mission to gather intelligence on how many warriors they would be fighting the next morning.

Hiding behind a small log, the two men slowly moved upstream against the current to the Yahi camp. At that hour, most of the Yahi were asleep. Surprisingly, the Yahi had not posted any guards, though they had several posted during the day. If lookouts had been posted, they surely would have taken notice of a log going upstream instead of downstream. As the log swept into shore with Anderson and Good hanging on, a dog suddenly rushed to the creek and began frantically barking. Anderson and

Good were both surprised because the Yahi did not normally keep dogs. This particular dog had been taken from a nearby ranch and was destined for the cooking pot.

Most of the exhausted Mill Creeks were sleeping out under the open stars on a partially moonlit night. Ishi was born into this band—and it was believed to have been a large band—but nowhere is the actual number ever mentioned. Probably the band did not exceed forty because Ishi mentioned that only once in his life did he ever see forty Yahi together.

The dog became frantic, staying on the creek shoreline but constantly lunging at Anderson and Good. Both men held their fire, hoping the dog would just leave. Several of the warriors sat up in their blankets. One shook a young son awake, telling him to go get the dog and to keep it quiet. The boy searched for some rope and then dutifully walked down to the creek. Anderson and Good, hiding as best as they could behind the log, watched the sleepy-eyed boy approach. The log was now only a few feet from the shore and only a few short branches gave any concealment. If the warrior had come down instead of sending his son, the fight would have been on. Instead, Anderson and Good took a deep breath and went under, their pistols kept hidden behind the log.

Most likely, as many of the Indians rolled over and went back to sleep, the Mill Creeks believed the dog to be barking at some wandering deer or raccoons.

In his 1909 book titled, *Fighting the Mill Creeks,* R.A. Anderson wrote this about the dog at Three Knolls: "Suddenly a dog broke forth into wild barking close in front of us, and, springing toward the bank, bayed furiously into our very faces. We could feel his hot breath and could have struck him with our six-shooters had we wished."

The young boy looked around and pulled the dog back, moving him away from the creek. He tied the dog to a nearby tree and began petting him and scratching him behind the ears. Soon, the dog calmed down. Anderson and Good waited another half-hour in the freezing water and then slowly pulled the log back into deeper water and across to the other shore. The two men, with teeth now chattering so loudly they were afraid of detection, quickly made their way back to their companions who were in hiding about a half-mile away. Putting on their clothing, they gave the layout of the camp and even marked locations of the sleeping Yahi.

The Guards would attack early the next morning, hoping to catch the camp still asleep. Fifteen men would attack the Yahi camp including an estimated six or seven from the Concow Valley, where Ishi's band of Yahi had murdered and raped two women and one man. The two women had been mutilated so badly that the Concow men could think of nothing but vengeance. They communicated this to R. A. Anderson who gave them "Free will to do as they pleased."

The next morning, limping with pain from a ripped off toenail, Good took six men and went upstream above the Yahi camp while Anderson took the remainder of the men and made a long circuitous route downstream. Anderson then climbed up a small hill and hid about thirty feet behind one of the three knolls while waiting daybreak. Behind him, standing amongst the trees or crouching down behind the rocks, were the other Guardsmen.

The three knolls were very close to the stream, and only mere feet away from the banks of the stream were the sleeping Indians.

Anderson's flintlock was cocked and primed as he drew a bead on a sleeping Indian.

Good was actually the first to open fire upon the unsuspecting Indians, followed by volley after volley from all the other Guardsmen. According to Anderson, "Into the stream they leaped, but few got out alive. Instead, many dead bodies floated down the rapid current."

One of the Guardsmen later estimated that between thirty-five to forty Indians were killed at Three Knolls.

It is known that two of those floating down the creek were Ishi, who was about nine years old at the time, and his mother. She and Ishi managed to escape, along with several others, by pretending to be dead. Most likely, Ishi's father fought the attacking Guardsmen and provided cover for their escape. Ishi's father was shot multiple times at point-blank range, with R. A. Anderson being the probable shooter. Anderson was one of the attackers closest to the creek, with the defending Indians on one side and the attacking Guardsmen firing away from the other side.

Several Indians were initially shot as they lay sleeping in their blankets. Others were shot as they scrambled for their weapons, but most were killed as they tried to flee their attackers.

Anderson never stated whether he killed his sleeping target or not.

Only a few Indians managed to survive and flee the murderous onslaught. The Concow men were there to avenge the deaths and atrocities to Mrs. Workman, her sister, Miss Smith, and an elderly man known as English John. Anderson had been elected Captain of the Guards for this particular raid, with Hiram Good named as co-captain. Anderson gave the Concow men permission, over Good's strenuous objections that "They were at liberty to deal with the Indians as they saw fit."

Anderson's declaration was code for, "It is okay to kill the prisoners." Good's angry objection was to the fact that women and children would now be killed. Anderson prevailed by reminding everybody of the horrible death suffered by the young Hickock boy at the hands of the Yahi children. Many of the Guardsmen—at this point probably not thinking too clearly—became enraged and tore into the wounded Indians—either shooting them or bashing in their heads with the butt ends of their rifles.

One of the captured warriors was wearing a large stovepipe hat that the Concow men identified as belonging to Mr. Workman. It was a hat identical to that worn by Abraham Lincoln. Several others were wearing white shirts also owned by Mr. Workman, who was not at home when the Indians attacked his ranch. Any Indian wearing Workman clothing was killed to avenge Mrs. Workman who was shot as she tried to escape and then had a large rock thrown against her chest. She survived in great agony for nearly twenty-four hours before dying from her wounds. The Indians had also taken some of her clothing.

In the last few minutes of her life, Mrs. Workman could not even cry out because she was choking on blood spurting from her mouth.

To avenge the Workman Ranch murders, some of the wounded Indian survivors were brutally killed by having their throats cut. All were scalped. So great was the rage over the deaths and rape of the Workman women that dead Indians were shot over and over and then had their throats slit.

"Captains" were elected by their peer group to lead the charge against the Indians. The Captain's word was law. The Captain or Co-Captains would create the battle plan, and the men were fully expected to follow the plan. Guardsmen only elected men as captains if they had experience, knowledge and proven prowess as Indian fighters. Both Hiram Good and R. A. Anderson had extensive leadership experience, and both always had the highest body counts from any attack upon the Indians. Some of the Guardsmen, in spite of their best efforts, never managed to shoot any Indians, while Anderson was documented to have once singlehandedly shot and killed nine warriors in just one hour of one battle. As such, the statistical probabilities are good that either Anderson or Good or both may well have killed Ishi's father, especially given their very front-line positions in the attack.

In the final aftermath of the fight, a toddler with six toes on one foot and "its" mother were spared—not out of any sense of compassion, but only because Hiram Good wanted the child. "It" was an "oddity," and Good wanted him. Anderson agreed to the request as a show of friendship and solidarity to a fellow Captain. As the Guardsmen and the child's mother headed away from the smoldering Yahi camp, the young woman soon sat down and refused to go any further. She just collapsed on the trail. Her eyes were vacant, and she kept shaking her head, seemingly "shell-shocked" from the brutal attack.

Everything she had ever known in her life—marriage, motherhood, family and tribe—a way of life that she loved had been suddenly and brutally stripped away from her.

Several attempts were made to get her to move, but she would not budge. She literally could not put one foot in front of the other, in part because she had been wounded in one foot. Some of the Guardsmen believed she was just being stubborn because her wound appeared to be minor. They were getting impatient. They wanted to get home in time for dinner.

Anderson whispered to a henchman by the name of Frank Curtis to go back and shoot her. Seeing the man approaching with a drawn pistol, the trembling woman first drew back and then, looking at her child, leaned forward and gave "it" a kiss good-bye. She was now crying with great sobbing shrieks rolling out from her thin body. Knowing what was about to happen, she grabbed the child's hand, pulled a shawl over her head and stretched out face down on the ground, squeezing tightly to her loved one as Curtis fired one shot into her head—right in front of her child.

Curtis then scalped the woman, tying her long hair around his saddle horn with the blood-soaked scalp brushing against his stirrup.

There are two contradictory footnotes about the toddler with six toes on one foot, whom Anderson could only refer to as "It."

Sim Moak wrote, decades after the massacre, that the child was a girl and that Hiram Good gave her to the pioneer Barrington Family. She took ill and died soon thereafter, according to Moak.

A. L. Kroeber, a University friend and mentor of Ishi, wrote in a 1911 newspaper article that the child was a boy. Ishi was most likely the source of that information, but Kroeber never identified his source. Kroeber's wife, Theodora, went on to write two biographies of Ishi and included her husband's published belief that the child was a boy, as well as Moak's identification that the child was a girl.

The attack at Three Knolls was over in twenty minutes, according to Sim Moak, but then the rest of the day was spent in looting and pillaging because the Indians were known to sometimes have large sums of money, which they obtained by raiding or trade.

The distinct footprints of one person having both a very large foot and a very small foot were never again seen after the massacre at Three Knolls.

Neither R. A. Anderson nor Sim Moak ever wrote down the number of Indians killed at Three Knolls, only writing, "Many." This was Ishi's band, probably one of the largest bands of the remaining Mill Creeks, and after the attack at Three Knolls and the Kingsley Cave Massacre, only a small number of Mill Creeks were now still alive.

THE ACTS OF A
COMPASSIONATE "HUMANITARIAN"

In April of 1871, the Kingsley Cave Massacre occurred. Four cowboys, J. J. Bogard, Jim Baker, Scott Wellman and their foreman, Norman Kingsley, were out looking for stray cattle when they stumbled across some thirty-three Yahi hiding in a cave. They found the hiding Yahi by following a blood trail from a butchered cow leading right to the cave. The cowboys quickly dismounted and, without any provocation, opened fire. The Mill Creeks were never given a chance to surrender.

The large cave was on a steep sloping hillside. The four men stood outside the open entrance and poured in one murderous volley after another. Within minutes, the defending Yahi warriors were killed. In an effort to protect their wives and children, the warriors threw themselves at their attackers only to be instantly cut down. After the warriors were killed, the cowboys took their time methodically reloading then executing the remaining women, children and the elderly. At one point, Kingsley came across a crying two-year-old clinging to his dead mother with both of his arms stretched across her back, clearly trying to protect her. In an interview given later in life, Kingsley revealed that before shooting this child and several others, he had to switch from his rifle to his pistol because his, "Big-bore rifle tore them up so."

Kingsley perhaps perceived himself as a "humanitarian" for his thoughtful consideration of the Yahi children.

Some whites, perhaps many, rightly believed the young cowboys massacred the Indians for no other reason than to make a name for themselves in the small pioneer community.

Ishi and his mother were not in the cave when the massacre took place. They returned to the cave later in the day—only to find all their friends and family murdered.

In accordance with Yahi tradition, Ishi and the remaining Yahi cremated the victims to release their spirits to the "Land of the Dead" where they would live in peace and friendship with all people for all eternity. Cremation was done at great personal risk because the four cowboys were still in the area. In spite of the risk of another attack, the Yahi survivors carried out the cremations. It was something they absolutely had to do. To not cremate the remains meant that the spirit of their loved ones would always be locked to the earth. The ghosts of those not cremated would seek out and haunt the survivors, bringing much fear and physical harm to them.

Neither Kingsley nor any of his men were ever charged or indicted for the killings.

The war against the Yahi ran from approximately 1850 until the Kingsley Cave Massacre in 1871. R. A. Anderson, to the surprise of many, always insisted that the war was not started by the Indians but was, in fact, started by early pioneer whites, such as the Ebben and Carty families. Anderson also firmly believed that a number of the Yahi were still living and hiding out in the Mill Creek area, even well into the Twentieth Century.

It seems the Carty Family fired some of the very first shots against the Yahi over a missing cow.

THE CARTY FAMILY COW

The Cartys* moved to Northern California in the early 1850s to start a ranch. Wherever they came from, they brought with them the prevailing attitude of prejudice against anyone not also white—especially Indians. Most Indians were widely regarded as "savages" by the community of settlers and not to be trusted under any circumstances—not even the friendly ones who worked on their farms and ranches.

One morning the Cartys noticed the family milk cow was missing. Somehow, they convinced themselves that the cow had been stolen and eaten by the Indians. They made no attempt to verify this; it was just something they intuitively knew. Angry, heavily armed, some twelve of the Cartys and their hired hands rode out seeking revenge. They found a group of nearby Indians camped along a stream. They snuck up and attacked the unsuspecting Indians with a fury, firing at them from behind rocks and trees. Two of the men, on horseback, rode a young Indian woman down. As she was running, the men began galloping their horses after her, one on each side. One of the laughing men reached out, his pistol almost touching the back of her head, and pulled the trigger. She tumbled several times. The bullet came out through her left eye. The men quickly dismounted and searched her for any valuables. Then they stripped and scalped her, tying her long black hair to a saddle horn—a common practice at the time. Scalps were widely viewed as trophies, proof positive of the courage and bravery of the man who possessed the scalp. Scalps were also worth five dollars, an average of about a week's pay.

Her body was left where she died.

Over the next several hours, the attackers shot and killed an additional seven men. Those deaths were apparently not enough to appease the family anger. They returned the next day to another village, already in deep mourning over the loss of family and friends from the first village, and this time killed fourteen men and one more woman.

In a two-day period, the Carty group took it upon themselves to murder twenty-three human beings over one cow.

The following morning, their missing cow turned up. The bawling cow had stepped through a broken fence and was found grazing upon a neighbor's pasture.

Not one member of the Carty Family or their employees was ever brought to trial, nor charged with any crime, for the killing of the Indians. The fact that the missing cow had been found mattered not at all to most whites. Instead, the Cartys were widely hailed as heroes for leading the charge against the "thieving redskins" even though the cow theft never happened. Most of the rough and tumble pioneer community, who lived in abject fear of Indian attacks, though few attacks actually occurred, truly believed the Cartys to be heroes, not killers. Still, many others in the pioneer community saw them for exactly what they were but, out of fear, kept their true feelings to themselves.

The whites had dealt the first serving of mass murder. Some twenty-one years later—right after the 1871 Kingsley Cave Massacre, there were now only fifteen to seventeen Yahi left. The small band of survivors went into hiding in one of the most inaccessible areas available to them, a place deep in a rattlesnake-infested canyon where the whites would never think to look. For the next forty years, the tiny dwindling tribe lived in complete seclusion, always looking over their shoulders, deathly fearful of any contact with the whites. Their last refuge was some five hundred feet up a sheer canyon wall, living on a small two-acre ledge, and hiding inside an abandoned bear cave known as *Wowunupo'mu Tena* (Bear's Hiding Place). They would only hunt and fish at night. Trips for freshwater were always made under darkness. Footprints would be swept away with brush. Rarely were they ever seen. One by one the group died off, either from old age or accidents. The loss of each valued tribal member took a terrible toll upon the small community. It was more than just dying, for that was an understood part of life; rather, each loss sounded the death knell of a once-proud nation.

Late in life, Ishi made only one statement to ever having been married while in hiding. He apparently lost both his wife and child to a drowning accident. The memory so saddened and depressed him that he never talked about his family again, even to his closest friends.

Carty is a fictitious name used to protect the identities of descendants of the original Pioneer family still in California.

THE BUREAU
OF INDIAN AFFAIRS

I n 1830, President Andrew Jackson made a political decision, rubber-stamped by Congress with only a one-vote margin, to finally solve the ongoing Indian problem. It was a decision fraught with failure and one that cost thousands of Indians their very lives. The decision was to round up all troublesome warring tribes and ship them to newly formed reservations in the Western United States.

The legislation became known as "The Indian Act."

A number of young bureaucrats from the Bureau of Indian Affairs and related agencies decided that the best way to meet the Congressional mandate was to have the U.S. Army gather up the tribes and force the Indians to march westward. The Indians could then be "watched" on the reservations and, with the Army there to contain them, it was believed the various Indian attacks and wars would end.

It was a policy of "Out of sight—out of mind—end of troubles."

Most of the program planners in this "Final Solution" were often in their early twenties, and most had never been West of Washington, D.C. They wanted to meet the objectives of Congress by solving the problem as quickly as possible and at the lowest possible cost, which would reflect well on their respective federal agencies. Most of the BIA employees were well intentioned, but some of the more self-serving bureaucrats knew that by implementing the program at the lowest possible cost, their career paths would then be greatly enhanced. This meant recognition for their work, which translated into promotions and higher pay. While others might have had a nobler goal, such as saving lives on all sides, in the end the bureaucrats gave the Indian nothing but a rushed, poorly thought-out program created by inexperienced people that caused nothing but misery, sadness and death for Native Americans.

Thousands of Indians died due to President Jackson's decision, even though the Government repeatedly told the Indians that the program was for their benefit. To convince the Indians to move, they were promised abundant food and medicine to meet all their needs. That never happened. Some food made its way to the reservations, only to be sold on the "black market" by a handful of crooked Indian agents more concerned about lining their pockets than feeding the people. Some of the items not sold were simply inedible. The processed meat given to the Indians was sometimes crawling with maggots, while other foods were often covered with mold.

Special Agent Walton of the BIA, as he reviewed his Agency's history on a snowy afternoon, was appalled at some of the Agency's mishandling of their charges. "No wonder," he thought, "that senior management wants to keep all this old stuff hidden away."

After the Civil War, the bureaucrats decided that the best way to end the Northern California Indian Wars was to gather up the bands of troublemakers and ship them to the Nome Lockee Reservation. The Yahi became the primary target because they caused the most problems.

Rounding up the Yahi was yet another colossal failure, as the bands of Mill Creek's fled to the high Sierras and went into hiding. For months, the Army combed the valleys and mountains but could not find one single warrior.

Meanwhile, the Yahi were constantly changing their hiding places in their rugged homeland. They always had the Army under watch. The Army was burdened down with horses, wagons and inefficient leadership. The Yahi had no horses or wagons. Their entire lifestyle was one of guerilla warfare. It was all they knew. Superb war chiefs who always had the best interests of the tribe at heart led them. Whenever they heard the Army advancing toward one of their camps, the bands would disburse and melt away into the forest where they would quickly set up another camp.

This placed the U.S. Army in an embarrassing situation, as the Government now had an unoccupied reservation. So the Army rounded up Indians from the peaceful tribes and sent *them* to the reservation. The Army then declared victory but, after a few months at Nome Lockee, most of the now-starving Indians simply wandered off and walked back to their traditional homeland.

Several years later, with only a handful of Indians remaining, Nome Lockee closed. Today, few in the BIA even know where the reservation was originally located.

Special Agent Walton of the Bureau of Indian Affairs carefully closed the yellowed file detailing the Government's pursuit of the Yahi Indians.

"Incredible," he thought. "Those poor people—hunted down and killed by the Guards, then chased for months on end by the Army to force any survivors to a reservation."

Page after page in the file detailed surprise attacks upon the Yahi and then recorded the body count. At first Walton suspected the count to be inflated but then realized that band after band of the Yahi were being systemically killed, often with an entire band perishing in one day. The same names kept appearing over and over as Indian fighters: Bill Ebben, R. A. Anderson, Hiram Good, Pentz (later known as "Pence"), the Carty Family, Sandy Young, John Breckenridge, Bully Bowman, and the Moak Brothers.

The Moak Brothers were in a different class from the others. They were not leaders but were hangers-on, like today's "groupies" with rock stars. Sim Moak wrote a book about being a Guardsman and fighting the Yahi, often under co-captains, R. A. Anderson and Hiram Good. The book was titled, *The Last of the Mill Creeks and Early Life in Northern California.*

For the most part, it was a book of adulation about Hiram Good and R. A. Anderson. A lot of the material supported or duplicated what Anderson had written about in his own book of fighting the Mill Creeks.

For Sim and his brother, Jake, killing the Yahi apparently was great sport. It was a game—one in which the Guards often held the prevailing hand. Dangerous, yes, because the Yahi fought back against insurmountable odds. Sometimes the Yahi won, surprising the Guardsmen and ambushing them, killing and wounding the occasional Guardsman, but mostly it was the Guardsmen who carried the day.

The one person Walton had a hard time figuring out was Hiram Good. Only two pictures were known to exist of Hiram Good. Both pictures showed a tall, well-built man with a strong look and belief that what he was doing was right. Walton admired Good's principles of never attacking women or children, but he just couldn't square that with Good's dogged pursuit, sometimes for weeks or even months, of tracking down and killing Indians. While Good drew the line about shooting women and children, if he couldn't find any Yahi warriors, he would attack peaceful Indians from other tribes to collect warrior scalps, which he then proudly displayed by knotting them to a tree outside his cabin door.

Plain and simple, Jackson's "Indian Act," was a miserably failed Federal policy operating under the guise of protecting settlers from Indians. It was not even a well-intentioned act. The entire piece of legislation was cobbled together to solve a political problem for people in Congress. Thousands of Native Americans died so that politicians running for re-election could tell their constituents that the Indian problem ". . . was now solved."

Walton made a phone call to a friend in the FBI, Special Agent Patrick Adams. Together, the two men had solved several of the homicides that had occurred on Indian Reservations. The FBI was the lead agency in working felony crime in Indian country, and Agent Adams was always a good guy to have as a partner.

Walton would send him the Yahi file; then the two would meet. At the very least, they might solve the case of the missing hunter and, ideally, find the hiding Yahi, which was rapidly becoming a top priority for both State and Federal agencies.

ISHI IN HIDING
1871 TO 1908

O nly five Yahi were documented to have actually lived into the Twentieth Century. The survivors were Ishi, his mother, his sister, an uncle and one older warrior. One of the two older warriors, believed to be Ishi's uncle, then died in a drowning accident. Though an entire Industrial Revolution was now sweeping the nation, the Yahi lived as they had always lived—as a Stone-Age tribe, surviving by the bow and arrow, surviving only on what they could hunt or gather.

While the few remaining Yahi knew of the reservations, they wanted no part of reservation life, which meant giving up their freedom and traditional way of life. Surrendering also carried with it the highly probable risk of being killed by the whites.

Yet each day, the four surviving Yahi would stand on a high, rocky crag, look to the West and see iron wagons traveling throughout the delta farmland. Civilization was fast approaching their mountain stronghold.

In 1908, long after the Indian wars had ended, a group of surveyors from the Oro Light, Water and Power Company, led by a local rancher named Jack Merle Apperson and his two sons, Fred and Merle, were close to the hidden Yahi camp. The Appersons and several other cowboys had been hired as guides for the surveyors. The power company wanted to build some high mountain flumes to transport water to generate electricity at a nearby-proposed dam. Jack Apperson was scouting out the next day's route with surveyor Charley Herrick, and began climbing up a wickedly steep embankment. He and Herrick had walked right by Ishi without ever seeing him. Slipping, Apperson leaned forward to grab some brush at the very moment that Ishi fired an arrow at him from behind a nearby tree. Ishi was aiming for Apperson's head, and the arrow just barely missed, grazing the underneath brim of his hat. Ironically, at that very moment, Herrick had been vehemently arguing with Apperson that it was impossible for any Mill Creeks to have survived into the Twentieth Century.

Two members of the survey party told Herrick and Apperson that they had spotted a naked Indian fishing with a long harpoon only the day before. Apparently, Herrick did not believe them.

While Herrick may have been in error about surviving Mill Creeks, he no longer was in doubt, according to Herrick. The arrow, which Apperson snagged while running away, caused a major change in Herrick's thinking.

Though no one knew it at the time, Ishi literally fired the very last arrow in nearly four hundred years of Indian warfare.

Ishi fully intended to kill the rancher to protect his tiny band, yet Apperson was providentially spared. Apperson and Herrick immediately fled and alerted the nearby survey party. On the next morning, when the surveyors and their cowboy guides returned, they all were heavily armed. They carried both repeating rifles and double-action pistols. One of the surveyors was even given a semi-automatic pistol for his protection, which he did not know how to operate.

Ishi met Apperson again in a 1914 University-sponsored trip to Ishi's old homeland. The two men smiled and shook hands. Both seemed to feel awkward about the shooting incident. An old, grainy, black and white picture exists with Jack Apperson resting one hand on Ishi's shoulder and a very uncomfortable Ishi leaning away from Apperson, perhaps in part because Apperson was still wearing his old cowboy pistol.

Since time immemorial, the Yahi took a survival cue from the animal world and would always freeze upon chance discovery, remaining absolutely motionless, knowing that the slightest movement might reveal their presence. High on a sheer canyon ledge they remained in deep hiding. Fearful of the heavily armed whites coming toward them—especially the cowboys from nearby ranches—the Yahi hiders simply froze as they had safely done so many times before.

This time things would not work out quite so well.

According to the surveyors' own words, had they walked just a few yards to the left or right, they would have completely missed the hidden Yahi village.

The band of Indians lived in three tiny huts made from tree branches and covered with brush, also concealing the entrance to a nearby small cave. All four Yahi occupants remained in hiding until the last possible moment.

As the surveyors and cowboy guides stumbled into the camp, an older Yahi man and a younger woman, later identified as Ishi's sister, suddenly broke cover and were seen running to a hidden trail. The brush-filled trail was an escape route down the steep canyon wall to a nearby creek pinery.

Ishi at the same moment was hiding in some thick growth, covering their escape with his bow. Just moments before running into the brush, Ishi managed to throw some old animal skin blankets over his crippled mother, completely hiding her. Several of the blankets were made from bobcat capes all sewn together. Several others were made from rabbit skin.

The ruse did not work.

Three snarling dogs that were accompanying the survey party began to strain against their leashes, tugging and fighting over the animal blankets. Within moments, Ishi's mother was discovered.

Ishi made ready to shoot at the party, hoping to kill one or more of the whites before they killed him. Even though his mother could not walk, Ishi was hoping that his sacrifice might allow her to crawl off and hide in the brush. Crawling away into the brush and hiding was something they had done decades before, and both had survived while tribal and family members all around them were brutally executed.

Ishi was terrified that the whites were now getting ready to kill his mother. It was, after all, what had *always* happened whenever the whites discovered the Yahi.

As a warrior, Ishi knew that he would have to kill the whites in order to protect his tiny band. He held back for just a moment, trying to decide which of the whites to shoot first. Instead, to his surprise, the young men tried to comfort his mother, as she was shaking uncontrollably. Unable to stand, her legs heavily bandaged with old scraps of cloth, the tiny, crippled woman began crying and pleading for her life in her native tongue. So intense was her fear that she was actually pulling out small clumps of her white hair while begging for mercy.

Several from the survey party guessed her to be over one hundred years old due to her cracked, lined face and wispy grey hair. Realistically, she was probably somewhere in her late seventies or early eighties, given Ishi's age. She had at most two more days to live.

The scene was heart wrenching, and Ishi decided he had no choice but to attack. He knew he would be killed, but maybe if he could kill one or two of the whites before they shot him, the others might run off. His mother might then be saved. He pulled back on his bow just as one of the men offered his mother some water. Ishi held off as the men tried to converse with her, but she did not know any English or Spanish, and they did not know any of the Indian languages. Ishi also did not understand or speak a single word of English. All he knew was that after forty years of hiding in the wilderness, the heavily armed whites had finally found them and were now going to kill them.

He remained completely hidden in the brush—only several yards away from some of the survey party—his bow fully drawn and pointing at one of the surveyors. He clutched several arrows in his bow hand and had a full quiver on his back. At one point, his arm began to weaken, and he nearly loosed an arrow upon the intruders, but his mother was now in a direct line of fire.

To Ishi's surprise, the surveyors did give his mother some water. The accompanying cowboys meanwhile commenced to loot the entire village of bows, arrows, clothing, snares, baskets—and even food. Several of them later said that they took *some* souvenirs, not to force the Indians into starvation, but because the artifacts taken would be of historical value due to the Mill Creeks being a "lost tribe." Within one hour, they stripped the surviving tribal members of their entire wealth and food bank. Nothing was left.

Talking amongst themselves, the surveyors resolved to come back the next day with a wagon and carry the elderly woman down the mountain to a doctor for treatment of her crippled legs. It was, according to their thinking, the least they could do.

Jack Apperson, according to author Theodora Kroeber, searched his pockets for something to leave as a "trade item" for what he and the others had taken. The only thing he had was his pistol, which he kept.

In a moment of excitement, flushed with the finding of a long-lost tribe of Indians and laden down with booty, several of the young cowboys began yelling and screaming, all the while repeatedly firing their rifles and pistols into the air.

When the survey party came back the next day, all four Yahi were gone.

After the intruders had left, Ishi ran to his mother and carried her down the hidden trail to the creek below. They decided to flee to the forests of Mt. Lassen. At one point in their escape, they had to cross a busy highway now filled mostly with farm wagons and a handful of iron wagons. Several times they tried to cross, only to be forced back by the sudden appearance of yet another vehicle.

Two days later, while carrying his mother uphill on his back through the forest, she whispered for some water. Late in life, Ishi told friends that he placed her against a tree and ran to a nearby stream. When he returned a few minutes later, she had died. Coyotes began to gather, starting to feed upon her body. Ishi killed one with an arrow and drove the rest of them off, literally using his bow to beat the starving animals away.

Overwhelmed with sadness, fatigue, fear and sorrow, Ishi forced himself to begin the ceremonial prayers for the dead. He began gathering branches for his mother's funeral pyre and lovingly cremated her remains. Even if it cost him his life, he was determined to follow Yahi tradition and release her spirit to the spirit world. There, all her pain and suffering would be over, and she could rest in eternal peace. Soon after, she was gone, the burning embers mixing with her ashes, all-blowing upward to the Yahi Land of the Dead.

ISHI'S SEARCH FOR FAMILY

After several days, still in shock and deep mourning, Ishi forced himself to several pre-arranged meeting spots, searching for his sister and her companion. He never found them. For months on end, he traveled throughout Deer Creek and Mill Creek looking for his family or any other remaining Yahi. Leaving the delta canyons, he returned to Mt. Lassen and wandered aimlessly through the vast wilderness, searching for any telltale signs left by survivors. He left small rock cairns at well-known trails as signs that he were looking for them. Hidden food and weapon caches he found undisturbed.

Returning to the canyons, he searched all up and down various streambeds in case they had drowned. He traveled from one deserted village site to another—even taking the risk of calling out to any hiding survivors. He searched everywhere and eventually concluded that something terrible must have happened. He came to believe in his heart that the other two tribal members had either drowned or been killed or captured by the whites.

He truly believed himself to be the last remaining Yahi.

What Ishi did not know then, and never found out later, is that he was under constant surveillance by his sister and the older warrior. They never revealed themselves to Ishi because they knew him to be a ghost, ready to exact terrible vengeance upon them for not cremating his remains. As such, Ishi would never know peace because his spirit would forever be locked to the earth, not to the Yahi Land of the Dead.

With all the gunfire and celebratory screaming from their discovered camp, they knew he could not have possibly survived.

Ironically, the two in hiding were more afraid of Ishi's ghost than of roaming armed whites.

Two years later, now with small children, Ishi's sister decided that for the safety of her family they must flee Northern California and head north, far from Ishi's ghost. They had been hiding deep in the Mt. Lassen forest but, time after time, Ishi had nearly stumbled upon them, once passing a mere twenty feet away while they hid behind a pine tree. For the first time in their lives, his sister, her companion and their children left the only homeland they had ever known and started to walk north.

Two days into their journey, a heavy rain fell, forcing the family to seek shelter under a small rock outcropping. Crawling through the brush to the overhang, they were surprised to find a Yahi widow with five small children also in hiding. All were shivering from the cold rain. The children were wearing threadbare scraps of clothing. For the first few moments, all parties were concerned that the others might themselves be ghosts. Finally convincing each other that they meant no harm, the two families spent much of the night talking, and by early morning they decided that they would all travel together to the remote Oregon wilderness.

The adults and their children walked for days on end until finally reaching the high mountain plateaus of Central Oregon. With abundant game for food and vast forests for hiding, the tiny band felt that they had finally arrived at a safe and secure place where they would be able to live out their lives in peace.

Two and a half years after initial discovery, on August 28, 1911, Ishi was captured in Northern California near Oroville, nearly naked, alone and starving. His hair was burnt to his scalp in mourning for his family. He had deer bones dangling from each ear and a wooden plug through his septum. He carried no weapons and had only a few dried berries and several pieces of smoked venison for food. A picture was taken of him in a poncho given to him by his captors. He looked as if the world had come crashing down around his ears.

Ishi stepped out of the hidden past and became the last known American twentieth century stone-age warrior. For the remaining four years and seven months of his life, he learned the mysterious ways of the white man. He would live his life in an exemplary way to bring honor to his people.

Unknown to Ishi was that hundreds of miles to the north, a small band of Yahi survivors were now carving out a new homeland for themselves, one forever free of the Englishmen and from the terrifying power of ghosts.

SNOWBOUND

EARLY NOVEMBER

Three young cowboys sit in a small line cabin near Paulina Mountain, deep in the Ochocos. The men are drinking beer, playing cards and taking turns keeping the small wood stove roaring. Two of the men are brothers, Darrell and Randall. Both are ranch hands. Their father had been a ranch hand, and his father before him a ranch hand. The whole family, for nearly the past hundred years or so, at one time or another had buckarooed on most of the big ranches in Central Oregon.

The brothers are both hard-working men, who know cattle, horses, and the ins and outs of ranch life.

The three had been snowed in for several days and were getting on each other's nerves. Cold days filled with smothering snow bothered them. They were all used to long hours of hard work because ranch work never, ever ended. Even the two brothers, who rarely disagreed, were on edge, not so much with each other, but more so with the new hand.

Turning to the new man, Jesse, Darrell said, "I don't believe it."

"You better believe it," said Jesse, "I know what I saw, and I know what happened."

Jesse was starting to get angry, causing Randall to wryly observe, "I think any parent who names their kid Jesse James has pretty much carved out that child's future."

Jesse slammed his open palm down on the card table, knocking cards and beer cans to the ground.

"I've never been convicted of any felonies, and the most I've ever done has been a little bit of county time. Got it?"

"Only because you were bragging about pleading your charges down to misdemeanors, and what you're proposing right now is a serious, world-class felony," said Darrell.

Darrell and Randall were a little older, more experienced and both were much bigger than Jesse. Still, being challenged did not sit well with Jesse. What the two "Doofus Brothers" Jesse's favorite description of them, though not one he shared with them, did not know was that Jesse always carried a pistol hidden beneath his coat. Though he had never used his pistol, Jesse felt it helped to compensate for his somewhat small size. If push ever came to shove, Jesse felt that at least he would be able to hold his own.

Before the snows came, Jesse was high up on Paulina Mountain looking for strays. If a rancher ran three hundred head of cattle in the Forest Service wilderness, he had to expect to lose a few animals each year to depredation. Jesse was merely looking for any unbranded calves or "mavericks" that he could sell on the black market. The ranch owner would not be any the wiser, and Jesse would be bringing his pay level up to what it should be—according to Jesse.

Jesse often thought the selling of "unbranded calves" to be his personal 401K Plan.

In another era, this was called cattle rustling, and cattle rustlers when caught were sometimes summarily hanged. That also did not sit well with Jesse. He truly believed that finding lost, unbranded calves just sitting around in the woods with a stupid look on their faces was nothing more than an income-redistribution plan, minus all the messy business of hanging.

Jesse knew of only two states that still allowed hanging for selected crimes—Washington and Utah—but he also knew that some ranchers were peculiar about cattle theft and would from time to time take the law into their own hands. Jesse was convinced that a cousin of his down in California had met such a fate for his practice of "thinning the herd." One day his cousin announced that he was going to a remote, high mountain ranch to look for some unbranded calves, and he was never seen again. Not only did the rancher make his cousin disappear, but also his horse was gone, never to be seen again.

Jesse really regretted telling the two brothers what he saw when he was out looking for "strays." Jesse was also pretty sure that the two had both been kicked in the head by their respective horses because he was giving them pure gold, and they were treating it like cow slurry.

"How old is she," asked a smiling Darrell, even though Jesse had already told him she had white hair.

"I don't know how old she is, Darrell. It's not like I could get up close and personal to her and calculate out her age."

Darrell and Randall were truly dumber than a sack full of hammers, thought Jesse. He was offering to let them in on a million-dollar idea, and they just couldn't wrap their simple "pea brains" around it.

Jesse kept looking at his watch, as if he could somehow end the snow. He was jumpy, with places to go and things to do.

Randall jumped in with, "But you did say she was a fast runner, right?"

"Fast and sneaky," said Jesse.

"Is that how she got the drop on you?" asked Randall.

"She did not get the drop on me," snapped Jesse. "If you remember, I told you I was up high looking several hundred feet down when I spotted her. She was alone and carrying a bloody deer leg all covered up with hide. She took it over near a rock outcropping and dropped it. Then she ran away. I don't know how she knew I was there, but I waited a few minutes and went down to see why she had dropped that deer leg. Next thing I know, she's above me and throwing big rocks down at me. Damn near knocked me out but I ran off.   Not exactly what I would call, 'getting the drop on me'."

Darrell simply observed, "Who got hit and who didn't?"

Jesse turned a beet red, but Randall calmed him down by quietly asking, "Jesse, how do you know that she's really from a lost tribe of Indians? I was born and raised here, and I've never heard of any such lost tribe."

Jesse said, "I rodeoed up in Prineville last year with a couple of Indians from Warm Springs, and we were sitting in my truck having a few beers when they told me. Seems those stories about wild Indians up in the Ochocos have been going around the Rez for years. My Indian friends were pretty straight with me, and I believe them. Now let me ask you a question. You tell me why some old lady all dressed in Indian garb would be running around in the middle of the wilderness carrying a deer leg?"

Darrell and Randall both shrugged their shoulders.

Jesse paused to gather his thoughts and spit some tobacco chew into an old coffee cup.

Randall turned to Darrell and loudly exclaimed, "Remind me to never use *that* cup again!"

Smiling now, happy that he knew something the others didn't, Jesse ignored Randall and said, "There was a whole bunch of bones scattered all around where she dropped that piece of deer. That's why I think she'll be back. I know the general location, and something's going on there. I believe she's some type of wild Indian hiding out from everybody. All we have to do is lasso her, and we get her on TV and split the profits—forty percent for me and thirty each for you two. We would be on the news, on all those daytime reality shows, maybe even Oprah. I bet we could make a million dollars out of this," said Jesse.

"You do know that Oprah retired many years ago," said Randall.

"She would come back for this," said Jesse, "like a special or something."

"What's the Indian lady's percentage of these divided profits," Darrell dryly asked.

"She doesn't get any," said Jesse, emphatically, "because she has never seen or heard of TV. Or money. So there's no need to cut her in for any money when she has no place to spend any money or any right to any money. After we're done milking this for everything we can get, we just take her back here and cut her loose to her people."

"We capture and kidnap her, and we don't get arrested for this? How do we even know who her people are?" Randall asked, looking squarely at Jesse.

"I know who they are," said Jesse, "They're Mill Creeks—part of the renegade Yahi tribe up from California. They hid down there for forty years, got found, and they've been hiding up here ever since."

Darrell asked, "So you think we just lasso this lady and put her on TV, and we fairly divide up the profits?"

"You got it," said Jesse.

Randall asked, "Your math is off about the splitting of profits, by the way, but how come, again, we never heard of the Mill Creeks?"

"Most folks haven't, but I grew up on a ranch near Helltown, California, and we surely heard about them down there. Everybody did, especially when their last warrior, a man named Ishi, gave it up and surrendered."

Jesse announced he had to drain off some beer and quickly stepped out of the tiny cabin, pleasantly surprised by the appearance of a blue sky.

Randall and Darrell were quietly talking amongst themselves when Jesse returned.

"Stopped snowing," said Jesse, "guess we go back to work."

Randall and Darrell nodded in agreement. Though riding through deep snow was not their favorite thing to do, it had to be better than being cooped up with Jesse.

"Listen," said Darrell, putting his face mere inches away from Jesse's face, "should you find any of these 'lost' Indians, include us out of your hair-brained scheme. We want no part of it. Understood?"

A chagrined Jesse, silently fuming, could feel his face again redden as he mumbled, "Understood."

Darrell and Randall suited up for the cold and went out to feed the horses. Jesse swept the remaining beer cans to the floor. He hadn't been talked to like that in years. He would find that old lady and somehow put some real money in his pocket, whether it was from Oprah or Project Oregon, it didn't really matter to Jesse. Once he had money, he could move back to California, far away from the Doofus Brothers, who apparently were too lazy to better themselves.

The men split up to resume work, and Jesse immediately rode out to the trailer office of Project Oregon. Jesse visited once a week for a weekly retainer fee of fifty dollars. He would meet with the project manager, only one of two people on-site, to let him know what, if anything was going on in the Ochocos.

The manager was constantly worried about somebody finding some obscure weed, plant or bug that might bring a screaming halt to the company's geothermal plant. The nine hundred-million-dollar project was to be constructed in the Newberry Caldera, right in the heart of the Paulina wilderness. The plant would create an estimated fifteen-hundred family-wage jobs. If the Spotted Owl could stop all logging in Oregon because it was endangered, then a tribe of lost Indians living in the Ochocos would surely bring the geothermal project to a screeching halt. Millions of dollars in both research monies and permit filings would be forever lost. Project Oregon was determined to see the plant through to completion. They were not in business to lose large sums of money. The geothermal plant, using underground steam to generate electricity, would happen in spite of growing opposition.

Jesse kept spurring his horse through the deep snow, knowing that with what he had to report, the project manager was about to experience some major heartburn.

STORM WARNINGS

Warden Ryan, Mason and Buster stood outside the ODFW office, discussing the emergency meeting. All three felt it had gone well. Deputy Johansen initially had to be convinced that the film was real and not solely for his benefit, but he quickly came around. The five Federal Agents were headed back to their respective offices. BIA Special Agent Walton was especially looking forward to an extensive re-read of the yellowed Yahi file. To the best of his knowledge, his was the only federal agency with an open, active file on the Yahi.

Deputy Johansen, meanwhile, was heading back to the Sheriff's Station for a briefing on a nearby marijuana farm found in Shevlin Park—a large, heavily timbered county park, only ten minutes from downtown Bend.

Cold snow clouds began spilling over from the Cascades. The local Z21 weatherperson was predicting major snowfall for most of December. Already the temperature had dropped twenty degrees, and the skies were clouding over. Mason zippered his heavy parka, then looked over at Buster who stood outside in just his shirtsleeves, earnestly talking to Ryan about coordinating a trip to the Paulinas.

"How is it that I, a beautiful creature of the forest, with a superb insulation package, am freezing, and you're out here like you're in Southern California?" asked Mason.

"I dunno," said Buster. "I never really feel the cold that much." Looking at Mason's red bandanna, Buster suggested, "You should wear a hat. Most heat loss is through the head, and a hat reduces heat loss."

"But I have a hat," said Mason. "This is an Indian hat, see?"

With that, Mason unfurled his red bandanna and quickly fashioned it into a stocking cap, covering most of his thick, black hair. Groaning, Buster returned to the office, muttering to himself about finding new friends.

"When are you going up?" Mason asked Ryan, referring to the Paulinas.

"The Governor wants me to put together an action plan for making contact. That's something I can really use your help on. This isn't cast in concrete, but he's thinking at the very least that we should see if they need any assistance and what we can do to help. Legally, as you know, being Native Americans, they have the right to hunt on ceded land. Hell, treaties aside, most of Oregon is ceded land, so they can hunt and fish just about anywhere they want."

Ceded land is public land that Oregon tribes used for hunting and fishing. Native Americans retained aboriginal rights of hunting and fishing on all lands that had historically belonged to or were used by the tribes. Some of the tribes, however, accepted lump-sum pay-outs for their ceded rights.

"True," said Mason, "But I don't think these people really need any help. It looks to me like they have been doing pretty good for themselves all along. Tell you what. I'll discuss this with the tribal chiefs and elders to see what their suggestions are. As you know, our reservation is quite large—bigger even than some New England states. I believe we could find a little space for them. We just need to designate some land for their use. It's up to the Hiders, but I know our three Confederated tribes would welcome them with open arms—taking them in, of course, being a part of our traditional way of life.

"Listen, if this thing should prove out," Mason added, talking about the DVD, "and if they choose to come out of hiding, I'll be the one asking for help. As it is, I'm having lunch with Buster in Redmond tomorrow," Mason said, "It's his turn to buy. If you're free, join us, and we can talk this over. Plus you get the extra benefit of watching Buster's hand shake as he reaches for his wallet. I'm not kidding," said Mason, "it is truly a sight to behold. I always skip breakfast—the most important meal of the day—when it's his turn to buy so I can fill up with lunch on Buster's nickel."

Before getting into his police truck, Mason, in a more serious vein, asked Ryan how Chance was doing.

"We just take it one day at a time," said Ryan. "It's all we can do. We both miss her very much. I am glad to see this snow coming in, though. This should make for a nice base when we make a Christmas tree run. I'm guessing sometime in mid-December—maybe even a little sooner."

"Tell Chance, come springtime, I'm counting on him for some help with that Appy colt. Plus the girls keep asking when he's coming up," said Mason.

"I know he's looking forward to it because he's mentioned it several times. I think he's planning on waiting until the river warms up, though," said Ryan.

Several years earlier, Mason taught Chance a traditional way to train a Mustang without breaking the spirit of the horse.

"Tie the wild horse off between two tame horses, and then get them into a strong river current. Put a young cowboy on the horse in the middle. All he has to do is hang on for a few minutes while the horse bucks and does his best to throw him. It is impossible for the horse to continually fight the river. You do a couple of river sessions, and the horse will not throw the rider. Yet the spirit of the horse remains intact. It is the old way of gently breaking a horse without violence."

As an afterthought Mason yelled to Ryan, "Hey, don't forget your tree permits. It would be embarrassing, you being the Game Warden and all, to get written up by the Forest Service for no permits."

PROJECT OREGON

Geologists discovered rich rivers of boiling hot water and steam deep beneath the forest floor of the Paulina Wilderness. Initial studies indicated a geothermal potential of enough energy to provide electrical power to hundreds of thousands of homes. A large plant would be constructed onsite, and thick transmission lines would carry the power to all parts of the state and beyond. Plant revenues would eventually be in the billions. Fifteen hundred new jobs would be created. The holding company that owned Project Oregon embarked on a public relations program emphasizing that the plant would only use naturally generated steam, which would replenish itself from the boiling rivers heated by underground magma. As community approval was vital to getting plant start-up, the project was presented to the public as a win/win for the environment. The traditional methods of damning up rivers or creating nuclear power or burning coal, gas or oil to produce electricity would no longer be needed and how fortunate Oregonians were to have such a find within the state.

"Not so fast," said a wide variety of environmental activists. Millions of board feet of timber would have to be cut down to provide necessary room for the huge plant. Similar amounts would have to be cut to make way for the transmission lines that would have to travel through hundreds of miles of designated wilderness to bring electricity to the marketplace. Both Deschutes and Klamath Counties would be forever drenched in sulfur smell, an unfortunate by-product of bringing underground steam to the surface. The traditional migration path of the great herds of deer and elk would most likely be severely compromised.

The litany of environmental complaints was endless. Every time one issue was resolved, another two would spring to the surface.

Both sides marshaled an army of lawyers to fight over every proposal and counter-proposal. Both sides were keeping close score on wins and losses, with the environmental side initially winning most of the support. Then Project Oregon took out a series of media ads stressing residential electric bills would skyrocket unless the plant was built.

Oregonians then started to shift sides. Much as many folks did not want the plant and the accompanying damages to the eco-system. They for sure did not want their power bills to double.

Things were starting to get nasty. If a little, butt-ugly minnow found in some obscure stream barely a foot wide could bring a halt to a badly needed hydro plant in Southern Oregon—as once happened—then anything environmental could stop the entire project. One only had to look at the Spotted Owl fiasco, which cost thousands of loggers their jobs.

The holding company of Project Oregon repeatedly stressed to its project management team that they would not tolerate any such delays. The geothermal plant was to go through at all costs.

Senior management believed in the concept of an "iron fist in a velvet glove." Build the plant, and bonuses would be paid—bonuses that would dwarf anything paid to Wall Street traders. Fail and those deemed responsible would be quickly fired and not given the chance to save face and resign, which meant little or no opportunity for similar employment elsewhere.

The ultimate burden of making all this happen fell to the project manager and his assistant who were living and working in a trailer at the proposed plant site. They were constantly surrounded by a flow of company lawyers, scientists and engineers, with everybody flying into the forest site by company helicopter from the Redmond Airport.

Fifteen-hour workdays for the two managers were the norm. Warren Eldon, the Assistant Vice-President of Plant Development, especially would not allow anything to get between him and his bonus. Getting the plant built became his "holy grail."

The Hiders were also keeping a careful watch on all the growing activity so close to their lodge. Something was going on, which meant something would have to be done. They did not understand the iron lodge with two men living in it and especially why so many whites were coming and going in their noisy flying wagon. Whatever was going on would not be of any benefit to the Indians, and what did not benefit them could only hurt them.

Night after night, the Hiders sat around the campfire, deeply worried, trying to figure out if the whites were going to attack them, or if they should take the initiative and either attack the whites or flee to the east. Either way would probably result in the loss of Yahi life. In spite of all the talk about attacking the whites, Chief Tuliyani had to face up to one irrefutable truth: he had only three warriors capable of taking the fight to the enemy. They were Jumping Bull, He Who Stands and the youngest, Kicking Horse.

The Yahi were vastly outnumbered and, in spite of all their talk, in no position to launch an attack. Yes, they would all fight to the death if attacked, but in terms of only three warriors mounting an offensive attack on outsiders, that realistically was not going to happen.

When AVP Eldon met with Jesse in his office, he thought it would be just another routine meeting with Jesse having little to report. Truth be known, Eldon did not like Jesse. He believed Jesse to be just another opportunist out to line his own pockets. Sometimes in life, to make things work, one had to occasionally hold one's nose and get on with the project, and this was one of those times.

Eldon reached across his cluttered desk, handing Jesse a thin, flat envelope containing one fifty-dollar bill.

"Cheap intel," thought Warren, as Jesse typically had little to report, other than the occasional wildlife sighting, which Warren insisted Jesse write down and date in case Warren ever had to go to court over a wildlife problem.

Jesse pocketed the money and then filled AVP Warren in on the fact that there was now a very serious threat, possibly even a permanent delay to building the plant.

Just hearing the words "permanent delay" caused Warren Eldon's stomach to boil. He began flipping files around his desk, searching for his tablet. He had to settle for pen and paper.

AN ENHANCED BONUS PROGRAM

After twenty minutes of near frantic writing and with a visible sheen of perspiration upon his face, Assistant Vice-President Eldon put the paper down. He was so busy writing he barely had time for questions. Of all the things he had to worry about that might delay or permanently block plant construction, never in a million years would he have guessed that it might be a tribe of prehistoric Indians living in the Ochoco Mountains. Such a presence, if true, would be a deal breaker, if word ever got out.

Warren Eldon was determined to make sure that this word would never get out. To minimize *any* kind of negative publicity, he had all kinds of scientific experts on his consulting payroll. He had plant doctors and bug doctors and Doctors of Forestry all do extensive research in their respective areas of expertise. He had hydrologists study rivers and streams and calculate the cubic outflow of water, both winter and summer to the *nth* degree. All the expert findings were submitted to both the Federal and State Departments of Energy to make sure that nothing phony could later be created by the opposition to stop or delay plant construction.

AVP Eldon believed that he had covered all his bases. He had resources, options and solutions for any conceivable problem the opposition might bring up. The one thing he never thought of, nor did any of his advisors, was stone-age Indians living right smack where the plant was to be built. This was a problem of monumental proportions and would have to be dealt with immediately.

Bug and plant doctors were not the answer. He might have to go with a very different group of people—people, he had been told, who were problem solvers and could get any job done.

Warren was aware, as was senior management, that wolves were returning to Oregon. Wolves he could deal with. Out of a nine-hundred-million-dollar-plant budget for the first phase, a full fifteen million was set aside for land reclamation. Eldon's plan was for Project Oregon to enhance the prey food supply well away from the plant, mainly by planting browse. Where the prey animals went, the predator animals would go. If anything, the overall animal numbers would increase, and everyone would be happy.

Company biologists had also advised Warren that the occasional grizzly would sometimes wander down to Paulina from Washington or cross over from the Hells Canyon area on the Idaho border. When that happened, Warren could expect volumes of negative publicity to break loose. Warren knew that the presence of such an animal would bring an immediate halt to plant construction until big-game biologists from various Federal Agencies could study the animal. A study always involved months of tracking, darting, collaring, drawing blood samples, and examining bear poop to see what the bear was eating.

Warren was convinced that such events were just an excuse for an aging bunch of government employees with their John Lennon glasses and graying beards to spend time in the wilderness, sleeping under the stars and yukking it up at taxpayer expense.

"Bears eat animals and fish and bugs and plants and all kinds of disgusting dead things," thought Warren. "We already know what they eat, and to do more research on bear poop is a colossal waste of time and money. It would be just an excuse to stop plant construction, especially as bears have been eating the same things since time immemorial."

In most cases whenever a grizzly visited Oregon, it was only for a few months or so until the bear was either killed or it returned home on its own. Warren couldn't wait that long. Plant costs would skyrocket with every delay. The company "bean counters" estimated that it would cost Project Oregon a minimum of one million dollars per day for every day of delay.

That type of a loss would crimp the bonus program.

To save the company large sums of money, Warren reached an unwritten agreement with Jesse on a "shoot and shovel" policy. For $2500 cash, Jesse would make any grizzly around Paulina disappear. All he had to do to collect was bring the ears to Warren and bury the carcass. Jesse couldn't agree fast enough.

"Wild Indians?" asked Warren.

"Wild Indians," said Jesse.

Jesse repeated what he had just told Warren. He told Warren he believed the Indians to be a band of Yahi who fled Northern California and were now hiding out in Central Oregon. He also warned Warren that the Yahi were renowned guerilla fighters who would stop at nothing to protect their tribe.

Warren asked if any of the project people might be in danger, and Jesse surprised him by simply saying, "Yes."

"Back in the frontier days," Jesse said, "Whites always killed the Yahi whenever they could because the Yahi would always attack and kill the whites. It was kind of a circular thing. I think that old Indian lady I saw out in the woods was doing her level best to kill me by throwing heavy rocks at me. That's what makes me think she is a Yahi. They were never bashful about killing whites. It seems like it's almost an honor-bound tradition with them."

Jesse went on to expand upon the Mill Creek war and how, after hiding for forty years in California, the survivors moved to Oregon to escape from the whites.

"I can't prove that, but it's what makes sense to me. I'm also saying that because they are Yahi you can expect some big problems," Jesse predicated.

Warren had learned early in his career that whenever he brought a problem to management, he was fully expected to also bring a solution. He expected no less from Jesse or anyone else on his payroll.

"How do you propose to deal with this," asked Warren, emphasizing that nothing, absolutely nothing, would get between Warren and his bonus.

"Simple," said Jesse. "I do believe I can convince them to go back to California. There are probably not more than a handful of them, and once I explain that no one is hunting for them in California or anywhere else, I think they would consider returning to their homeland. I think they are stuck in some kind of a time warp here, and they have absolutely no concept of life in the Twenty-First Century."

"And you know their language to communicate with them?" asked Warren, somewhat incredulously.

"I don't think anybody today knows their language," said Jesse. "But I can sign a little— probably enough to get my point across."

Eldon was convinced now more than ever that Jesse was a simpleton. The only reason he even kept Jesse around was to be his eyes and ears in the forest. Surprisingly, as it turns out, he now really needed him.

Warren went over and closed his office door. "Jesse," he said, "we are going to give this lost tribe whatever they want. That's the kind of incentive program that works. As of right now, I am putting you on the payroll at five hundred dollars per week. You have only one thing to do: Find these people and report their location back to me. You are to report in to me every day, either in person or by phone. You can keep your cowboy job and your cowboy pay with the Circle G. Riding through the woods looking for cattle will give you the perfect cover to be searching for these Indians. Find them, notify me, and we'll get the right experts to reason with them. Your job is not to reason with them. You're only task is to locate them. We'll take it from there."

Warren wrapped his fingers around his chin while in deep thought. "If this tribe wants to return to Northern California, we will buy their old homeland for them. If they want an apology from the Governor of California for past misdeeds, we will have the Governor go before them and apologize. We'll take out full-page newspaper ads filled with apologies. We'll provide scholarships for any of them who want to go to school. In short, we will do anything we can to appease them. The only thing we ask is that they leave here, and go back to California. Now, do I have the right person for the task?"

As an afterthought, AVP Eldon added, "Here's how important this is: I'm thinking a ten-thousand-dollar bonus for you if you can just lead me to where they live. I've got experts who will take it from there. All you have to do is find them, and then point them out to me. You do that, and you will be ten thousand dollars richer."

For a moment Warren had a sickening thought: "What if Jesse stretched the assignment out for months on end to stay on the payroll? Be just like him," thought Warren, who then told Jesse, "Make this happen in the next two weeks, and I will get you an additional five thousand dollar bonus on top of the ten. Deal?" he asked.

Jesse practically leaped across Warren's desk to shake on the deal, carefully. He did not want Warren's tablet to slip from his coat.

OREGON ARMS

Jesse was barely out of the office when Project Oregon's Assistant Vice-President Warren made a search for a private number given to him by top management. It was the unlisted number for Oregon Arms, a small Portland-based company made up mostly of former Seals, Rangers and Special Forces who provided personnel for dangerous missions to the U.S. Military around the world. Warren was patched through to the Operations Director, introduced himself, and made the terse comment, "We have a problem." The two men discussed the lost tribe of Indians hiding out in the Paulinas and of Jesse's task to find the Indians.

The two began brainstorming some solutions.

The Operations Director of Oregon Arms finished with, "If your guy can't find them, I'll send a few Rangers down there to help with the search. They can also do the negotiations and aid you in case things get dicey."

That was the kind of help that Warren had been told he could count on. To negotiate with the Indians, he must first find them. Then the Operations Director added, "Let me be crystal clear about this problem. I know we want to solve this quietly but, should our negotiations with these Indians fail, you will still need the problem solved."

"We do need this resolved," said Warren, still thinking discussion and incentives.

"Understood," said the Director, "We problem-solve on behalf of our clients, and we do not let our clients down. Rest assured that we will find these renegades and negotiate with them. If they refuse to move or otherwise accommodate you, we will have to consider perhaps some more difficult alternatives."

AVP Warren's stomach was already roiling from Jesse's info. Now it sounded like the Operations Director was leaning toward something much more than persuasive discussion between the parties.

The genie had been let out of the bottle.

Warren took a handful of *Tums* to calm his stomach.

PAULINA WILDERNESS

SIX MONTHS EARLIER

Whisper, an elderly, white-haired Indian woman, was the first wife of Chief Tuliyani, tribal leader of the Hiders. Her sister, Nopanny, was the Chief's second wife. According to Indian custom, Chief Tuliyani married Nopanny when her husband, Pullissa, died.

Marrying a sister of the first wife was a tradition in place since the ancient times of early Stone-Age life. A marriage of two sisters minimized the disruption of bringing in a total stranger to the Chief's lodge. Such a marriage often kept the widow from literal starvation, while the Chief's image and status in the tribe was greatly enhanced because he was in a position to support two wives. An additional fact was that both sisters often benefited by the mutual sharing of all the work, which was seemingly endless.

For thousands of years, this type of arrangement worked well. True, there were always problems, but most of those were amicably worked out.

Early one morning when it was still pitch dark outside, Whisper shook Nopanny awake.

"Nopanny," she urged. "Let us go to the Little Valley and dig in the meadow for some tubers."

Nopanny groaned and turned away from her sister, saying she had a headache.

"You go," she said, "and let me sleep."

Whisper sensed the beginning of yet another disagreement. It wasn't Nopanny's refusal as much as it was the way she said it. Whisper fully understood headaches; she just didn't like being brushed off. As sometimes happens, living in such close proximity, the sisters would occasionally fight, this being one of those times. Several harsh words were exchanged and Whisper rushed off, feeling that once again she had to do all the work, while Nopanny would get all the rest.

Though Nopanny and Whisper genuinely loved one another, there existed a strain of jealousy between them that sometimes caused difficulties, especially as Whisper was the younger sister. To safeguard her position as first wife, Whisper worried about leaving her sister with her husband. Whisper knew Nopanny to occasionally be a gossip and was fearful about Nopanny talking about her behind her back, especially to their husband.

Whisper grabbed her knife, digging stick, basket, an old, yellowed cowboy hat, a handful of pine nuts, and a hunk of warm venison from the communal stew pot.

Peeking outside, she found it to be a beautiful summer day with the beginnings of an immense blue sky and just a hint of a chill in the air. The peace and beauty of her surroundings began to melt away her anger. As was her practice, before digging she would feed the grey squirrels some pine nuts. If the squirrels were not around, she would eat the tasty nuts herself.

Wrapping her breakfast carefully in a tanned hide, she began walking to the meadow. When she arrived, several squirrels were running about high in the trees. One with a torn ear she recognized; he had become something of a pet. Resting now, with her back against a large pine tree, Whisper reached into her burden bag and scattered a few pine nuts on the ground. Typically, the squirrel with the torn ear, braver than the others, would scamper down the tree and gather the nuts. Always cautious, he would gather a few nuts, then quickly turn and race up the tree, sit out on a limb, eat the nuts, and then come back for more.

Whisper now felt bad at her anger toward her sister. Much as she valued her "alone" time, she wished her sister had come along. She would have enjoyed feeding the squirrel with the torn ear.

The squirrel was perched high above her, constantly running back and forth on a long limb, chattering excitedly. Though it had not happened yet, each time they met, he was getting more brave and adventuresome and would soon be eating out of her hand.

This time, however, the squirrel refused to come down. His usual behavior was to race down the tree for some treats. Whisper tried to entice him by throwing out even more nuts. Normally by this time, he was finished with his first course and back for his second. Whisper stretched out her hand and began gently calling him. She had some pine nuts in her hand. He raced along the branch and, for just a moment, Whisper thought he was going to come down.

"Finally," she said.

Instead, his chattering stopped, and he instantly froze—remaining absolutely motionless. Then he suddenly ran around to the very back of the tree trunk and within seconds scampered to the top. All the other squirrels were all doing the same.

Looking up through the thick limbs and brush, Whisper could barely see him. He remained completely frozen in place.

"Something scared him," she thought with a growing sense of unease. Barely moving her head, Whisper carefully looked all around. She did not see anything. She knew that whatever had disturbed the squirrels was not an owl or eagle because if it were, the squirrels would never have run to the treetops, making themselves easy prey. It had to be something else.

"It is not a bear," she thought, as bears are big and clumsy, and she would have definitely heard a bear.

"It might be a cougar, but a squirrel to a cougar was a mere snack, simply not worth the time and effort to get, especially if it involved climbing a tree."

A cougar had once stalked Whisper many years ago. While walking down a trail, she sensed that something was behind her. She quickly whirled around and came eye to eye with a cougar. For just a moment the animal froze, and that gave Whisper enough time to immediately raise her hands high over her head and to rush directly toward the cougar, screaming at the top of her lungs. The cougar whirled around and instantly bounded away.

Whisper kept slowly turning her head, looking all about to see what had scared off the squirrels. Born in the wilderness, she had learned to completely trust her instincts, and right now her instincts were telling her that she was being stalked. Something was after her.

With the sun now breaking over the high mountaintops, Whisper was momentarily blinded. Looking to the east while shading her eyes with the old cowboy hat, Whisper thought she saw an animal break out from a rock pile and start running toward her. She quickly rose to see if it was another mule or burro lost in the wilderness.

Last year a tribal member had found a lost mule grazing in the meadow. That very night the mule was in the communal pot, helping fill empty bellies for a full week.

The tribal larder was starting to fill. Baskets of smoked salmon ran alongside one wall. Thousands of pounds of acorns were being ground and rinsed to make flour for both gruel and bread. Numerous deer and elk had been hunted and their meat smoked for the long season of snow.

Whisper wanted nothing more than to gather some nutritious tubers to flavor the stew pot. An animal running toward her gave her a moment of pause.

"It's not a bear," she thought, shielding her eyes from the rising sun, "and it's not a cougar."

For a few seconds, Whisper thought it might be a black burro running toward her—maybe an animal that had broken loose from a tourist pack train.

Several seconds later, Whisper knew that it was not a burro. It was moving too fast and heading right toward her. The wind blew a scent her way, like that of a wet dog. The Hiders never kept dogs for fear that their barking might attract unwanted attention. From time to time, Whisper would see lost or stray dogs in the wilderness, and they always gave off a powerful wet odor.

She knew whatever was running her way was not a coyote because coyotes were too small and cowardly to attack people.

The black creature was heading directly toward her, its yellow eyes fixed on Whisper, lips starting to curl over rows of gleaming fangs.

Instantly Whisper thought, "This is not a dog. This is a wolf."

Whisper had never seen a wolf in her entire lifetime of hiding in the forest, surrounded by wild animals. As a child growing up, she would sit by the campfire and listen to the old stories. She knew about wolves but had never seen one—until now.

Immediately, she jumped up, yelling and raising her arms over her head. The wolf never even slowed down. He was covering a lot of ground, and Whisper had only seconds to spare.

Whisper instantly grabbed a tree limb and began climbing. She clawed her way up but her dress kept getting snagged in the branches, slowing her down. The wolf's scent was now overpowering. He now stood directly below her, getting ready to leap. The wolf moved around the base of the tree several times looking for a clear path through the tree limbs to Whisper.

Whisper knew that if the wolf managed to pull her from the tree, it would be all over. The only weapon she had was her knife. Frantically pulling the knife from her belt, the knife got tangled up in the branches, and she dropped it. The knife bounced harmlessly off the wolf. The wolf instantly grabbed the knife in his mouth, shook it several times, then dropped it to the ground and sniffed it. Whisper then threw down the only thing she had left, her breakfast. The venison rolled several times on the ground. The shadowy figure quickly ran to the venison, sniffed it, looked up to Whisper, and then took the chunk of venison in its mouth and ran back to the forest.

Whisper was shaking so hard from the encounter that she had to wrap both arms around the thick tree for support. She climbed as high as she could possibly go, afraid that she might fall but even more afraid that the wolf would come back for her.

She didn't realize it until later, but she had climbed almost sixty feet up the tree. She caught sight of the wolf several moments later running up through the forest and across the meadow to a pile of rocks, carrying the venison in his mouth. Then he just disappeared.

Hours later Chief Tuliyani and Jumping Bull, heavily armed with bows and spears, walked out of the dense forest and cautiously looked around. Whisper called to them and climbed down from the tree. Chief

Tuliyani could see that she had been terribly frightened. Wrapping his arms about her, he held her as she sobbed out her story.

"There," she said, pointing up the mountain to where the wolf disappeared, "He ran to there."

That night the Chief stood before his tribe and told of Whisper's brush with death. "We must be vigilant," he said, "This wolf is a new enemy to us. Our parents and grandparents for generations back have lived with wolves but always very carefully. Now we must protect ourselves as they once did."

Before he could continue, several of the tribal members were interrupting with questions. Rarely did the people interrupt in Council, but the Chief understood their fears.

After hearing their questions, the Chief responded, "Our elders taught us that wolves will always run away from people. What happened this morning is not the normal way of the wolf. He might have mistaken Whisper for a deer or for some type of prey animal, but I do not think so. We have always looked over our shoulders and listened for the enemy, but now we must be even more careful."

Late that night the Chief and his closest advisor, the tribal Shaman or Medicine Man, the *K'uwi*, sat by the campfire, stirring the glowing embers. The Shaman observed, "I think that maybe Whisper had a vision and that she should take the black wolf as her totem."

Soon after, the Chief lay down next to Whisper and quietly told her what the Shaman had said. Whisper shook her head, "No." It was not a vision. It was very real, and Whisper now knew what she would have to do in order to protect herself from this new invader.

The tribal members called the black wolf, "Shadow."

A CRIMINAL UNDERCLASS

It was mid-December, and hunting season was finally over. Warden Ryan had issued a record number of tickets to people for hunting without any license or tags, for shooting across the roads, for shooting cow elk when their tags were only for bull elk, and for public intoxication.

One hunter wanted to go the hard way. Ryan had to repeatedly warn him to place his rifle on the ground or go to jail. Armed, angry and drunk, weaving back and forth, the hunter said that Ryan did not have any legislative authority to tell him what to do. He knew his constitutional rights, and Ryan was violating them. The hunter finally placed his rifle against a tree and hitched his pants over his plus-sized frame. Then, in spite of his two friends telling him to back off, the hunter charged Ryan. Ryan neatly sidestepped him while at the same time sticking his size twelve boot out in front of him. The dazed hunter went down like a sack of potatoes and quickly found himself in handcuffs. His two companions kept apologizing for his behavior.

Fire season was over, too, as the entire forest was now blanketed with more than two feet of snow. Tree limbs were sagging under the snow's heavy weight. Thick branches were breaking from huge old-growth pines and in some cases dropping over a hundred feet to the ground. The aspen trees were now completely bare. Just two short weeks ago, their brilliantly colored yellow and red leaves were covering the forest floor.

Hunting season was over, and all hunters had quickly cleared the woods as the snow continued to pile up. Snow was good for tracking, but too much snow made hunting nearly impossible.

With the heavy snowfall, artifact hunters could no longer get into the high country to rob and pillage Indian gravesites.

Certain crimes appeal to certain criminals of a certain age. Marijuana growers are mostly in their twenties. Meth labs are operated by former marijuana growers now in their thirties and forties. Timber thieves are in their forties and fifties—stealing firewood to sell, usually to support *their* habit of marijuana and meth.

Artifact hunters tend to be in their sixties and seventies. These are not the same people who, when out walking the family dog find an occasional arrowhead and take it home. Hard-core artifact hunters dig up gravesites with heavy machinery looking for bows, knives, war shirts with scalps, old coins and whatever else is available. They can crater an entire area in one day in their quest for artifacts. One couple went so far as to not only steal everything they could find, but they even advertised an ancient skull for sale on the Internet. Another thief used a jackhammer to chisel off Indian petroglyphs that had been in place literally for thousands of years.

Fortunately, the thieves were caught when advertising their "finds" on the Internet.

For the next five months, with the exception of an occasional poacher and some snowmobilers or cross-country skiers, the forest would be mostly uninhabited.

The Wolf Recovery Task Force had put together a simple action plan for making contact with the Hiders. Dividing the wilderness up into small grids, they would continuously patrol each grid with snowshoes, snow cats or snowmobiles until they found the tiny tribe. Every wisp of smoke would be investigated. Snowshoe tracks leading into the thick brush would be followed. Blood trails or any large animal carcass would be examined closely for clues. Weather permitting; they would do flyovers with either Oregon State Police or Forest Service helicopters.

The Task Force would not rest easy until contact had been made. The resources of Federal, State and local authorities were now in full support of the mission. The Governor agreed to further amend his gag order so that other necessary parties could become involved on a need-to-know basis.

Authorities began a careful "smoke and mirrors program," leaking info about the wolf recovery but keeping any news about the Hiders close to their vests.

Once the tribe had been located, Mason would be brought in to make the initial contact. Everyone seemed to be in agreement that probably a number of meetings would have to take place to build a bond of trust. At some point, the Hiders would have to make a decision as to what they wanted to do. Mason would be the point man. He was an Indian, he was easygoing, and he was always smiling. His imposing size would certainly impress those in hiding. The people would be offered a number of choices—pretty much anything they wanted to do. Unlike the Washington, D.C., bureaucrats of the Nineteenth Century who forced all Indians onto reservations to "solve the Indian problem," the Hiders might elect to stay right where they were and to continue living as they always had. If that was their choice, then that would be respected. If they chose to step into the Twenty-First Century from the Stone Age, tribal members from the Warm Springs Reservation would help mentor them in their transition. Or, alternatively, if they wanted to return to their native land of Northern California, then that could also be easily arranged. Another choice was that some might want to learn the white man's ways, while others might choose to continue their traditional way of life.

It was whatever the lost tribe most wanted. Mason cautioned the task force that the wishes of the tribal chief and elders were what most tribal members would follow, according to Indian custom. If the consensus were to stay or to leave, most would follow the wisdom and wishes of the chief and elders. Most but perhaps not all.

Timeframes were established, deadlines set, and the Governor gave his approval to the plan. The thought was that by early spring, at the very least, some form of initial contact would have been made.

As is always the case, the best plans sometimes go awry.

IN SEARCH OF THE
PERFECT CHRISTMAS TREE

Ryan woke his son early that morning. It was the first day of Christmas vacation for Chance and he wanted to sleep. "It's cold. It's snowing. It's dark outside. It's too early. Nobody gets up this early. Leave me alone. I don't want to go."

Ryan knew that Chance really did enjoy getting the family Christmas tree; it's just that he didn't want to go quite so early. Ryan decided to let Chance sleep in for a while. If anybody had a right to complain, though, it was Ryan. He had just finished five long days of patrol and paperwork. This was his first day off, and where was he going? He was going right back up to Paulina. What made this trip different is that Chance would be with him. It would be a fun trip, just like they always had. Ryan made sure to stock up with Chance's favorite foods, hot chocolate; tons of trail snacks and thick Paninis.

As Chance always said, hot chocolate and Paninis were "Pretty much a health-food breakfast."

Even though it was his day off, Ryan planned to keep an eye out for any clues that might bring about contact.

While Chance was finishing up his typical nine hours of sleep, Ryan was busy packing the truck. He first hooked the snowmobile trailer to the back of his four-wheel-drive truck. Fuel supplies were loaded, along with a shovel, small chainsaw and axe. Helmets and snow gear were loaded into the truck canopy, along with bottles of water and two down sleeping bags, just in case. Though he had toenail tires on the truck, Ryan made sure to pack snow chains.

As a state trooper, Ryan was required by Oregon law to always have his service weapon with him. As a warden, Ryan had learned to carry extra handcuffs and several spare clips of ammo at all times, just in case. Given the above-average snowfall for so early in the season, Ryan brought along his avalanche locater. He brought it along almost as an afterthought. He also packed a spare inhalator for Chance, in case of an asthma attack.

They were ready to go. All that Ryan had left to do was the Herculean task of dragging Chance out of bed. He walked in with a steaming mug of hot chocolate and began the process.

Four hours later, they pulled into Paulina Lodge and started the snowmobile trip to the summit. Paulina Lodge sits on the very edge of Paulina Lake, some two hundred and fifty feet deep, filled with Kokanee and record-breaking German Brown Trout. A black forest and high mountain crags surround the remote lake. An old logging road, the Paulina Trail, leads to the summit. In any direction, it was forest as far as the eye could see.

"An hour up, ten minutes to get the tree, and an hour back. Then home. Then what? Phone time with Ashley?" Ryan asked.

Chance nodded in agreement. He and his friends, several of them literally from his pre-school days, planned on snowboarding every day during winter break at Mt. Bachelor.

Chance wanted Ashley to try snowboarding. Newly arrived to Oregon from California, she quickly said yes, which surprised him, because he was thinking she liked shopping more than outdoor activities.

In truth, she did. Ashley's thinking was, "If you have seen one tree you have seen them all." But then again, Chance was tall, good-looking, and athletic. She especially liked the fact that he was always smiling. The decision, from Ashley's point of view, was a no-brainer.

One day at Summit High School, Chance and Ashley were holding hands while hurrying to their next class. Chance noticed three guys bullying a friend of his from Junior High. Saying nothing, Chance released Ashley's hand and walked over to his friend and placed an arm around his shoulder, giving him a hug and greeting.

The friend mumbled a low, "Thanks," and immediately left. Two of the three bullies became silent but the third one, who towered over the others, got mouthy. Chance quietly stared at him while the insults flew.

Ashley tried to intervene by saying, "Chance, c'mon, we're going to be late for class."

Then the bully started to mock Chance by repeating what Ashley had said in a very high-pitched voice. Still saying nothing, Chance instantly reached out to the bully, grabbed him by the shirt, swung him around and slammed him hard into the lockers. The surprised bully, with the breath momentarily knocked out of him, slumped to the ground while several nearby students laughed. Regaining his footing, the bully brushed himself off as if nothing had happened and pushed his way through the jeering students, followed immediately by his now-humbled posse.

A stunned Ashley asked, "Do you always do that?"

"No," said Chance, again smiling, "But I promised my friend I would have his back. This is not the first run-in he's had with those losers. The loudmouth guy has been bullying people for years. I think he's embarrassed now more than anything else. Hopefully, he'll think of this as a wake-up call to stop bullying others. I'm not counting on him having a change of heart but that little tune-up might help.

"Tune-up?" Ashley asked. She added, "Weren't you afraid?"

"No, not really," Chance replied. "My Dad taught me that bullies will never pick on people who fight back," he added. "In spite of all their tough talk, deep down they really are afraid of anyone who will stand up to them."

Chance never was one to start a fight and, given his size and strength, he had only a few fights in his lifetime. Conversely, he never backed away from a fight, either.

"What I especially like about him," Ashley later confided to a friend, "is, in his own quiet way, he takes action. I texted a friend in L.A. about what happened, but I made the mistake of including a picture of him. Now *she* wants to move up here."

Ryan nudged his son from his daydreaming, asking, "Okay?"

"Okay, what?" asked Chance.

Ryan replied, "You just agreed to get the snowmobiles out of the trailer. Make sure to lift with your legs, not your back."

THE MISSING ELK HUNTER

Taking a hot chocolate break from snowmobiling, Chance and Ryan talked about the Yahi and how they had remained in hiding for so long. In history class, Chance had recently completed Theodora Kroeber's biography of Ishi entitled, *Ishi: The Last Yahi—A Documentary History.*

Chance said that Ishi believed his sister and her companion had died by drowning after the power company surveyors found their high ledge camp.

"Go where the evidence takes you," said Ryan, who had read the first Ishi book decades earlier by the same author. "In part Ishi was saying that, because he never found their bodies. It is possible that they might have drowned and that their bodies were washed down to the Sacramento River. But now there is another school of thought, which suggests that— instead of drowning—they fled to Oregon, and their descendants have been hiding here ever since. I suspect once Mason makes contact, those questions will be answered."

"What I don't get," said Chance, "is how those settlers could feel right about killing all the Indians. I mean, that could have been Mason and his family."

"Trust me on this," responded Ryan, "I've see Mason in action. He once cleared a bar brawl in about two minutes. If ever attacked by the Guards, he would have been the only one left standing."

"Okay then, different question—before I forget. I see coyotes all the time. If they are about the same color as a wolf, how do you tell the difference?"

"Easy," said Ryan. "A wolf is three or four times the size of a coyote. A wolf has a long snout; coyotes have a much smaller face, almost like a fox. Coyotes yip, wolves howl. Coyotes have short legs; wolves have long legs. Plus you can smell a wolf pack from several hundred feet away. They smell terrible. One whiff of a wolf pack, and you had better head for the nearest tree. Once you find that tree, keep climbing because wolves can jump a good fifteen feet into the air. Go high and go fast."

"Okay, back to the Indians. How come you have never had any reports about them, and how come they have never attacked anybody here?" asked Chance.

"Pure luck that Buster got them on his camera traps. Otherwise I don't think anybody even suspected that we have a lost tribe up here. They have a lifetime of experience in hiding from the whites. It's what keeps them alive. I think you and I might have a near impossible situation of hiding and living in the woods, camping out literally for every day of your life, but remember that this is what these folks have been doing for thousands of years. It's not like they are just now learning how to set out snares for deer or to stalk an elk. Those skills have been passed down from generation to generation, since forever. They are the best at what they do. They are so good that the U.S. Special Forces even adopted some of their guerilla tactics. That's about as good as it gets." Ryan explained.

Ryan appeared lost in thought for a moment, and then he continued, "I also don't know that they have never attacked anyone in Oregon. Now that I think about it, we did have a mysterious disappearance of a hunter just a few years ago. At first, we treated it as a missing person, and then I started to think that maybe some foul play was involved. Apparently this missing hunter treated elk camp as his own little fiefdom. His hunting partners told me that he drank from sunup to sundown, refused to help split wood for the fire, wouldn't take his turn at cooking or cleaning and was given to long bouts of angry behavior. He repeatedly said he wasn't, 'the camp bitch,' and refused to do any of the camp chores. When he turned up missing, two in his hunting party just assumed he was off sulking someplace and would eventually show up. The other two guys, when I later interviewed them, seemed pretty shaky about the whole incident. They started out hunting with him that day and came back without him. My focus was on finding the missing hunter. I figured once I find the hunter, everything else would fall into place. Unfortunately, I never found him. To this day he is still missing."

"Why did these guys even hunt with him?" asked Chance.

"I'm told he was a good hunter and very generous with his share," Ryan responded.

Thinking of the sequence of events, Ryan added, "That night, all four guys reported him missing, but only two were willing to go back out looking for him. The other two refused, even though they had walked out of camp with him that very morning. Their excuse for not going out and searching is that they were too exhausted from hunting. If anybody found him, great, otherwise he was on his own. Then one of the other guys told me that these two guys spent part of the day in their tent and didn't hunt at all. They just seemed very jumpy and nervous and whispering to each other about something. It seemed like pretty strange behavior to their friends who tried to reach out to them but to no avail."

Ryan turned to Chance to emphasize his point.

"I took the initial report that night about the missing hunter, and I alerted Deschutes County Search and Rescue. We all met that night up at their hunting camp. I always thought it a little odd that only two of the hunters joined in the search while the other two went home because they were tired. We were all tired, cold and wet, but a man's life was at stake. Two guys going home just didn't seem right. We pressed on for a full two days, rotating personnel in and out on the search. We found one of his Jim Beam bottles, some cigarette butts on the trail plus his orange hunting cap. There was a definite smear of blood on the hat, and a subsequent DNA test showed it to be his. Thing is, we could never find his body. You can almost always find a body in the woods because scavengers leave little bits and pieces behind. We didn't find anything. No clothing, apart from his hat, hunting equipment or body parts. That's what made me so suspicious. I booked everything we found into the evidence locker and really focused on his two so-called friends who couldn't even bother to search for him."

"Do you think the two guys who went home might have killed him and dumped him down into a canyon or something?" asked Chance.

Deep in thought, Ryan said, "I dunno. Maybe. The whole thing just didn't pass the sniff test, though. The two guys who didn't help search alibied each other, which led me to think that maybe they both had a hand in his disappearance. Just their shaky attitude said that they knew more than what they were telling me. That and they were dropping 'tell' sign all over the place. They were constantly fidgeting during the interview, their story kept changing, and what struck me is that when I offered them a lie detector test, they both refused and lawyered up.

"In every case, I mean *every* case that I've ever investigated; there is always means, opportunity and motive—the MOM theory. These two guys had the means and opportunity but apparently no motive. At least, nothing I could find. They did not have any shared business investments, no one was fooling around with anybody's spouse and there was no insurance fraud of any kind—nothing. They were just casual friends who went hunting together. They included the missing guy because, in spite of all his faults, which were legion, he consistently filled his tag and maybe even theirs. This meant meat for everybody. At the same time, no one really wanted to be around this guy when he was drinking. One minute he is your best friend, the next he wants to fight you over some perceived slight."

Ryan took a deep breath and continued, "I got really busy on a commercial poaching operation, so I had to turn the whole missing hunter thing over to our Detective Bureau. One of my buddies kept me in the loop and said that while they were suspicious about the circumstances, they couldn't find anything. They were continuing the investigation which is where we stand now."

They continued on in silence for another minute, and then Ryan added, "Something happened, I just don't know what."

"Do you think we might see any Indians up here?"

"I doubt it, son," said Ryan. "With all this snow, they are probably holed up somewhere in a nice warm lodge, which is probably nothing more than a lava cave."

"What about wolves?" Chance asked.

"Same," said Ryan, "Plus, I think the minute they hear snowmobiles; they just turn tail and run."

Based upon his experience as a game warden, Ryan was not in doubt, but he was just a few hours away from finding out that he was very much in error.

HOW **NOT** TO GET ALONG
WITH OTHER PREDATORS

S everal male wolves were resting in the back of their den; a small cave with multiple openings. It was late fall and the pack had feasted that morning on an elk calf. Shadow stood, yawned, and then walked to the male wolves. The rest of the pack was stumbling over each other to get out of Shadow's way. Sniffing the males, he selected two by pressing his nose against their noses, turned and pushed his way out of the lair. The other two immediately followed.

The three wolves began loping through the dense forest. Shadow was in the lead. The wolves ran for several miles on end, mostly uphill until they reached a rock overhang, only eight feet in depth and barely two feet high. Sniffing around the cave entrance, Shadow and the two wolves then hid in some nearby brush. Not one made a sound. Not one made a movement. The three were on the hunt.

Several hours later, a large adult cougar came up the trail carrying a rock chuck in its mouth. Normally, the cougar would make several leaps up the rocks to a flat ledge where in safety it would devour its kill.

Smelling the wolves, the cougar froze. He dropped the rock chuck to the ground. He couldn't quite place the scent because he had never before encountered wolves. The overpowering smell spelled danger. The cougar looked all around, sniffing carefully, trying to see if the wolves were still there or were just passing through. The cougar bent down to retrieve the rock chuck and to seek the safety of the ledge.

Just as the cougar placed dinner in his mouth, the nearby brush exploded and three snarling wolves instantly surrounded the cougar. The attack was vicious and fast. All three wolves were biting the cougar, trying to place a kill-hold on the back of the cougar's neck. The cougar had the rock chuck ripped from its mouth. Defending itself, the cougar was now sitting upright on its hind legs. With lightning strokes, the cougar began furiously slashing at the wolves. He managed to snag one wolf's leg and sink his fangs in to the bone. The wolf howled in pain and pulled back, giving the cougar just enough space to attempt a leap for a nearby tree.

Shadow and the cougar leaped at the same time. Shadow managed to catch the cougar by a rear flank and completely spin the animal around. Shadow then grabbed the cougar by the back of the neck and crunched down. The cougar began air slashing, trying his best to break free. The two other wolves helped Shadow pin the cougar to the ground and, within one minute, the cougar rolled his eyes back in his head as his body went limp. Shadow continued crunching down until he was satisfied the cougar was dead. The three wolves sniffed the cougar's body, turned and started the long, loping run back to the den.

They left the rock chuck next to the cougar.

ON THE PAULINA TRAIL

Rigged out in their thermal snowsuits and heavy helmets, Ryan and Chance resumed their snowmobiling through the thickening snow. The logging road was so full of deep snow that they could barely get their snowmobiles up the trail.

"Stay right behind me, and just follow my taillights," said Ryan. "Make damn sure you stay away from the edge as it is several thousand feet straight down. If we should, for any reason, get separated, just stay where you are, and I'll come back and find you."

"Yes sir," said Chance, ribbing his Dad about the State Trooper attitude.

Ryan straightened up, surprised that a smiling Chance was nearly eyeball to eyeball with him.

"Good," said Ryan, "because one more wisecrack, and I'll be having an extra Panini for lunch. As we only have two, you can quickly figure out where that second one is coming from."

"O.K., O.K.," said Chance. "Not the Panini. I take it all back—anything but the Panini!"

For the first time since the death of Suzanne, father and son were enjoying a good laugh together. They slowly began working their way to the summit of Paulina Mountain. After a long, arduous trip, Ryan pulled over to an old logging landing at the very end of the tree line. Chance followed. Though Chance could barely see due to the roiling storm clouds, he knew they were somewhere close to the mountain top, probably well past the eight-thousand-foot level.

A few feet away, almost invisible through the falling snow, was a piece of yellow police tape wrapped around a small, fat, bushy pine tree.

"One of the perks of the job," said Ryan, smiling, "I found this tree a few weeks ago and knew it was the perfect one for Mom. If she were here with us, I just know that this is the tree she would want."

The snow was coming down so thick that Chance nearly stumbled trying to help Ryan fell the tree. One quick swipe with the chain saw, and the tree hit the ground. Together, father and son tied the tree onto the backseat of Ryan's snowmobile and made ready to go down.

Ryan brushed the snow off his thermometer and pointed.

"Twenty-nine degrees and dropping," he said, "I don't want to get stuck up here. Let's just head back to the lodge, and we can eat in the truck." Chance nodded.

"Blink your lights if you need me to stop. I don't want you too far back so you can't see my taillights, but don't be riding my rear in case we hit any ice. And remember . . ."

"Stay away from the edge. I got it."

Ryan started to slowly wind his way down the road. Chance was following behind him, just close enough to barely make out the taillights. The thick, heavy snow continued to cover the mountains, blocking out nearly everything in sight. At its peak, the snowstorm was dumping more than a foot of snow per hour, setting a new mountain record.

Chance began inching up behind his Dad's snowmobile. "Should the need arise," he thought, "There is no way Dad would ever see me blinking my lights between that tree shielding his view and all this falling snow."

A loud, cracking sound startled Chance. Another tree limb had fallen to the ground. Darkness came early in the high mountains. The cloud cover and falling snow had already severely reduced their visibility.

In tandem, the snowmobiles slowly continued their descent. From the windswept mountaintop of eight thousand feet, they began threading their way down through the forest. Every time Chance's mind started to drift, he would hear another limb snapping from a tree. Each breaking limb startled him, moving him ever closer to his Dad's snowmobile. After a while he could tell whenever his Dad was approaching the edge because he reduced his snowmobile to a mere crawl. Once past the danger zone, his Dad would ever so slowly pick up his speed.

Chance had a rough idea of where they were, guessing about fifteen hundred feet or so above the lodge, which sat at roughly sixty-five hundred feet. They still had a very long way to go. Then he began thinking about Ashley, wondering what she was doing. If he had phone service, he would call her but no sense in even trying. It would not bode well to slide off the mountain talking to Ashley. The State Trooper would be more than a little annoyed, and Chance would probably be grounded for the rest of his life, if he even survived the fall.

The snowfall was creating a winter wonderland but, after looking around, Chance could not fathom a lost tribe hiding out in the wilderness. He understood, he thought, why Indian survivors would go into hiding, but that was so long ago. The world had completely changed. It had changed back even in the early Twentieth Century with the advent of electricity, cars, planes and trains. The electronic age was in full bloom in the Twenty-First Century. People were taught in all the schools not be suspicious or prejudiced against others. Proof was in the pudding: his Dad and Mason had been best friends for years. Every time the families had a barbecue, his Dad and Mason would sit off in one corner talking and laughing about different things but mostly talking about the job.

The Hiders simply had no idea what the new world was like.

Last term, when their history teacher broke them up into small discussion groups for the Ishi book reports, one of the first questions that came up was how could otherwise good people participate in and sanction such atrocities as some early settlers had carried out on the Indians?

There was no easy answer. Their teacher explained that fear played a big part of it. The Indians attacked farms and ranches because they themselves were being attacked in their camps. No one pushed the Yahi around because, whenever threatened, they would fight. It was their only means of survival. Yahi warriors were the defenders of family and tribe and when the government repeatedly broke their promises to the Indians and sent in the Army, or Militia, the only recourse the Indians had was to fight. If they didn't fight, they and their families would surely die.

Ironically, settlers living on remote ranches had identical fears. They were deathly afraid of Indian attacks. Many felt that if they didn't strike first, that the Indians would kill them. It was just a short leap to the idea of killing all the Indians—even the friendly ones—to make all of Northern California safe for the whites.

The decision was cemented when the Mill Creeks brutally murdered the Hickock and Lewis children. Murdering innocent young children pushed many whites right over the edge—a bit of an irony when some of these very same whites were killing Indian children and then wondering why the Indians were killing white children.

During the same time frame as the American Westward expansion, whites in Canada were also moving from East to West. There were few Indian conflicts in Canada because the Canadian Government had the backbone to honor their treaties with the First Peoples. With rare exceptions, whites did not kill Indians and, conversely, Indians did not kill whites. When problems did arise, Mounties were quickly rushed in to settle disputes. To the credit of the Mounties, they settled in the Indians' favor as many times as they did for the whites. It wasn't always easy, but the fragile peace was somehow maintained.

Genuine fear on both sides was one of the main causes of conflict going back literally to the very first English settlements in Virginia. As such, war between whites and Indians in America had been raging on for hundreds of years. While most pioneers were decent, law-abiding folks just looking to make a better life for themselves, several frontiersmen were young, impulsive drifters, poorly educated, often unemployed, often exploited, often taking the law into their own hands, especially when *they* felt threatened.

One of the study groups asked the teacher, "In your opinion, from the Indian point of view, which one of the pioneers committed the worst atrocities?"

"What we regard as atrocities today was considered acts of bravery yesterday," replied the teacher.

The students refused to accept that. They wanted a real answer.

"All right, the same names keep coming up for those who fought against the Indians. Most of the pioneer community widely viewed these folks as selfless heroes, willing to risk their very lives to protect their community—Ebben, Anderson, Good, Young, Breckenridge, Bowman, the Moak brothers, the Carty family. Take your pick. I think that over a period of time, these Indian fighters became extremely frustrated and took more and more matters into their own hands. Pretty soon they were killing any and all Indians. The Guardsmen were embittered about fighting a twenty-one-year war against the Indians. It seemed to them to be never ending and getting worse instead of better. My honest answer is, I don't know what pushed otherwise good people into making bad decisions, other than rage and fear. I don't think we know enough about them to know what was driving them. Still, if I had to pick just one man who regularly took the law into his own hands, I would guess Mr. Pentz."

MR. PENTZ'S ABJECT FAILURE
AT ANGER MANAGEMENT

In the early 1850s, Mr. Pentz and several companions were walking up a narrow trail alongside Concow Creek, deep in Indian Territory. The small creek separated Concow land from Yahi land.

They encountered a solitary Indian Chief walking toward them. One report, written decades later, states that the man was a Concow Chief, another that he was a Yahi Chief. None of the reports explain how they knew the man to be a Chief.

Pentz and his companions were probably the first white people that the Chief had ever seen. The whites stopped and stood in the middle of the trail, motioning for the Indian to move aside. The Chief stopped, surprised by the sudden appearance of the whites and then shook his head, "No." They signed again for the Indian to move. Again, he refused. If anyone should get off the trail, it should be the whites. He was a Chief, this was his country, his trail, and why should he defer to a group of total strangers?

Mr. Pentz began angrily questioning the Indian over his refusal to move and early into the one-sided conversation detected a "surly and belligerent attitude." The solitary Indian, who most likely did not understand one word of English, apparently failed Mr. Pentz's attitude test. Pentz decided to take it upon himself to punish the offending Indian by hanging him. Pentz believed that simply yelling at the Indian would not be enough. The Indian would have to be punished, and it was up to Mr. Pentz, as the aggrieved party, to carry out the punishment.

In the early pioneer days, for a white to simply shrug his shoulders and walk around the Indian would be a great loss of face. This was absolutely unacceptable to Mr. Pentz.

The Indian, however, did not care about the loss of face for Mr. Pentz. He had "right" on his side, and he was not going to move off his trail—not for anybody. A furious fight ensued, and it took all four of Pentz's men to hold him down while a rope was thrown over a tree limb.

The Indian fought with everything he had, but Pentz and company managed to overpower and hang him.

The body was left hanging several feet off the ground, now blocking the trail, causing Pentz and friends to get off the trail and walk around the swaying body. It was a moment of irony that apparently eluded Pentz and his men.

At that time, frontier communities started paying a bounty of five dollars for every Indian killed. A scalp was proof of the deed. It is unknown whether Pentz and his men scalped the Indian after hanging him. Most whites scalped Indians to prove the courage of the whites. The five dollars was an extra bonus, often equaling a full week or more of work.

In 1853, like his nearby friends, the Carty family, Mr. Pentz discovered several of his cattle missing. He gathered some ranch hands and some Mexican War veterans and went looking for the Yahi Indians. None were to be found. So Mr. Pentz and company rode some forty miles south of the Yahi country and soon stumbled across a band of Maidu. Several hours later, according to one of his men, the Pentz group finished killing some fifty to sixty men, women and children.

He and his men then killed another twenty-five Indians near Dogtown, California.

In all the killings, they captured only one Yahi—a man known to the pioneer community as "Express Bill." Pentz and company promptly hanged poor Bill.

Every time the Indians killed a farmer, teamster or settler, meetings were immediately held at the Pentz ranch. The Pentzs and Cartys would join forces, arm whatever drifters they could find, and set out on a bloodlust of killing Indians. They never came back without scalps, and most often the scalps were from Indians who wanted only peace with the whites.

Most likely the scalps were turned in for the bounty.

One thing the Yahi were good at was to trick the whites into killing Yahi tribal enemies. The Yahi would travel some thirty or forty miles outside their normal homeland, kill an unsuspecting prospector or traveling teamster, and then quickly retreat to their mountain hideout. The whites would angrily respond by killing the wrong band of near-by Indians, believing them to be responsible for the murders.

The Yahi made sure that whenever they killed a settler or rancher, it was usually in the homeland of an enemy tribe, giving power to the old saying, *"The enemy of my enemy is my friend."*

Neither Mr. Pentz nor anyone from the Carty family nor any of the people they employed was ever brought to justice for all the murders and atrocities they committed.

Conversely, all Northern California Indians paid for the actions of a few by vigilante justice.

THE MISSING ELK HUNTER

TWO YEARS EARLIER
(PAULINA WILDERNESS)

Jumping Bull and Kicking Horse crawled from the lodge through the brush-covered entrance for an early morning hunt. Their tribal Chief and several others joined them. Each hunter carried a pack board plus a bow and full quiver of arrows. Each had a long knife for skinning out and carving the game up for carrying back to the cave. In their grandparents' lifetime and, for all the years before that, the men would hunt and kill; the women would carry the meat home, allowing the men more time for more hunting, plus their most important job—protecting the tribe. The old ways and the division of labor had been put aside to allow for the tribe's survival into the Twenty-First Century. Now the women were as skilled with the bow and the lance as the men, and the men were carrying back the game to the lodge. Some of the very best warriors that the small tribe had were women. But, in fact, none of the Hiders, either male or female, had ever been tested in combat like their ancestors, except for one very recent encounter.

So careful were the people in their hiding that their only contact with an enemy combatant occurred when a white hunter saw them and, staggering forward, started shooting at Chief Tuliyani. It could have been the fact that the Chief was dressed all in buckskin, and the hunter mistook him for a deer. Or it could have been that whites always shot at and tried to kill the Yahi. As it was, the Chief was wounded with one pass-through shot to his upper shoulder. Immediately, several of the Chief's hunting party rushed out of the nearby brush to shoot the attacker full of arrows.

Two companions of the hunter watched in horror as their friend raised his rifle to shoot at the Chief. Both yelled to not shoot. The man fired anyway and within seconds, before he could even get another shot off, he was filled with arrows. His two friends could not believe their eyes as their companion dropped to the ground. He appeared to be mortally wounded. The white snow around him was turning a bright crimson. They turned and ran as the shouting Indians fired volley after volley of arrows at them, just barely missing.

The two hunters ran off with several Indians in pursuit. The Indians ran just far enough to retrieve their arrows and then returned to assist their tribal Chief.

Fearful of discovery by others, the Indian hunting party quickly diverted a nearby small stream, dug a deep hole in the narrow streambed and placed the hunter's body, clothing and gun into the gravesite. The muddy hole was filled in and heavy boulders pushed over the burial site. Then the Hiders re-diverted the stream back to its original course and threw more rocks around. All traces of the brief encounter were brushed away and, with the stream back in its original bed, no one would ever find the body. The people would be protected.

The tribal members assisted their elderly Chief back to the lodge.

No one in the outside world, now seemingly filled with the Englishmen, would ever know of the attack, which was over literally in seconds. The Hiders watched as searchers went about looking for the missing hunter; then as the snows fell, the searchers simply stopped coming. The Hiders felt that the searchers would not be back until the springtime—if ever.

By then, because of the troubles brought by the flying iron wagon, the people would have to move even deeper into the wilderness.

Their Chief fully recovered from his wound.

A PREDATOR ATTACK

PRESENT TIME
(PAULINA WILDERNESS)

After the Chief's shooting, all tribal members would very carefully push the brush aside to look all around before leaving their hidden lodge. Outside the lodge meant danger. Outside was where the cowboys, Guardsmen and hunters were. Inside was the safety of family and tribe.

As very young children, they had all been trained by their parents to stop, look and listen before venturing out. The Chief's shooting had reinforced their worst fears.

Jumping Bull and Kicking Horse sat by the cave entrance for a full minute, straining to hear the slightest sound. They were on high alert for outsiders. Not hearing anything, the warriors started to very quietly move some brush aside to peek outside the cave entrance, knowing that if any enemies were there, the Hiders would most likely not be seen. When satisfied that no one was around, they would push against the brush, exit and replace the brush to conceal the entrance to their lodge.

Jumping Bull crawled forward and slowly removed enough brush to make room for both he and Kicking Horse to exit. Leading with his left arm while crawling out, he suddenly felt tremendous pain as his arm was suddenly grabbed and nearly crushed with a powerful bite. He could feel skin and tendons literally compress down to his wrist bone. He screamed in reaction to the pain. Gritting his teeth to keep from screaming anymore, he dropped his bow and reached for his knife. In an instant, he was completely pulled from the lodge.

The onslaught began. Rolling on the ground and trying to escape from his attacker's powerful jaws, Jumping Bull was frantically slashing and cutting. One slash opened a cut on the attacker, but it was not enough to drive him off. Jumping Bull was pulled another twenty feet from the Lodge entrance as the attack continued. Bleeding heavily, almost passing out from the pain, Jumping Bull kept thrusting and slashing with his knife.

Each time, the animal managed to easily sidestep him, loosening his grip and then instantly repositioning to deliver the killing bite.

Kicking Horse cried out to his tribesmen for help and then tore through the brush to charge the animal. He rushed forward to help his father and delivered several powerful blows with his bow to the head and face of the attacker, momentarily driving him off. Several tribal members and Kicking Horse half carried and half pulled the mauled hunter back to the safety of the lodge. The frightened tribal members gathered around and asked what happened. Before slipping into unconsciousness, Jumping Bull mumbled, "Shadow."

Shadow ran off under a hail of arrows—all of which missed him.

The women cleaned Jumping Bull's wounds and applied poultices to his arm while the Shaman prayed over him with a sacred eagle feather and blew Juniper smoke over his body. For nearly three days, he drifted in and out of consciousness and then slowly started to regain his strength.

Shadow now knew where they lived.

THE FIRST ENCOUNTER

The snowmobile began sliding on a patch of icy trail. Ryan slowly stopped, leaned far to his left, looked back and waved at Chance, motioning to him to be careful on the ice. Chance returned the wave, and Ryan continued the steep descent. Chance followed closely behind. From this point to the lodge, the trail was a treacherous mix of snow and hidden patches of ice beneath the snow. All of Paulina Mountain was being buffeted by high winds and falling snow. Instead of a one-hour trip back to the truck, it was turning out to be more like three. Snow-laden branches were constantly falling, quickly turning the winter wonderland into a disaster area, making it all the more difficult to safely navigate.

For one brief moment, looking down, Chance could see the brightly lit Paulina Lodge. The lodge and nearby log cabins were all decorated with red and white Christmas lights. Seconds later, the swirling snow and darkening clouds erased the entire scene.

Black snow clouds continued rolling in from the Cascades, bringing an early darkness to Paulina. The two snowmobiles were barely moving downhill when Ryan, now worried about the worsening weather, ever so slightly increased his speed.

"Good," thought Chance, "About time." At the rate his Dad was going, it would be midnight before he would even get lunch, which did not sit well with Chance, who was—no surprise—now starving. Chance eased up on the throttle a little and reached behind him for a snack from his saddlebag. He could just make out his Dad's taillights ahead of him.

Chance suddenly found his snowmobile drifting in a slide to the right, bringing him to the very edge of the high mountain trail. He immediately steered to the left but overcorrected for the black ice beneath the tracks. His snowmobile began sliding away from the edge but heading straight for a massive pine with a deep snow well surrounding the base. Sliding on the ice, Chance was unable to regain control of his machine and, in slow motion, the snowmobile started up and over the berm into the snow well. Jumping off, Chance's snowmobile finished a lazy turn and then did a nose plant, trapped deep inside the snow well.

Looking down the trail, Chance could see his Dad's snowmobile slowly continuing downhill. Chance began frantically yelling and waving but within seconds the taillights were gone. Chance tried to pull his snowmobile out, but the heavy machine would not budge. He wondered if a tread hadn't broken and wrapped itself around a dead log, holding the snowmobile firmly in place. For sure, it would take both he and his Dad to drag the snowmobile from the snow well.

A discouraged Chance sat on the edge of his snowmobile, devouring his snacks, waiting to hear the roar of his Dad's snowmobile returning to help.

"Five minutes before he comes back," thought Chance, "and then we can either pull the snowmobile out or we'll dump the Christmas tree, and I can ride behind him."

He hoped his Dad would understand about the ice patch. Accidents happen and, for sure, he was not speeding. That his Dad would know. Maybe they could even hook up a line and pull the snowmobile out. Maybe his Dad ought to hurry up and get back because being stranded all alone in the middle of a snowstorm with all kinds of limbs crashing to the ground was definitely not a good thing.

Twenty minutes later Chance was thinking, "He must know I'm not behind him. He's probably just looking for a safe place to turn around."

Another twenty minutes later and Chance was swinging his arms and stamping his feet to keep warm. The thermometer on his snowmobile read twenty-five degrees. Nightfall was near, and Chance knew that the temperatures would plummet. When the snow first began falling, it was mostly a dry powder; now it was a heavy, wet snow, causing tree limbs to crash to the ground. Chance began shaking from the wind and ever-increasing cold.

"Hypothermia," he thought, "What a great way to start the holidays."

He began looking around for a deep snow bank to hollow out a snow cave as a shelter. The snow cave would protect him from the wind and gradually increase his body temperature. The problem was, the deepest banks were at the base of the Ponderosas and, for sure, he did not want a heavy limb crashing through his snow cave.

For the next few minutes, the forest fell under a blanket of silence. The roaring wind would come and go but, for now, it was absolutely quiet. The snow kept coming down. Finally, far off in the distance, Chance could hear noise from a snowmobile. Like the wind, it seemed to rise and fall in intensity. Listening carefully to gauge how far his Dad might be, Chance removed his helmet to better hear. At first he shook his head in disbelief, then a shock of panic started to set in for it was not an engine; it was the howling noise of an approaching wolf pack.

The hair began to rise on the back of his neck. Seconds later, Chance could feel his throat muscles constrict with the onset of an asthma attack. His breathing became strained as he frantically went through his pockets looking for his inhalator. The more he forced himself to breathe, the harder it became. Finding the inhalator, he sat in the snow and pressed the button down, holding his breath for as long as possible. His throat muscles began to relax. His breathing became less labored. He took another long pull of medicine and again held his breath.

"Stupid asthma," he thought, "I never had this until Mom died."

Ryan, meanwhile, continued his downhill descent, completely unaware that Chance was not behind him. Twice Ryan almost pulled off to check on Chance but not seeing any signaling headlights, kept pressing on, knowing that the sooner they got to Paulina Lodge, the better.

Going over the day in his mind, Ryan was pretty sure that, had he known the weather would be this severe, he would have postponed the trip for another time.

In the meantime, Chance stood, now a little lightheaded and wobbly, and brushed the snow from his visor. He listened carefully and convinced himself that he had just imagined the howling wolves. His Dad had told him they would be holed up in a lava cave somewhere.

Then, he heard the howling again, this time definitely closer. Visibility was bad enough, but now the very edge of darkness was setting in. Though he had already tried his cell phone, he tried again, but there was no service. His only hope now was his Dad showing up, armed and ready. As a game warden, he would instinctively know what to do. Most likely, the wolves would all run when they heard his snowmobile. That gave Chance an idea. He reached over and pressed the starter on his snowmobile, thinking that if the wolves would run from his Dad's snowmobile, they would certainly run from his.

Instead of the roar of an engine, all Chance heard was the *click, click, click* of a dead battery. He turned the key on and off several times, all the while pressing the starter button. More clicks, no engine. Chance was pretty good with mechanical things, but he could not understand why the battery died. Maybe due to the cold weather, but then it dawned on him. His engine stalled out when he hit the snow berm, but Chance had forgotten to turn the ignition off. He had left the headlight on, which was now buried deep in the snow. His battery was completely drained.

At that moment, Chance heard the baying and howling of the entire wolf pack. They sounded terribly close. Chance didn't have time to climb a tree, nor could he even reach the lowest branches of any nearby trees. He quickly began rummaging through his saddle packs for any kind of weapon. All he had was a small Swiss Army pocketknife and a weak flashlight.

Broken tree limbs were now all around and they were his only hope. Chance reached out for a fractured limb only a few feet away. It was a thick, stout branch, almost seven feet in length with a long partial point where it had split off from the tree. The snowmobile was in front of Chance and the old growth Ponderosa behind him. His back was protected and to some degree his front. He hefted the heavy pine limb. If one or more of the wolves decided to attack, maybe he could hit them hard enough to drive them off. Then he remembered that wolves never attack people. They were afraid of people.

Suddenly, there was a loud crashing to his left, and four does came bounding through the snowdrifts only mere feet away from the snowmobile. They seemed terribly stressed and appeared exhausted from running. The snow was greatly slowing them down. For the few seconds that Chance could clearly see them, all four appeared ragged and wild-eyed. They would leap, run a few feet through the snow, and then leap again. They jumped past Chance and continued struggling downhill on the old logging road.

Chance remained frozen in place. He could now hear the soft padding of the wolf paws crunching through the snow. They were on the hunt and almost on top of the does. They were no longer howling. Seconds later they appeared, following directly in the deer tracks. Running toward Chance, he could see their tongues hanging out from the long pursuit.

The pack leader was a huge black wolf, just like his Dad had told him. He was taking long leaps through the snow, and the other wolves would do their best to keep up. They were so close that Chance could smell the entire pack.

Chance did not move—remaining absolutely motionless—hoping that the wolves would be so focused on catching the deer that they would run right by him, not even seeing him. Besides, what else could he do?

Spotting the last of the fleeing deer, the black wolf redoubled his efforts. He looked neither to the left or right, just kept his bright yellow eyes focused intently on the running deer. As he ran parallel to Chance, he seemed to slow for a moment, looked over at Chance and, for one brief moment, curled his lips over his fangs, looked back and forth between Chance and the deer and continued running down the does.

The black wolf didn't even miss a stride. None of the other wolves so much as looked at Chance; all were struggling to keep up with the pack leader.

In an instant both the deer and wolves were gone.

Chance just stood there, trembling and exhausted. It took him two full minutes before he could even move. He had never before been this frightened in his entire young life. The running wolves had passed so close that Chance could have reached out and touched them with the broken tree limb. He kept telling himself that wolves were afraid of people, but so were coyotes, and he had recently read about a pack of coyotes attacking and killing a hiker somewhere in the Midwest.

The lead wolf was everything his Dad had described. As he was running by, Chance could see the powerful muscles rippling underneath his skin as he made one long leap and bound after another. As the lead alpha male, all the other wolves were panting hard, trying to keep up with him.

A badly shaken Chance looked upward and asked his mother for her help.

"Send Dad," was all he asked. His Dad would know what to do.

PAULINA WILDERNESS

PRESENT TIME

It was a very tired and surprised Ryan who dismounted at the truck. He stretched, working the kinks out of his lower back from hours spent on the snowmobile. Chance was not behind him. He kept checking all the way down, but not once did he see Chance flashing his lights. Ryan felt sure that he would have known or sensed if something had happened.

Ryan unlocked the truck, started the engine and dug into his Panini. If Chance did not show up in the next few minutes, Ryan would head back up after him. He was hoping that if Chance could see the cabin lights that maybe he just slowed down and was taking his time getting there, which would be in character for Chance, as he was most likely thinking about Ashley.

Ryan did not have cell phone service. Several times he tried to call the dispatch center from his truck radio but could not get through. He went into the lodge to use a landline but was told that power and phone lines were down, not just in Bend but also in most of Deschutes County. The Lodge and guest cabins were operating only on generator power. Falling trees had gone down through power lines everywhere. It would be hours—maybe even days—before electricity and phone service would be even partially restored.

Under normal circumstances, even on his day off, Ryan would have reported for duty at the Bend office to assist with patrol. Things were different now. Chance had still not shown up, and Ryan was getting worried. Snowmobiles could be fickle, and Ryan began thinking that most likely Chance's snowmobile might have broken down, and he was stuck somewhere up on the mountain. With temperatures dropping and the heavy snowfall continuing, Ryan quickly stashed the Christmas tree into the truck bed, topped off the snowmobile fuel tank and loaded up with extra food and water.

Ryan started back up the mountain, but it was very slow going. His plan was to go a few hundred feet, turn off the engine, remove his helmet, yell out for Chance and listen. When he first started patrol as a State Trooper, his training officer had told him to always patrol with the windows partially down. "I don't give a rat's ass how cold it is outside," said the grizzled trooper. "Keep the heat on and the windows down in case some taxpayer is out there screaming for help."

Ever since, even on the coldest nights, Ryan always kept the two front windows mostly down on any police vehicle he was driving.

The higher up the mountain, the more worried he became. He kept scanning the road to see if the snowmobile had gone off anywhere. He worried that if Chance had gone off the road, he might try to walk down the mountain. It would be too easy for him to get lost, especially as the road was now just a mass of snow.

By the time he was more than halfway to the top, Ryan had made numerous stops, constantly calling out for Chance but to no avail. Several times the howling wind had died down and then would instantly pick up. If Chance was anywhere near the road, Ryan hoped that he would either hear the snowmobile or his Dad calling.

Ryan increased his speed ever so slightly, knowing that Chance had to be somewhere close by. His headlight shone brightly against the falling snow. He came to a small, slight bend in the road with deep snow banks on either side. As he slowed for the bend, he immediately braked to a hard stop. Right before him was a freshly killed deer. The carcass had been partially eaten and was surrounded by wolf tracks. This was definitely not there on his way down. Ryan guessed that the deer had been killed maybe a half hour ago at the most. The falling snow had covered nearly all of the blood but, as Ryan examined the carcass, it was still warm. Looking around, Ryan could see where the running deer had jumped off the snow bank to escape the wolves. A few feet off the road, just inside the forest, Ryan could see another deer, then a few feet past that still another.

Great chunks of meat were missing from all of the deer. To Ryan, it looked like a fourth deer left a blood trail as it was dragged off into the forest.

Ryan guessed he had just missed the wolves.

The wolves had ripped the deer apart, scattering torn legs and entrails all around the kill sites. Judging from the size of the nearby tracks, Ryan guessed that the fourth deer belonged to the pack leader and that he dragged it away to keep the others from getting any of the meat.

Alpha males will share but only after they have had their fill.

Ryan yelled several times for Chance. He dragged the deer remains to the side of the trail, strapped his helmet on and started the snowmobile. His plan now was to go full-bore up the mountain until he found Chance. It wasn't that far to the top, and Chance had to be on the road somewhere. If he didn't find Chance or the snowmobile, he would come back to the deer marker and follow his original plan of stop and shout.

One thing he learned as a game warden—you have to change your plan to meet changing circumstances.

Confident he would absolutely find Chance; he was also developing an alternative plan—just in case. If necessary, he would snowmobile to Hwy. 97 and then use his cell to call out Deschutes County Search and Rescue, assuming he would have service. The more eyes looking for Chance, the faster he would be found.

Ryan now began to worry that maybe Chance had some type of run-in with the wolves and was waiting for Ryan to find him. In a way, though, that didn't make sense. Ryan knew that there had never been a documented case of a wolf attack in Oregon. Not ever. On the other hand, if it was just a broken snowmobile, Chance could always make a snow cave and wait to be rescued. He had plenty of warm clothing, water and trail food.

Just as Ryan started to turn the throttle, he was suddenly hit with what felt like a freight train. He never saw it coming. It happened so fast that he lost control of the snowmobile, and it literally tipped over on top of him, pinning him to the ground. Ryan instantly felt a sharp, cracking pain in his chest. For the first couple of seconds, he thought a falling limb hit him. Then he heard the snarling of a wolf and felt tearing pain as the wolf clamped down on his right arm and tried to drag him out from under the snowmobile.

Ryan nearly passed out from the pain. His chest hurt so bad that it was all he could do to breathe. Through the thick insulation of his snowmobile suit he could feel his arm being wrenched around behind him. He had only seconds to act or he would lose his arm. Using his left hand he pulled out his Glock and, pressing it directly into the wolf's chest, began firing.

The wolf's chest cavity blew apart from the high-powered bullets. Ryan was trying to get out from under the snowmobile when he heard heavier panting. Another wolf had come up from behind and slammed into him, trying to get its jaws around Ryan's neck. The snowmobile helmet blocked his way. Ryan knew that wolves killed by clamping down on the neck, suffocating the prey. Now nearly flat on his back with the grey wolf behind him, Ryan looked up directly into the wolf's face, extended his arm and pulled the trigger. He put two rounds into the wolf's head, killing him instantly.

Ryan could feel warm blood trickling down his arm. With every breath that he took, it felt like a vise was clamping down on his chest. He knew that the remaining wolves were there, but he couldn't see them.

Then, standing near his feet, was the immense black wolf. The snowy background framed him. The other wolves stood behind him. They were terribly nervous, stamping their feet in the snow and whimpering. Loud gunfire was new to them. In the space of just seconds, they had lost two pack members. One young wolf, at the very end of the line, made several false charges toward Ryan. He would lunge forward a few feet and then stop, snarling and turning the whole time.

It took every ounce of his strength, but Ryan slowly raised the Glock and pointed it directly at the black male. His hand was shaking uncontrollably. He knew if he could take out the leader, then the rest of the wolves would run off.

Try as he might, Ryan could not fix the iron sights onto the alpha male. His gun hand was shaking too much. It didn't matter. At such close range, all he really had to do was point and shoot.

He fired three rounds off in a rapid-fire sequence. The black wolf just stood there, not making a sound. His yellow eyes were seemingly filled with rage. Strangely enough, all the other wolves, with the exception of the very last one, just kept staring intently at the black male.

Somehow, Ryan had missed. In an instant, the pack leader was gone. He turned, leaped up the snow bank and disappeared. The other wolves were right behind him. Ryan could hear the pack running off into the forest. For a few seconds, he could hear them crashing through some brush and then nothing.

Ryan convulsed several times with pain. Though the temperature had now dropped to twenty degrees, beads of sweat were dripping from his face onto his parka and then freezing. Every breath he took wracked his body with pain. Between short breaths, he tried to calm down. He knew he was slipping into shock.

He was also terribly worried about his son. Chance breaking down on the trail in the middle of a severe snowstorm was one concern, but now Ryan was worried about the wolves finding him. Ryan started out looking for Chance, but now he was counting on Chance finding him.

Ryan felt very faint. He guessed he had some broken ribs at the very least. He might even have a concussion. It was impossible for him to push the snowmobile off. He felt himself on the verge of consciousness.

Pretty soon he would be completely covered with snow. Reaching to his chest, he pushed the red button on his avalanche locator. Instantly a GPS signal was sent pinpointing his exact location to the County Search and Rescue Coordinator. An alarm would sound at the Sheriff's Office, and the Search and Rescue team would respond with volunteers on snowmobiles and the County snow cat.

No matter what it took, Ryan would somehow get through this. He would survive. "This too shall pass," he thought. He was all that Chance had left. He knew that Chance was counting on him—now more than ever.

At all costs, Ryan had to survive.

YET ANOTHER WOLF ENCOUNTER

The escaping wolves kept porpoising up the mountain behind their leader. The pace was frantic, accelerated by the violent deaths of the two pack members. All the wolves were well fed and wanted nothing more than to return to the den to sleep off their meal and recover from the trauma of the day. It was a struggle for them to keep up with the black wolf. To not keep up would cause them the most severe of problems, which none of them wanted.

It seemed that the alpha male had other plans. He was making a beeline for where he had spotted Chance. The pack gamely followed behind. The safety of the pack depended upon all the wolves acting as one.

Chance never heard the wolves coming. To conserve battery power, he would turn the flashlight on, make a quick 360-degree scan and then turn it off again. He started a scan when he noticed several shadows silently moving through the woods. The wolves now stood some fifty feet or so before him, quietly lined up behind their leader. The black wolf fixed Chance with a stare while the other wolves, with one exception, kept their eyes solely on their leader. The one exception was the young wolf at the end of the pack. Several times he would make a false charge toward Chance, running a few feet forward and then instantly turning and returning to his place in line. Chance noticed he was the only wolf who never looked at the alpha leader.

Chance remained absolutely motionless, one gloved hand wrapped around the sharp lance, the other holding his small flashlight.

The flickering flashlight seemed to bother the pack leader. Several times he looked away to avoid the light.

The pack seemed smaller. Chance worried that several of the wolves might be moving in on him by his blind spots. He slowly turned his head to the left, and as he began to turn to the right, he noticed the last wolf working himself into a frenzy. The wolf would lunge forward, then stop, then begin running in tight circles. Several times he repeated the process, all the while edging ever closer to Chance. Suddenly, without warning, he bolted, charging head-on straight at Chance.

Chance had only seconds to act. The wolf was now only several leaps away. For just one moment—instead of panic—Chance could actually feel the fear go away. He could handle this. Every cell in his body was surging with adrenalin. He instantly tried to decide if he should hit the wolf with the heavy end of his stick or try impaling him with the sharp end.

He had only one goal; to stop the attacking wolf.

The decision was made for him.

As the young wolf was about to leap, the pack leader attacked him.

The black wolf cleared almost twenty feet of distance with one bound and grabbed the young wolf around the throat. He literally lifted him off the ground, viciously shaking his head back and forth. The young wolf put up a tremendous struggle but, with all four feet completely off the ground, he could not get any purchase. He was frantically snapping at the throat of the alpha male. He tried tearing into the flesh, but the black wolf was crunching down on the back of his neck. The fight continued for a full minute, and Chance could see the young wolf's eyes slowly roll up literally back into his head, followed by a loud cracking noise. The wolf went limp and stopped struggling, but the black wolf held him for another full minute, slowly dropping him to the ground.

The kill took place only yards away from where Chance was standing.

Disobedience was simply not tolerated. If the other wolves ever sensed even the slightest weakness by the pack leader, they would instantly turn on him, doing their best to kill him or, at the very least, to drive him out of the pack. Either way was a death sentence. To stay alive, the alpha leader had to maintain the strictest of discipline.

The wolf he just killed was his own son.

Blood was now gushing out from the dead wolf's throat and mouth. His long legs were limp, and his head was completely flopped over to one side.

The black wolf sniffed him several times and then raising his head to the sky, he gave a long, mournful howl. The other wolves all joined in. The howling continued for a full minute and then stopped. The alpha male gave Chance a final look, turned and started running, leaving the dead wolf near Chance's feet. The dwindling pack instantly followed.

Chance again remained absolutely motionless. For several minutes, he just stood there in total shock. This was the closest he had ever come to being in complete danger. Strangely, he was now beyond scared. He was completely energized by his pounding heart. Chance felt that if attacked, he could have taken on the entire pack and killed each and every one. For that one moment in time, he was absolutely invincible.

Then shock started to set in. Reaching for his inhalator, he quickly took two pulls, holding his breath until the medicine stabilized his breathing. He simply could not believe what had just happened. The snow all around was red from the leaking wolf. Chance stepped out from behind his snowmobile and began prodding the wolf with the tip of his lance. The wolf's blood completely covered the long end of the sharp limb and began to freeze. Chance poked the wolf several more times until he felt it was safe enough to push the body away.

He wisely decided that he did not want the dead wolf around in case the other wolves came back.

Pushing didn't work, so Chance stood in front of the wolf's stomach and with one hand grabbed the tail and with the other grabbed a front leg. He managed to pull the wolf back a good hundred feet, and then he returned to the snowmobile and collapsed, violently shaking from his encounter. He could not figure out if the shaking was from the cold or from the wolf attack.

Never before had he ever experienced anything like this. Still trembling terribly from what just happened, he then began to wonder if there was any way he could keep the wolf hide. Maybe he and his Dad could skin it out and take the pelt home, or, at the very least, the teeth. It's not like *he* killed a federally protected animal. The wolf died a natural death, sort of, and he was just recycling it—in a matter of speaking.

He could hardly wait to tell Ashley what had happened.

PAULINA WILDERNESS

TWO WEEKS EARLIER

It was a bitter cold night. The Hiders had just finished a communal stew of venison, greens, cooked tubers and a dessert of huckleberries spread over warm Indian fry bread made from crushed acorn flour. Another deep snowfall appeared imminent, with black storm clouds forming over the mountains to the west.

The Hiders broke into small family groups and sat around the fire, talking softly amongst themselves. From time to time, someone would throw an extra log onto the fire, causing a flurry of sparks to rise to the cave ceiling. Most of the people sat or stretched out from sheer exhaustion, recovering from the labors of the day.

One woman started singing an ancient song, the same song that her grandparents and great-grandparents sang while hiding from the whites in Northern California. Several others joined in, all singing quietly. To sing the old songs was a way to give praise and remembrance to all those who had gone before them.

Storytelling and singing were the only forms of entertainment that the tribe ever knew; so busy were they at just barely keeping alive and hidden from the Englishman.

Various tools, weapons and heavy clothing were strewn about the cave. All the Hiders carried their long obsidian knives. Both men and women used their knives many times during the day, either for food preparation, cutting animal hide, or shaping their weapons. Knives were sometimes joined together and used as scissors with the butt ends held in place by a small peg of wood tied off with deer sinew. Lances, bows and arrows were stacked all around the cave. A winter's supply of firewood was neatly placed in immense rows at the very back of the cave. Pegs pounded into the lava cave walls held fiber baskets filled to overflowing with smoked fish and elk meat. The tribe of twelve, most of them quite elderly finally had enough food stored to see them through to the spring.

Outside, a vast array of brilliant, blinking stars peeked out through the snow clouds. The stars were so close one could almost touch them. A strong wind blew through the treetops. Storm clouds moving in from the Cascades were now reaching the Ochocos. Several of the tribal members shivered and moved in even closer to the fire.

The Guardian, always a warrior in his prime, sat next to the brush-filled cave entrance. Several times he glanced over his shoulder, occasionally hearing the snapping of several small branches. Like so many times before, he assumed it was nothing more than some ground squirrels or mice seeking either warm shelter or escape from bigger predators.

Mere feet away, a gray timber wolf was quietly pulling the brush apart. Strong smells of meat and fish filled his nostrils. Inside was enough food to see the entire pack through the long winter, but they were not there for the food. Standing at the very rear of the pack was the large black wolf, yellow eyes on fire, as the other wolves nervously paced. They were waiting for the cave to be opened. Several of the younger wolves were salivating long streams of drool.

The drools were from anticipation—not fear.

The Guardian soon noticed a strong, powerful smell and poked his cousin, telling him that he again had eaten too much venison and now the whole tribe would suffer. His cousin laughed, denying the accusation but also noticing the smell. Both men, suddenly growing alarmed, turned to the cave entrance. At that precise moment, the first wolf crashed through the brush and all the wolves rushed into the cave, snarling and slashing in every direction at once. The wolves spread out and went for victims of opportunity.

Bringing up the rear was the large black wolf. He was the guarantee that no one would get out alive.

This was not to be a short-lived attack. The wolves were there to kill. Everyone started screaming. Whisper dropped to her knees as the black wolf ran toward her. Shadow paused for one moment, staring at her, and then leaping; he sailed right over Whisper and clamped his powerful jaws around the neck of an elderly warrior, dragging the screaming man back to the cave entrance. Crunching down, he held the man in place until he finally stopped moving. He searched for his next target and spotted a young female standing by the fire, momentarily frozen in place by the ferocity of the attack.

Both the Guardian and his cousin were now pinned to the ground by attacking wolves, and both men were bleeding heavily as the wolves raked them with tooth and claw. Each man had his knife out and was repeatedly stabbing at their attackers. For the Hiders, for the first time in over one hundred years, their lodge was under attack in what would clearly be a fight to the finish.

He Who Stands and Jumping Bull each grabbed a lance from the cave wall and charged toward the wolves, yelling and screaming at the top of their lungs. The wolves were momentarily startled but held their ground. The young woman managed to grab a piece of burning wood from the fire and began swinging it in front of her. An elderly man picked up the stew pot and threw the boiling hot contents upon two wolves running toward him.

Kicking Horse and Chief Tuliyani both managed to grab a bow and send a swarm of arrows at the attacking wolves. Most of the arrows missed, bouncing harmlessly off the cave walls, but three arrows struck home and the stricken wolf turned to flee. Chief Tuliyani grabbed a lance and thrust it deeply into the wolf's chest, killing him instantly.

The remaining wolves were furiously slashing and biting the people. There was no respite from their attack. Over the snarling of the wolves could be heard the screaming of the people. One of the younger wolves, so crazed with the attack, actually began biting another wolf.

The black wolf stared at the young woman, his yellow eyes searching her out. He watched as she kept the other wolves at bay with the burning log.

Jumping over the body of the now-dead elderly warrior, the alpha male dropped down into a crouch and made ready to leap. The woman had just enough time to scoop up a pot of red-hot embers and, as the wolf leaped toward her, she threw the ash and embers directly into the wolf's face, momentarily blinding him.

The pain from the fire was intense, and the pack leader howled with rage. He ran in several small circles, pawing at his face, trying to shake off the burning embers. Moments later, he again found the female who had managed to pick up a nearby lance.

In a fury, Shadow ran toward her. She began to frantically jab the empty air in front of her to keep Shadow at bay. After one such thrust, Shadow reached up, crunched down hard on her lance, and snapped it in half. He ignored the older, easier targets running through the lodge. For now, he had only one target, and that was the one who had caused him so much pain.

The young girl held on to the thick end of the lance and grabbed a deer cape, which she managed to wrap around her arm. The black wolf was upon her, and she held him off with her wrapped arm squarely in his mouth, all the while beating on his head with the short, heavy end of her broken lance. Her defense against the wolf was merciless. Her furious blows were so fast and powerful that the alpha male was nearly knocked unconscious.

The black wolf suddenly turned and ran from the cave. The surviving wolves instantly followed, leaving behind the one dead wolf.

After the wolves departed, most of the elderly tribal members collapsed to the ground. Several others, bleeding heavily, leaned against the cave walls for support. One man reached out for his wife, and she collapsed in his arms.

Chief Tuliyani quickly took charge, directing his three standing warriors to guard the lodge entrance in case the wolves returned. The men quickly piled heavy lava rocks, one on top of the other, to block the cave entrance.

The Chief saw his childhood friend stretched out near the cave entrance, dead from the attack. Other tribal members, both male and female, were moaning and bleeding heavily from their wounds. The young girl sat on the cave floor, holding her arm, hysterically crying over the loss of an uncle. Deep sobs wracked her body. The dead warrior was one of her favorite great-uncles.

In the middle of the cave was the body of a dead timber wolf. Several of the precious food baskets had been tipped over and the contents now covered with dirt and ash. Whisper ran to her husband, visibly trembling and held on to him for support. Nopanny, bleeding heavily from a gashed shoulder, was struggling to reach her sister and their husband.

In over one hundred years of hiding, the tribe had never gone through anything like this. The Chief had the fallen warrior's body covered and after trying to comfort his friend's shocked wife, herself badly bitten, made arrangements to release his friend's spirit to the land of the dead in the coming morning. The Chief knew that none of the tribe would get any sleep that night, and it was best for all to have the cremation immediately. That was the proper Yahi way to handle death.

The dead wolf would not go into the communal stew pot. Kicking Horse and his father, Jumping Bull, would skin the wolf out, carry the meat far from the cave and leave it for the forest scavengers to find. The wolf hide would be dried and left stretched inside the cave entrance with the hope that the scent of the dead wolf would prevent any more wolf attacks. The pack was now nearly cut in half with only five wolves remaining.

BIA HOMICIDE INVESTIGATION
PRESENT TIME

Special Agent Walton finished his third complete reading of the Yahi file. He managed to speed-read the file over a two-day period. "No wonder these poor people fled California," he thought. "If they stayed, they all would have been murdered." Still, in spite of poring over every page, the most Walton could glean was that if under attack, the Indians always fought back. They were proud warriors, and fighting was their entire tribal history.

Walton thought that, "Maybe, just maybe, these folks might be involved in the disappearance of the missing elk hunter."

Walton decided it was time to re-interview the four elk hunters, especially the two who had lawyered up. Hiring expensive defense attorneys was usually not something most people did, unless they had something to hide. Decades of knowledge and experience had taught Walton that all he had to do was find out what they were hiding.

The two men who refused to help or explain what had happened to their missing friend had the right to have their attorneys present during any interviews. Walton also had some rights as an investigator, starting with the right to have the FBI present during an interrogation. Under Federal law, the FBI investigated homicides on Federal land. "They can voluntarily come down here with their attorneys," thought Walton. "Or the FBI and I can go to their place of employment and have a heart-to-heart with them there."

Either way would work.

Walton reached for the phone to start the process. He would give the attorneys a courtesy call and have the attorneys contact their clients. That would start the ball rolling. He would separate the two persons of interest during the interrogation process, suggest that he and the FBI knew more than what the potential defendants were saying, then point out that whoever shared first would get the best deal, and the other guy would be left holding the bag.

He would take the lead on one interview, and FBI Agent Adams would handle the other.

It was time for the truth to come out.

RYAN'S RESCUE
PRESENT TIME

Mason Many Crows and Deputy Johansen met Buster Higgins at the ODFW Headquarters in Bend. Buster loaded the Jeep Cherokee with emergency supplies while waiting for Mason and Johansen to arrive. He had the chains on and an ODFW snowmobile trailer hooked up and ready to go.

Hwy. 97 from Lolo Pass up and over the divide to Bear Springs Road all the way down to Northern California was choked with snow. Numerous cars were sliding off the road into the drainage ditches. Big trucks were simply stopping in the middle of the road, and as far as the eye could see, the highway was lit up with the emergency lights of police cars, fire engines and tow trucks.

The signpost for the small town of Maupin was completely buried under the snow. Maupin was named after the late Harold Maupin who shot and killed Chief Paulina in April, 1867, because Paulina was eating one of Maupin's cows. Maupin was so proud about the kill that he nailed Paulina's scalp to the side of his barn.

Several unemployed loggers sat by the side of the road with a sign offering to put chains on for so much per set. They were swamped. Small recompense for losing their jobs to a little mouse-pooping owl that permanently closed all Oregon public lands to logging. The environmental theory was that the Spotted Owl would never nest again if its nesting tree were cut down. The scientific reality was that the owls simply moved a few hundred yards away and made a new nest in another tree.

Earlier, Mason was busy working the phones, making wellness checks on elderly tribal members living on outlying remote ranches to see how they were doing. From time to time, he would dispatch one of the tribal woodcutters to deliver an emergency cord of firewood to someone in need. The Confederated Tribes of the Warm Springs Indian Reservation covered nearly twenty-four hundred square miles, making it one of the biggest Indian reservations in the entire nation. It was a lot of territory to cover, and some of the tribal members did not have any landline or cell-phone service at all. Mason especially liked to compare the reservation to Rhode Island. "Rhode Island," he once observed, "Has about eleven hundred square miles with a population base of over one million or more. Our reservation is two thousand four hundred square miles with only thirty-nine hundred people living on the entire Rez."

Vast tracks of forest, mountains and meadows filled the reservation. From the high mountain Douglas fir and pine forests in the West to the deep, arid canyons of the East, Mason knew that there were parts of the Reservation that no one had ever seen or explored, simply because the locations were so remote and inaccessible. The rivers were all clean and pure and, aside from the occasional isolated ranch, most of the mountainous land was uninhabited.

Between phone calls, one of his assistants, Cindy Kalama, slipped a note to Mason that Buster was anxiously holding on line 2. Mason immediately took the call, and a stressed Buster told him that Ryan's avalanche locator had gone off high in the Paulinas, and no one had been able to reach him. Mason said he was on his way, and he and Buster quickly put together a list of items they would need.

"Start by getting that jar-head Johansen to join us," said Mason, "He's big, he's strong, and I know he's smarter than what he looks. We can for sure use his young eyes and muscle on a search and rescue."

Mason grabbed his heavy parka, his red bandana, and made a Code 3 lights and siren run down the centerline of Hwy. 97, arriving at Buster's office in less than one hour.

"Fill us in," said Mason, as he and Johansen squeezed into the Cherokee.

"I got the GPS coordinates from Search and Rescue," said Buster. "I looked it up on my topographic map, and he's way more than half-way up the Paulina Trail. We're coordinating with Search and Rescue, but some of their people can't even get out of their driveways. I think we'll be the first ones there. Paulina Lodge is our designated command center."

"What about Chance?" asked Mason.

"He's off snowboarding with some friends, according to my son," said a grim-faced Buster. "You get a snowfall like this, every kid in the world decides it's time to go out and play."

The talk turned serious as they turned off Hwy. 97 and started the slow, arduous trip up to Paulina Lodge. Several times they talked about ditching the Jeep and just taking the snowmobiles, but Buster prevailed when he pointed out that there were other tire tracks going up to the Lodge.

"Very good, Buster," said Mason, "We're going to make a tracker out of you yet. Then again, isn't it possible that those tracks might be coming down from the Lodge instead of going up?"

Buster thought about it for a moment and conceded that it might be possible but asked, "So what, and who cares? As long as we can get up there, we're good."

Mason turned to Johansen and asked, "*Semper Fi,* how do you read those tracks?"

Johansen quietly asked, "Were you in the Corps?"

"No," said Mason, "But I am a veteran. Being a poor, land-locked Indian, I wanted to see the world, but I didn't want to join the Navy, as I knew I would get seasick, delicate being that I am. So I joined the Coast Guard, and they put me on the Cutter Mackinac hundreds of miles off the coast of Iceland. I spent one entire winter in the North Atlantic counting whales and icebergs and managed to get seasick every single day."

Johansen decided to put Mason to the test. "What does *Semper Fi* mean?"

"It means 'Always Faithful.' Everybody knows that. It's kind of like everybody knows the true meaning of *Carpe Diem.*"

Johansen paused and said, "I don't know the true meaning of *Carpe Diem.*"

Mason sighed and answered with a question: "*Semper Fi* is Latin shorthand for *Semper Fidelis,* right?"

Johansen nodded.

"*Carpe Diem* is French. It's what Frenchmen say to each other. Two Frenchmen meet on the street, and they'll be all smiles and say *Bon Jour, Monsieur,* which means 'Good Morning, Sir.' Then they'll mutter under their breath, *Carpe Diem,* which means, 'Hope you have a crappy day'. This is the nature of Frenchmen. They don't like other people. They don't even like other Frenchmen. I thought everybody knew that."

A smiling Johansen said, "I walked right into that didn't I?"

"Yep," said Mason, "But it's good for you. Good police training. Always question what people tell you because some people will lie through their ass some of the time, but all criminals will lie to you all the time. It's like they can't help it. I don't know if lying is part of their DNA or whatever, but it is what it is."

Almost as an afterthought Mason added, "*Carpe Diem* is Latin for 'Seize the day'."

The three then began laying out their search plans for Ryan.

One hour later, they were snowmobiling their way up the Paulina Trail. Mason was in the lead. The Global Positioning Satellite coordinates were entered into his Bushnell and, using the Lodge as the first way point, created a straight line to the blinking X, which was Ryan's location.

Mason slowed as he rounded a small, narrow bend and came across what he first thought was a terrible snowmobile accident. Ryan was pinned under the snowmobile. Mason could just barely make out his chest rising and falling. As he brushed the snow off Ryan, Mason uncovered the two dead wolves. At the same time Johansen lifted the Glock off Ryan's chest. He ejected one live round and another two from the clip.

"Wow," said Johansen, looking down at the dead wolves. "He only had three rounds left. That's taking it down to the wire."

Buster frantically began scooping snow out from under Ryan. He managed to slip a wooden First-Aid board under Ryan and nodded to Mason and Johansen. The two men   grabbed the tipped snowmobile and lifted it high enough for Buster to pull Ryan out.

"Good job, guys," said Mason, while Buster did a cursory exam of the unconscious Ryan.

"I gotta stop this bleeding or we're gonna lose him. Just give me a few minutes to get him bandaged up," said Buster.

Mason was already on his satellite phone making arrangements to have an ambulance meet them at Paulina lodge.

With the heavy weight of the snowmobile off his chest, Ryan seemed to breathe a little easier, although his breathing remained very shallow and labored.

While Buster and Johansen continued with the First Aid, Mason removed his old wheel gun, a long-barrel.45-caliber Smith and Wesson, and began a search of the area. He started with the two dead wolves and then walked in growing circles, mentally mapping the barely visible wolf tracks and torn-apart deer.

Mason cleared the area in a few minutes. Satisfied that the wolves were gone, he holstered his service revolver. He pointed out the dead deer to Buster and Johansen.

"Way I read this," he said, "I think Ryan came across the pack feeding on the deer. They attacked him to protect their kill. He tried to escape, and the snowmobile tipped, pinning him. Then these two came in to finish him off. He shot them, and the rest ran off. I can just barely make out their tracks heading uphill."

Buster didn't even look up. He kept pulling bandage after bandage from his First-Aid kit and continued working on Ryan's arm.

"You don't even want to see this," Buster said to Mason. "He's lost a lot of blood, and this arm is an absolute mess."

Mason was again on his satellite phone giving Dispatch an update on Ryan's condition. He had Search and Rescue give advance notice of Ryan's condition to the St. Charles Emergency Room and to the Bend office of the State Police.

Bundling Ryan up in a heavy blanket, the three men strapped him onto a First-Aid sleigh. With great effort and a lot of heavy lifting, the rescuers turned their snowmobiles around in the narrow roadway, preparing to tow the sleigh between two snowmobiles with a line tied off front and back.

The three agreed that it appeared Ryan was alone. There was only one set of snowmobile tracks on the trail and they were pretty much filled in with falling snow. Mason then made arrangements to have a State Trooper detailed to pick up Chance and bring him to the hospital.

All three were very worried about the extent of Ryan's injuries.

"I've seen this crap in Afghanistan," said Johansen, "and it ain't good. This poor guy is all tore up. Almost looks like an IED got him."

SAR was advised that Ryan had been recovered, and the volunteers could be called off.

As an afterthought, Buster said that as soon as the weather allowed, he was going to come back up and bring the wolves in for an autopsy.

"It might save Ryan from some rabies shots if those dead wolves test negative," said Buster. They would run DNA tests on the wolf blood from the scene and from bite marks on Ryan. If it all matched and turned out negative, then Ryan might not need the otherwise painful series of shots. Only a doctor could decide.

Mason said he would come down and give Buster a hand and that would give him an opportunity to drop Ryan's truck off at his house.

Then Mason abruptly changed his mind, saying, "No, I'll just follow you guys down in his rig," remembering that Ryan always kept his truck keys on the left front tire of his vehicle whenever out in the woods.

Six hours later, Ryan was in the Intensive Care Recovery room at St. Charles, having had emergency surgery for a collapsed lung caused by one of his three broken ribs piercing the lung. Heavily sedated, he had lost a perilous amount of blood, and the ER physician worried that he might also have a concussion. More tests were necessary. He also had ninety stitches in his right arm from the wolf attack.

"Not to worry, he will make it," said the attending doctor, "but he'll need some physical therapy to make him whole."

Mason sat in the ER room, head slumped down, exhausted from the rescue when he suddenly had a scary thought. Bolting upright he turned to Buster and said, "I just realized something. Following you guys down, I had a Christmas tree rattling around in the back of Ryan's truck."

A very tired Buster could barely mumble out a "So?"

"So, if his snowmobile was pointing up the mountain and Ryan already had the tree, why was he going back?"

Buster jolted awake and amidst a flurry of swearing said, "Chance. He was going back for Chance."

Both men began making phone calls. The State Trooper dispatched to Ryan's house went back and, after interviewing a nearby neighbor, reported that the neighbor had seen Chance leave that morning with Ryan. The woman added that she and Chance had even waved to each other.

Just to be on the safe side, the officer left Chance a note on the door, should he somehow arrive home, to immediately call the OSP Watch Commander. Before resuming patrol, the trooper threw a flake of alfalfa to Bailey and quickly fed the family dogs.

As word spread about the missing Chance, troopers coming in from exhausting twelve-hour shifts immediately volunteered to join the search party and help out. Chance was family, and they would stop at nothing until he was safely found.

AN UNPLANNED RUN-IN

PRESENT TIME

Chance was beyond tired. He closed his eyes for a brief moment. All he needed was a little power nap—just enough to get re-energized.

"I'm so close to the road that I'm sure I'll hear Dad's snowmobile," he thought. "Then we can get the hell out of here."

When he awoke, it was early daylight. Surprisingly, he had slept for several hours and found himself nearly covered with snow. He thought he heard some voices but could not make out what anyone was saying. Maybe his Dad had gotten help, and they were coming to rescue him.

The snow was still coming down heavily, but at least the wind had died down. Chance stood, stretched and brushed several inches of snow from his visor. Hearing more noise and wondering if it was a return of the wolf pack or, hopefully, some rescuers, he gripped the bloody tree limb and carefully looked around.

What he saw was even more incredulous than a returning wolf pack. A young Indian girl was skinning out the dead wolf. She had the pelt almost completely removed when she looked up and saw Chance, then pointed out Chance to the men with her. All were surprised at the sudden appearance of the "snowman." The men stared at Chance with solemn, angry faces, while the young girl finished pulling off the wolf hide and tying it to her pack board.

Ignoring Chance, she continued gutting the wolf and then cutting the carcass up into four parts. She put one quarter section on her own pack, while the youngest of the three men helped her tie off the remaining quarters to the other pack boards.

All four were dressed in buckskin with heavy bear fur draped over their shoulders. Each was carrying a bow and quiver of arrows, and each had their own wooden snowshoes.

The girl was the only one wearing a hat, which appeared to be made from white rabbit fur.

Chance simply did not know what to make of this. He wondered why they were out in such bad weather. He thought, if they were the Hiders—and who else could they be—that maybe they could help him get down to the Paulina Lodge. He was at first fearful about approaching them, but then again he had no one else to turn to. Maybe if they had been walking around the woods, at the very least they could tell him if they had seen his Dad.

Chance yelled out a greeting and waved, but there was no response. He yelled again and carrying the lance loosely in one hand, started to plough through the snow to the group.

The two older hunters immediately stood in front of the young girl while the younger hunter, now looking very menacing, nocked an arrow to his bow and began raising the bow to the advancing Chance.

Chance stopped, standing nearly three-feet deep in the powdery snow. He placed the lance across his chest in a defensive position. The young girl pointed out the blood on the lance and then looked down at the slain wolf. She turned to the three men and, in a language that Chance had never heard before, kept repeating herself, forcing the young man to finally lower his bow.

An argument broke out amongst all four. The men seemed to be arguing against her, but she held her ground, walking to Chance over their angry objections and then tried taking the lance away from him. She pulled it; he held on, and then she twisted it right out of his arms. Carrying the lance back to the group, she pointed to the dried blood on the tip.

There was more arguing until the oldest of the group simply raised his hand and spoke quietly. The two other males reluctantly agreed. They motioned for Chance to follow them. The youngest tried one more time to persuade them otherwise and again raised his bow, pointing an arrow at Chance. The young hunter was sharply rebuked by one of his elders. Then he finally lowered his bow, picked up his pack board and was given the blood-covered lance to carry.

The two older men and the young girl turned and started to walk back into the dense forest. The young hunter, whom Chance guessed to be only a year or two older than him, stood behind him and started jabbing him forward with the sharp stick.

It was not an easy hike. With Chance not having snowshoes, he and his guard began to fall further and further behind. It took a great deal of effort and energy for Chance to walk through the deep snow while his captor merely glided across. Each time Chance slowed down, he was given another hard poke to go forward. Twice the young hunter slammed the butt end of the sharp stick into Chance's helmet whenever he felt Chance was not going fast enough.

The blows surprised Chance. He was going as fast as possible. This was rapidly turning into a scary situation.

One hour later, Chance guessed that they had barely gone a mile.

He wondered if they were taking him to his Dad. He asked several times, but each time he asked, he was again hit with the lance. He wondered if maybe they had captured his Dad but then thought, no, that would not have happened.

After taking several more hard-hitting blows, Chance spun around and shouted in his captor's face, "No!" He clenched his fists and moved toward his tormentor. The young Indian stopped in his tracks. He appeared both surprised and perplexed. He stopped hitting Chance and motioned for Chance to move forward.

Seconds later, Chance could feel the sharp stick pressed between his shoulder blades as he again followed the others.

"I'm a head taller than this guy," he thought, 'One more poke, and he is going down, and I'll make a beeline for the roadway. The others are carrying so much they wouldn't be able to catch me, and when Dad shows up, that will turn things around."

It wasn't much of a plan but Chance felt it was better than being taken captive.

Slowing their pace, the other three were now barely a hundred feet ahead, with the young girl in the lead. Chance could hear the swift flow of a river, but all he could see was a field of white and part of a river channel.

This time of the year, most of the high mountain rivers were barely ten feet across and no more than three or four feet deep. In the springtime with all the snow melt, those same rivers would be some twenty feet across and five or six feet deep, brimming with pan-sized trout.

For now, whole sections of the small river were freezing up with snow and glasslike ice.

Chance suddenly heard a scream and watched in horror as the young girl slipped into the river and was pulled under a long clear plate of ice. At one point he could actually see her being pushed along by the strong current under the ice, tumbling end over end. The two men with her were struggling to get their snowshoes and packs off.

By now, Chance had reached the riverbank and could see a layer of newly formed ice by the river's bend. The current was pushing her downstream. Chance could see her coming and, without a moment's hesitation, he jumped into the icy water, almost slipping and going under himself. The current was rapidly pushing her toward him.

For one brief moment, Chance could see the fear and horror written on her face. She was only seconds away as Chance quickly removed his snowmobile helmet and, grasping it with both hands; he raised it over his head and with one powerful blow fractured the sheet of ice. Reaching down, he caught her tumbling by.

He started to lose her and pulled on her collar with all his might. Just as the collar ripped from her coat, he managed to get both arms under her and pulled her to the surface. She came up coughing and sputtering. For a split second, he almost lost her again but now managed to grab onto her pack board.

The two older men were yelling as they rushed to the river. Chance pushed the young girl to the outstretched arms of the men, and they pulled her ashore. One of the men than ran along the riverbank until he reached Chance; he and Chance's tormentor pulled him from the icy water.

As he was being pulled out, Chance saw her white hat pop to the surface. He grabbed it and threw it on the riverbank.

The girl was shivering terribly. The oldest of the three covered her with his heavy furs. He looked over at Chance and briefly nodded. Leaving two of the pack boards behind, he began half dragging, half running her through the woods.

It seemed like she could hardly move.

Chance felt the cold as if a thousand bees were stinging his wet legs. Luckily, from the waist up, he was somewhat dry, with the exception of his arms. The other two motioned for Chance to follow.

The young Indian took the girl's dripping pack board and slung it over his shoulder. Without thinking, Chance grabbed the other pack board and slung it across his back, figuring if nothing else, it would keep some of the wind and cold off. Almost as an afterthought, he bent down and grabbed her white hat.

Several hundred yards ahead, Chance could barely see the man and young girl quickly pull and tear some brush apart and then drop to all fours and crawl into the brush.

When Chance and the two other Indians arrived at the same spot, one of his captors knelt and motioned for Chance to crawl through the brush. Chance started through with both men following behind, rearranging the brush. Within a few seconds, Chance had crawled through the brushy opening, which led directly into a large, concealed lava cave.

Going through the brush and entering the warm cave made Chance think of what it must be like going through an igloo. Once he got into the cave, he could see that the cave ceiling was some thirty- to forty-feet high and that the cave itself was several hundred square-feet in circumference. Several small fires brightly lighted the cave, and in the middle of the cave was a large fire pit with a roaring fire. Several stew pots were placed high over the fire.

Hanging from different wooden pegs around the cave were bows, lances, baskets, clothing, rolled Tule mats for bedding and in one far corner, an immense woodpile.

The young girl was shivering before the large fire, surrounded by a half-dozen or more men and women, all of them elderly. They turned from the girl to Chance, staring at him in near absolute amazement.

No children were about. The tribal members all had a deep look of fear and seemingly everyone began talking at once. Several of them were visibly shaking as nothing like this had ever happened before.

For the first time in over one hundred years, they were directly face-to-face with the dreaded Englishman.

The girl was fighting back tears as her companions were explaining what happened. They kept pointing to Chance, his lance and the quartered up wolf pieces. The young girl seemed on the verge of collapse when she turned and spotted Chance.

Several of the women had wrapped her in thick animal skin blankets. Holding the blankets with one hand, she walked over to Chance, placed one hand on his chest and completely broke down, sobbing uncontrollably.

Chance did not know what to do. He knew that she was trying to thank him, but he was overwhelmed by everything that had taken place from that very first moment his snowmobile had slid off the trail.

Fumbling around, somewhat embarrassed, he handed her the white hat. Though the hat was dripping ice-cold water, she nervously kneaded it in her hands.

She looked up at Chance and tearfully said, "Thank you."

She was quickly grabbed by several of the elderly women and taken back to the warming fire when an astonished Chance loudly asked, "You speak English?"

She nodded her head, yes, and yelled out, "Modoc."

CAPTAIN JACK'S MODOC WAR

The Modoc Indians lived in the immense Klamath basin of Northern California and Southern Oregon, a walk of only several days away from the nearby Yahi homeland. Their tribal Chief was Captain Jack.

Captain Jack's Indian name was "Kintpuash," which none of the local white traders from Yreka, a California border town, could either remember or pronounce so they nicknamed him "Captain Jack."

In the early 1870s, the Modoc fought a brutal, vicious war against the U.S. Army. It was a short-lived war—only a few months or so in duration. At the end of the war, the Army hanged Captain Jack and a handful of his inner circle for war crimes.

The Army took issue with the fact that Captain Jack personally shot and killed General Canby when the two sides were sitting at a peace table under a flag of truce.

Shooting General Canby, a Civil War veteran and the only Army General ever killed in an Indian War, did not sit well with senior Army officers.

As Captain Jack and several other Modoc were shooting the General, his last words were, "Stop. You have killed me."

During the war, fifty-two Modoc warriors were hiding with their wives and children in the lava tubes and caves of the Tule Lake area; part of the five thousand square-mile Klamath Basin. The Modoc were very fluent in English because for years they had openly traded with the whites in many Northern California towns, especially Yreka. They did not speak a broken "Pidgin English" like so many other tribes. Instead, they sounded exactly like one white conversing with another. Fluent English was a great source of pride to them.

The Modoc warriors used their knowledge of English to kill soldiers. At nighttime, under cover of darkness, several warriors would sneak up to where the soldiers were bivouacked. They would listen in on the next day's war plans, which helped them immeasurably, but even more importantly, they would learn the names of the nearby soldiers.

The next day, when fighting was at its heaviest, a warrior would crawl close to the enemy lines and cry out, using a soldier's name, "I've been shot. Help me, please. I've been shot."

The soldier, hearing his name being called out, assumed it was a friend in terrible distress. He and several other soldiers rushed forward to drag their wounded companion to safety, but instead they were shot and killed by hidden Modoc warriors.

It was the kind of trick that definitely worked once, possibly twice, until the front-line soldiers whispered to one another a one-word code that any wounded soldier was to use in case they did get shot. The code word was changed every day. If the other soldiers did not hear the correct code word, then they would open fire to where they heard the plea for help.

That also worked only once or twice. By then both sides had changed tactics yet again.

The fighting was savage by all standards of warfare. In December of 1872, the Modoc killed "Jump-Off Joe," and his entire militia of twenty-three men. Unlike the Guardsmen attacking the Yahi, the men of Jump-Off Joe's militia were not so lucky. One month later, the Army lost thirty-five combat-experienced soldiers who were killed in a daylong battle with the Modoc. The Modoc did not lose one warrior in either fight.

Some of the soldiers were killed by bow and arrow but most by rifle or pistol.

It was later learned that the Army had more than twenty-five percent of the entire Army in pursuit of just fifty-two warriors.

The U.S. Army revised its war plan. Historically, the Army had learned that the best way to win an Indian war was to find the tribal enemies of the warring tribe and hire them as mercenaries and have them fight for the Army as U.S. Army Indian Scouts.

Typically, the mercenary Indians hired could not believe their good fortune. The Army was willing to pay them an average of eight dollars a month for every month they were on the payroll, plus give them a new Winchester rifle, Colt pistol, horse and uniform—all of which they could keep after their enlistment was up.

All they had to do to earn their pay was to hunt down and kill their tribal enemies, which was something they were trying to do all the time anyway.

They were welcome to keep all the scalps they collected, plus their enemy's horses, wives, children and all other "war booty."

For centuries the Warm Springs Indians and the Modoc had been traditional enemies. No one really knew the reason why; it was just something that had always been.

The Army recruited a group of warriors from the Confederated Tribes of the Warm Springs Indian Reservation under the leadership of Chief Billy Chinook to fight the Modoc. Most of the enlistments in the U.S. Army Indian Scouts came from the Tenino area of the reservation, so the Army knew the warriors as the "Teninos."

The Warm Springs Indians were merciless in their attacks upon the Modoc. The Modoc were now suffering some heavy casualties and, greatly outnumbered, they quickly sued for peace.

Though enemies with the Warm Springs Indians, the Modoc were one of the only tribes the Yahi had never warred against because the Yahi widely regarded the Modoc as friends—often referring to them as "cousins."

Some Twentieth Century ethnologists believed that the two tribes were in fact distantly related. Several went so far as to publish that the Yahi were actually a splinter group of the Modoc and not at all related to the Yana. That particular theory was quickly proven to be incorrect.

By 1871, over four thousand Yana Indians had been killed, including almost the entire tribe of Yahi. After the 1871 Kingsley Cave Massacre, the Yahi had only seventeen men, women and children left. At that point they fled to the most remote, inaccessible area of their homeland and went into hiding.

In 1873, after the Modoc War was ended, a small number of Modoc, fearful of getting hanged like their tribal Chief and his advisors—

fled the Klamath Basin and went to Northern California to hide with their "cousins," the Yahi.

It took the Modoc several weeks of tracking to find the Yahi. Two years later, after things were quieting down on the Frontier, the Modoc started slowly drifting back to their ancestral lands in Oregon and California.

Today, most of the Modoc live in Oklahoma, where the U.S. Army sent them to a reservation. They were promised food and medicine in exchange for giving up their weapons. Once all the weapons were collected, crooked whites promptly stole their food and medicine.

When Captain Jack and four of his men were to be hanged, Chief Billy Chinook and his warriors rode for ten days to witness the hanging. The Teninos sat on their horses before the gallows. As a sign of respect for the bravery of the Modoc warriors, the Warm Springs Indians sang their death songs to the Modoc as they were led up the scaffolding and hanged.

Early on during the two years of hiding, a Modoc woman spent much of her time teaching English to one of her Yahi "cousins." The two would sit side by side for hours on end practicing English, all the while weaving baskets or scrapping elk hide to make into clothing. Every day the Modoc woman would teach new words and phrases to her friend, gently correcting pronunciation and inflection until the Yahi woman could speak English as fluently as anyone from Yreka.

This knowledge was passed down within that same family and, generations later, the only Yahi who could speak or understand any English at all turned to Chance and said, "Thank you."

ISHI

PORTRAIT OF A 20-CENTURY

STONE-AGE WARRIOR

Ishi was captured outside the Ward Slaughter House near Oroville, California, on August 28, 1911. It was late evening, and the exhausted Ishi was trapped—pushed up against a corral fence by four growling, lunging cattle dogs. Starving and totally fatigued without any weapons or water and only a few dried berries and deer jerky for food, Ishi curled up into a fetal position while several butchers, holding vicious hog gambrel hooks, pulled the dogs away. Ishi expected at that moment to be put to death by the whites.

Brutality at the hands of the whites was all Ishi had ever known for his entire life, starting as a young boy when he peeked through some brush and watched his father struggling with one white man when a second came up and shot his father in the chest. When his father collapsed to the ground, the two Guardsmen stood over him and repeatedly shot him in the head, face and chest. Then both Guardsmen grabbed a fleeing woman, pushed her to her knees and shot her. The dead bodies were scalped, looted and thrown into Mill Creek where they eventually washed down to the Sacramento River.

It is known that the leader of the Guards on that particular attack was R. A. Anderson. The attack took place early in the morning at a campsite deep in Yahi country called Three Knolls and later became known as the "Three Knolls Massacre."

Decades later, the burly butchers grabbed one of the last surviving Yahi and forcibly dragged him to the slaughter house. One of the men ran to a phone and called the local sheriff, excitedly telling him to immediately come to the shop as they had just captured a wild Indian.

Ishi slumped to the ground, waiting for the beating that would end his life.

While waiting for the Sheriff, the butchers softened and offered Ishi some water which he refused, fearing it might be poisoned.

At the time of his capture, Ishi's long hair had been burned to the scalp as a sign of mourning for the loss of his family and tribe. He was wearing nothing but an old, cut-off canvas poncho put on him by the butchers. Underneath, he had on a torn undershirt picked up in his travels from an old campsite. He had long, deer-bone ornaments hanging from each ear and a wooden plug piercing his septum. He was barefoot and shaking uncontrollably.

Within the hour, the sheriff and his deputy arrived in a horse-drawn wagon. They handcuffed Ishi and placed him in the wagon and transported him to the local jail. They repeatedly questioned him in English and Spanish, but Ishi did not respond. He put his hands over his ears while his eyes glazed over as he waited for them to shoot him. Why they were prolonging his death he simply did not know, but he also truly believed that it would occur within moments.

Ishi was placed in what he later called the Chief's lodge but was in fact the local jail. Word quickly spread in the small town of Oroville that a wild Indian had been captured and taken into custody. Literally within minutes people started to crowd around his jail cell, offering Ishi cigarettes, plugs of tobacco, food and water, all of which he refused. The crowd swelled to a large number, spilling out into the streets. Everyone wanted to see the "wild Indian."

By the third day of his capture, more than a thousand whites and an estimated several hundred Indians from all over Northern California had traveled to Oroville to see the Indian prisoner. The capture was newspaper headlines. None of the local Indians were able to successfully talk with Ishi except one elderly Yana survivor, and that one was able to converse with him only in a severely limited fashion.

The crowd made way for a little boy and his mother to look at the Indian. The boy stood before Ishi and smiled and waved. Ishi merely stared, trembling with fear, now believing that the large crowd had assembled for his hanging.

That belief increased when an elderly man, the former Sheriff of Butte County, pushed his way through the crowd and declared the Indian to be a Mill Creek; a tribe long thought to be extinct.

According to author Orin Starn, who wrote, *Ishi's Brain: In Search of America's Last "Wild Indian,"* the man was none other than, "R. A. Anderson, the renowned Indian Fighter."

Staring intently at Ishi, Anderson told a newspaper reporter that he had spared Ishi's life in 1864 when Ishi was a boy of about ten or twelve. Starn quotes Anderson as saying, "I think it is extremely probable that he is the boy, grown to manhood and now reaching the decline of life."

There is significant controversy over Ishi's birth year. While Anderson may not have been in doubt, he was possibly in error, as Ishi was reportedly, according to his biographer, only four years old in 1864—not twelve. It also would have been significantly out of character for Anderson to have spared a twelve-year-old Mill Creek boy because of Anderson's lifelong conviction that, "Nits become lice."

However, in this case, there is an even stronger possibility that Anderson was in fact correct.

Dr. T. T. Waterman, the university linguist whom Ishi first stayed with immediately after his capture, always maintained that Ishi's birth year was 1854. Ishi was the source of that information. Ishi and Dr. Waterman were in fact able to converse but only barely.

However, along those same lines, it's also possible that the 1854 date was perhaps a simple error of interpretation.

Theodora Kroeber, Ishi's biographer, wrote that Ishi was born in either 1860 or 1862, but Mrs. Kroeber never met Ishi. She never had an opportunity to interview him. She saw him only once in passing at UC Berkeley when she was an undergraduate. She stood outside a classroom for several minutes watching while Ishi sang several Yahi songs to the students. Later, she went back to the classroom wanting to meet him, but everyone was gone. Although both Ishi and Theodora frequented the same university buildings, she never again saw him. It is believed that Theodora's future husband, Dr. Kroeber, Ishi's university mentor and friend, gave his wife the information about Ishi's birth year. The source was again from Ishi. Why the discrepancy over the birth year is unknown.

No one recorded Ishi's reaction to seeing R. A. Anderson, who may well have shot and killed Ishi's father at the Three Knolls Massacre. Due to fear, fatigue, exhaustion and the passage of some forty-six years in time, Ishi may not have even recognized Anderson—then the sole-surviving Captain of the Guardsmen.

Meanwhile, people were shouting at Ishi in a babble of languages. Many were smiling and pushing food and a variety of trinkets to him through the bars. The Sheriff cleared the jail but allowed local Indians to stop by and talk with him, hoping for a communication break-through.

Many hours later, Ishi was in a near catatonic state as Indian after Indian approached and questioned him in their native tongue. As none of them could speak Yana or Yahi, he did not understand a word of what they were saying, but he may well have taken some comfort in knowing that the whites had not yet killed all the Indians.

It would take an elderly Yana Indian named Sam Batwi and Dr. Waterman, whose academic specialty was Indian languages, to be able to finally communicate with Ishi. Batwi was one of the few surviving Northern Yana and Ishi a Southernmost Yahi, but their language dialects were so significantly different that, while the two men could communicate, in reality, it was only with great difficulty. At the same time, Dr. Waterman's pronunciation of many Yahi words was also not understood by Ishi although the two could somewhat converse.

Batwi or Batwee would consistently fill in voids of Ishi's history as he saw fit, according to Theodora Kroeber. Initial reports by Dr. T. T. Waterman in a published article called, *The Last Tribe of California,* indicate that Ishi did not like Batwi because he felt Batwi was too pompous and too much of a braggart. Ishi also did not respect Batwi as an Indian because Batwi had a beard which made him too much like a white man.

According to Waterman, "It was a curious spectacle to see these two surviving representatives of an almost vanished race treating each other with the most distant politeness." Waterman also wrote in the same article that, "Ishi regarded him (Batwi) as a tiresome old fool, though he was too polite to say so."

Another contemporary report by an unidentified newspaperman published before Waterman's article states that the two men were friendly toward each other and got along fine.

From the moment of his capture until several days later, Ishi refused all food and water. Sheriff J. B. Webber, a kind, smiling man, was seriously worried that Ishi would soon starve to death. The Sheriff wanted Ishi in the best possible condition when Dr. Waterman arrived to take Ishi to Berkeley University. It was hoped that Dr. Waterman would be able to converse with Ishi and record his tribal history. Sheriff Webber was also going to ask the university doctor to find out where the rest of Ishi's people were hiding, if in fact any others were still alive.

All Sheriff Webber had to do now was keep his prisoner alive and well. The Sheriff picked up a rumor going around town that some people were talking about rushing the jail and lynching the Indian or turning him over to the few "Guards" still living. To prevent any such problems, Sheriff Webber posted his biggest deputy outside the jail armed with a double-barreled shotgun, a pistol in his holster and another pistol thrust into his belt. The Sheriff was not taking any chances.

The jail eventually was swarmed but only with well-wishers bringing food and small gifts for the "wild Indian."

Genuinely concerned over Ishi's deteriorating condition and sensing that the Indian was not eating because he was afraid of being poisoned, the Sheriff placed a bag of donuts and a jug of water, along with two empty cups on a tray.

Entering Ishi's unlocked cell, Sheriff Webber motioned for Ishi to eat. Ishi shook his head, "No." The Sheriff poured a glass of water and tried handing it to Ishi, which he refused.

The Sheriff then drank the full glass of water and reached out for a donut, using sign language to have Ishi point out which one to take. Ishi pointed, and the Sheriff reached down and ate the donut.

The Sheriff again motioned for Ishi to eat and drink. He poured Ishi a full glass of water and handed it to him. He signed for Ishi to take a donut. Hesitantly, Ishi drank the water, then immediately refilled his glass. He took a donut and ate it. Surprised and delighted at the taste, he quickly ate another. He liked the sugary taste of donuts so much that within the space of a few minutes, he finished off all the water and the entire bag of donuts.

For the rest of the day, Ishi ate meal after meal specially prepared for him until late that night when he simply could not eat any more. For the first time since his capture, he actually smiled and pantomimed by rubbing his stomach that he was full. He stretched out on his jailhouse cot and within moments was sound asleep.

In contrast, another contemporary report states that when Ishi was taken to the Oroville jail, he was so famished he immediately ate numerous bowls of beans and donuts and then promptly fell asleep.

One of the butchers who captured Ishi was a strong young man by the name of Adolph Kessler. Kessler heard a cry for help from a neighboring teen-aged boy hitching up horses for the butchers to ride home. Kessler ran out to the corral and, spying Ishi, tackled him and held him to the ground, gambrel at his neck, thinking he was a thief. Ishi remained absolutely frozen in place by the barking dogs and rearing horses.

The first night of his capture, author Starn writes, Kessler was the very last person out of the jail following Sheriff Webber. Kessler looked over his shoulder at Ishi and reported, "At the last look I got of him, he was still standing there. There was a little light in the cell. Still standing there looking out, I just wondered what in the world was going through his mind."

Later in life Kessler became the Police Chief for the Oroville Police Department.

Several days later Ishi would meet Dr. T. T. Waterman, and his life, as he knew it, would never be the same. Unknown to Ishi, he was rapidly becoming a famous celebrity stepping into the tumultuous Twentieth Century literally from the Stone Age. The fear and culture shock were enormous. Ishi was more afraid of what lay before him than when he singlehandedly killed a wounded bear with only a knife and a spear.

Being attacked by an angry bear was a dangerous and serious situation; living with the Englishman in early Twentieth-Century San Francisco was even more so.

Within one week of meeting Dr. Waterman, Ishi would ride on a train, in a car, on a ferry, see a play in San Francisco and stand on the cliffs of a beach—mesmerized by the thousands of people before him. He would initially stay in the Waterman house with hot and cold running water and doors and windows. He had never experienced that before or ever envisioned a lodge with central heat that people could turn on whenever they were cold. Matches and window shades he believed were magic inventions of the white man—just like trains and cars. Ishi told Waterman, in so many words, that the "Whites must have very powerful magic in order to keep trains and trolleys from falling off their tracks."

He loved pulling a faucet handle and having water suddenly appear, especially hot water. It was something he could almost never get over. He would turn on the water; watch it spill into the sink, then stand there, one hand under the running water, smiling in deep appreciation— yet at the same time shaking his head in absolute disbelief.

Ishi first found the Englishmen's food to be more than a bit of a mystery. He preferred his food dry, keeping with his lifelong eating habits. Englishmen, he noticed, were always pouring something on top of their food. Donuts and ice cream, however, he took to immediately—so much so that within a few months, he went from one hundred sixty pounds to two hundred pounds.

He found that losing the unwanted pounds was much more difficult than the gaining of the unwanted pounds. He went from never having enough to eat to now having too much. Dr. Waterman taught Ishi how to weigh himself, and he would stand on a scale watching the numbers roll up, mumbling all the while, "Too much-ee, too much-ee." Once he had shed the extra weight, like the Englishmen, he continuously struggled to keep the pounds off.

In that sense alone, Ishi had officially joined the Twentieth Century.

Ishi went into hiding with his mother, sister and other tribal members when he was about seventeen years of age, right after the 1871 Kingsley Cave Massacre. He spent the next forty years of his life in complete isolation, hiding with his dwindling band in a remote, dangerous wilderness. For the last fifteen of those forty years, he and four others lived on nothing more than a sloping two-acre ledge, five hundred feet straight up a sheer canyon wall. Several well-concealed trails led down to the valley floor and nearby Deer Creek. Ishi also made a long milkweed rope for an emergency escape, which he kept coiled by the cliff's edge, tied off to a pepperwood tree.

The tiny band felt safe and took comfort in the fact that none of the Englishmen would ever accidentally stumble across their hidden camp. Then one day came a surprise visit by some power company surveyors and their cowboy guides. On the day of discovery, the band numbered only four due to the prior death of one of the older warriors accidentally drowning in Deer Creek.

Ishi managed to rescue his mother on that day, but he never again saw his fleeing sister and her companion warrior.

According to best estimates, Ishi's mother died approximately two days later.

Ishi mentioned only once that he had a wife and child. Almost in tears he shared that they both died in a drowning accident. He never spoke of his wife or child again. His friends learned to never mention them because the few times they did, Ishi became morose and depressed for days afterward.

Still, some contemporary reports stated that the fleeing woman seen bolting from the hidden camp was not Ishi's sister but was actually his wife. This does not appear to be factually correct, especially as Ishi had confided in Dr. A. L. Kroeber about the drowning death of his wife and son. The confusion may have originated with the Yahi word for sister having multiple meanings, including cousin and/or wife.

For the next two and a half years after the camp break-up, Ishi survived entirely by himself. He spent months searching for his sister and her companion to no avail. He traveled from the deep canyons of Mill Creek to the snowcapped peaks of Mt. Lassen. He continuously searched for any hiding Yahi, roaming the vast forest, never again hearing from his sister or any other tribal member.

After his capture in Oroville, he could now see numerous whites with family and friends all around. It was information overload.

Within one week of his capture, Ishi traveled with Dr. T.T. Waterman to UC Berkley in San Francisco. Dr. Waterman also hosted Ishi in his own home for two to three months.

SAN FRANCISCO LIFE

Ishi overnight became a major San Francisco celebrity. The public adored him. Everywhere he went people would wave and shout out to him. The non-stop attention, though, made him feel very uncomfortable. He would often become rigid and stoic whenever surrounded by groups of whites—even small groups. It was difficult to shake the fear of being put to death. He would often wring his hands in anxiety while his eyes would constantly dart from one person to another. He never really felt comfortable in formal meetings, with one exception. At the University Museum where he was now living, Ishi would often spend several hours on a Sunday afternoon knapping arrowheads, which he usually gave away to wide-eyed young boys. After knapping the arrowheads, he would sometimes demonstrate his archery techniques.

One Sunday, to the delight of the crowd, Ishi shot a newly made arrow through a newspaperman's hat from an estimated distance of a hundred feet or more. The newspaperman reported that he was happy he was not wearing the hat when Ishi put his arrow through it.

Whenever friends or even people he just met had to leave, Ishi would sadly raise one eyebrow and ask in broken English, "You go?" When told, "Yes," Ishi would then resolutely say, "I stay."

He seemed to be understandably afraid of people but, at the same time, he desperately craved companionship from people. He fit into a classical approach/avoidance pattern. On the one hand he tried to avoid people; on the other hand, after living alone for so long, he would often surround himself with people but only when he could control the situation, such as a Sunday afternoon visit with well-wishers.

He never once said, "Good-bye" to those leaving and, while he disliked shaking hands, he came to gradually accept that this was a part of the white man's culture. He finally came to the point where he would in fact shake hands but always very softly and always with some reluctance.

So well did his tiny band do at hiding that Ishi was seen only a few times during the years from 1871 to 1908. Locals hunting or fishing rarely saw him but when they did, he would disappear in a flash. A picnicking family once spotted Ishi hiding behind a near-by tree, angrily staring at them. The family immediately left. Another time a young deer hunter, D. B. Lyon, saw smoke coming from a small campfire hidden in the brush. The hunter threw a rock into the brush and heard a smothered cry of pain. Years later Ishi told friends that it was he and several others who were hiding in the brush. He took the risk of building a campfire to ward off the bitter cold and did so believing that no one else was around. When Ishi and the others ran off, Ishi dropped his hat and arrow-making kit and some freshly killed lamb legs—all of which D. B. Lyon retrieved and kept.

As the years passed, Ishi put on strength and muscle. He grew from a spindly teen-aged boy into a disciplined, well-muscled warrior. He was now the defender of his tribe, as well as the main provider. He was skilled in warfare as was his entire tiny band. He learned all the old songs and the culture of his people. He learned what plants to use for a headache and what to do in the event of a sore throat or rattlesnake bite. He could identify any and all tracks he came across. And he excelled at making weapons necessary for food or survival.

Several local ranchers stated Ishi was a medicine man. Several others stated he was the chief of his tiny band. Ishi indicated both statements to be true.

He could successfully call a deer to within twenty feet of his bow. He did this by imitating the distress sounds of a fawn, which attracted both bucks and does to his hiding spot. He learned to call in rabbits as well as the animals that preyed on rabbits, such as bobcats and coyotes. Everything he hunted or gathered helped the tiny tribe to survive.

The Hiders knew to never make noise. Singing was at a near whisper. Cooking fires were small and always in an enclosed space to avoid detection. Tracks were carefully wiped away by brush. Snares were hidden. Animal entrails buried. The people did everything in their power to remain invisible to the whites.

Ishi lived most of his adult life with only four other people and as a result did not initially know of any number over five. Whenever asked for a number past five, he would typically respond, "No more." He did, however, know one other number, forty, which he believed to be the original size of his band before the Guardsmen killed most of them at the Three Knolls Massacre.

One week after his capture, Ishi was standing on a small hill overlooking the ocean. It was the first time in his life that he had ever seen the ocean although he had heard about it from both family and tribal elders. Theodora Kroeber reported that he barely paid attention to the crashing sea. Instead he was absolutely fascinated by the thousands of white people on the beach before him. He could not number or count them, but he kept whispering, "Hansi saltu, hansi saltu," his native tongue for "many white people."

From that point on, Ishi would slowly make his way into the white world. He did this with some degree of fear, eagerness, forgiveness, and always a smile as he marveled at all the clever inventions of the whites— especially his favorites, which were stick matches, calliope whistles and disappearing window shades.

Time after time, Ishi delighted in stick matches and wished he had them during his long years of hiding. That and hot water from a faucet.

He gradually learned some limited English but mostly in sentence fragments such as, "Him's good," or, "No good." At the time of his death, he barely had six hundred words total in his English vocabulary.

He learned to drink and appreciate coffee, which he called "kopee." Alcohol he stayed away from. His favorite greeting to both friends and strangers, always accompanied with a big smile, was "Everybody happy?" which he pronounced as "Evelybody hoppy?"

Mary Ashe Miller, a journalist writing about meeting Ishi only a few days after his capture, said in the September 6, 1911 issue of the *San Francisco Call,* "The Indian is wonderfully quick and intelligent; he has a delightful sense of humor; he is docile, cheerful and amiable, friendly, courageous, self-controlled and reserved, and a great many other things that make him a very likable sort of a person."

She went on to physically describe Ishi as, ". . . nearly six feet tall, well-muscled and not thin."

If this description is accurate, Ishi must have been a giant amongst his tribe, as most Yahi warriors were barely five feet, eight inches in height.

Though Ms. Miller did not specifically say that Ishi was handsome, he did have rugged movie-star looks. As pictures of Ishi appeared in various newspapers, he was soon deluged by letters from admiring women, several of whom stated that they wanted to marry him. Ishi believed such proposals to be very improper, dismissing them by saying, "No good."

He soon started calling policemen, "bahleecemen," and all Chinese people, male or female, "Chinamen." Another favorite expression he frequently used was, "Sure, Mike." Even his use of otherwise derogatory slang terms for Blacks, Italians, Irish and many other races was always accompanied by a disarming smile. They were terms he picked up from his street travels and he at first believed them to be proper.

What initially impressed Ms. Miller and all to whom Ishi came into contact with was his smile, his friendliness and the sincerity of his genuine forgiveness for the atrocities committed against Ishi, his family and his tribe.

Ishi soon realized that the easy-going nature and friendship of whites in the early part of the Twentieth Century was vastly different from that of the whites of the Gold Rush era. For most of his life; he had lived in constant fear of being killed by the whites. Now, he eventually came to believe his life to be much better in the Twentieth Century than in the Nineteenth.

Ishi stayed true to his Yahi religion, which he observed every day and at all different times during the day, such as giving thanks to Grandfather Creator for each and every meal, including snacks. He always wore clean clothes, bathed on a daily basis and soon started wearing shoes.

In the 1914 return trip to his old homeland, Ishi was introduced to J. Merle Apperson, the frontier rancher whom Ishi tried to kill by shooting an arrow at his head. Apperson and his two sons were among the cowboy guides for the power company surveyors who stumbled into and then ransacked the hidden Yahi camp in 1908. Recognizing each other, it appeared a rather awkward moment for both. As they were introduced, Apperson extended his hand in friendship to Ishi, and Ishi accepted the handshake as a sign of forgiveness. The two men simultaneously smiled as the old days were put behind them.

For the next several hours, Ishi and his companions sat in the same room with the entire Apperson family who kept asking Ishi if he really meant to kill Apperson Senior with the arrow or to simply scare him off.

Ishi smiled and said, "No die man,*" which was Ishi-speak for, "Yes, I shot the arrow but mainly to scare him off because I was afraid he would stumble across our campground."

*Author Richard Burrill, *Ishi Rediscovered*, from information supplied by Mrs. Apperson in her book, *We Knew Ishi*.

However, when the arrow was fired, Apperson had just passed the hiding Ishi and was climbing up the side of a hill when he bent over to grab some brush. Ishi, only several yards
away, fired uphill. The arrow narrowly missed Apperson's head by only one or two inches,
grazing the underneath brim of Apperson's cowboy hat. Had Apperson not bent over at the exact moment Ishi fired, it very well could have been a fatal encounter.

After reluctantly posing for a picture with Apperson dressed in his leather chaps and wearing his pistol, it then appeared to Ishi that all the horrible days of warfare and hiding were now completely over. It seemed to his university friends as if a great burden had been lifted from his shoulders.

Ironically, when the trip to his old homeland was first proposed, Ishi adamantly did not want to go back. Perhaps it was fear of painful memories or running into old foes such as Apperson or some of the still-living Guardsmen or being abandoned by his friends.

Ishi never directly addressed his fears but shared his main objection to going was—according to biographer, Theodora Kroeber—the weather would be "too cold." That argument fell on deaf ears as the planned trip was for late spring and early summer. Then Ishi said that there were no chairs or beds in the wilderness. He was also very serious, even a little fearful, that they would all starve because there was "no food."

Dr. A. L. Kroeber, Theodora's husband, calmed Ishi's many objections by assuring him they would have lots of bedding and camp chairs, and that mules would be used to pack in all their food. Finally, Ishi was told that if they ran out of food, they would eat the mules. Smiling at the persistent humor, Ishi finally agreed.

One of the main goals of the trip was to see if any other Yahi were still in hiding. The twelve-year-old son of Ishi's friend, Dr. Saxton Pope, begged his father to take him along. That first night at Deer Creek, Saxton Pope, Jr., positioned himself next to Ishi. Soon, everyone was asleep and, according to Pope, Jr., Ishi slipped out of his sleeping bag, whispering to young Pope that he was curious about something, and he wanted to make a search of the nearby canyon.

Ishi returned hours later and quietly told Pope, Jr., who late in life told Ishi's biographer, Theodora Kroeber, "It is good. None are lost. They found their way." Ishi never gave any further explanation to this comment and, to this day, no one knows exactly what he meant by it.

To date, no other hiding Yahi have ever been found in either Mill Creek or Deer Creek. From time to time though, even stretching into the mid-Twentieth Century, local ranchers would find small fires in hidden brush with bare footprints around the fire. Sometimes fishermen or hunters would round a bend and report seeing a naked Indian running for the timber.

Early on during the university camping trip, Ishi managed to bring down a large buck with just one arrow from a bow he had made, providing deer meat for the entire group. The bow was the Yahi preferred weapon, suitable for either warfare or a hunt.

From the beginning of the Indian Wars to the very end, hundreds of thousands of arrows—perhaps even millions—had been shot at the invading Englishmen. In just one hour of battle at Custer's Last Stand, both the scientific and historical community agree that more than twenty-four thousand arrows were fired at the Seventh Cavalry by both the Sioux and Northern Cheyenne warriors.

That's a lot of arrows for just a one or two-hour battle, especially when you consider that the majority of warriors were armed with both rifles and pistols.

Ishi has the historical distinction of firing the very last arrow of the Indian Wars at J. Merle Apperson the day before the surveyors and cattlemen stumbled across the hidden Yahi camp. Now, on the return trip to his old homeland, especially after meeting Apperson, Ishi sensed that the old days of hatred and fear were truly over.

While temporarily staying at the home of Dr. T. T. Waterman right after his capture, Ishi had his first bath ever in a bathtub. After the bath, he doused himself with talcum powder, which he came to call "Lady powder." When Ishi finished with his bath, his hostess ran into the bathroom, fearful that it would be a mess. To her surprise, it was immaculate with the towels and washcloths neatly folded and put away. So impressed was the hostess that she immediately showed the gleaming bathroom to her husband, asking why he, with all his advanced university education, was unable to do the same.

At the time of his capture it was considered rude and very poor manners to ask any Native American to share his or her tribal name with total strangers. For anyone outside of the family or tribe to say the name would be to rob that name of its power. Yet everywhere Ishi went, he was always asked his name, especially by newspaper reporters. As Ishi did not yet speak any English, he was dependent upon Dr. Waterman to translate for him. Ishi was quickly becoming a very popular celebrity in San Francisco, and he needed a name. Dr. Waterman would translate for Ishi that, "Because the Indian lived alone for so many years, he did not have a name, but he would gladly take one if someone had one to give him."

To that end, to help Ishi save face, Dr. A. L. Kroeber proposed the name, "Ishi," which is Yahi for *man*. The name fit and, for the remaining four years and seven months of his life, he was known as "Ishi."

Much of Ishi's life remains a closed secret, with only tiny nuggets occasionally coming to the surface. As a leader and the providing warrior for his tiny band, reporters sometimes referred him to as a "chief." He had extensive knowledge about healing plants and how to best treat a rattlesnake bite (you bind a toad to the bite and the toad's toxins dissipate the snake venom). Several newspapers sometimes reported him as a "medicine man." In a sense, both titles were appropriate.

In reality, most of his small circles of close friends were employees from the UC Berkeley's Anthropology Department, the Custodial Department, or from the next-door University Hospital.

Ishi gradually got over his fear that the whites were going to kill him, which took some time. Soon, with a growing but limited number of words and phrases, he even began to feel comfortable in the city. For the first time ever, he had a part-time job as a custodian at the University Museum and a monthly paycheck—a portion of which he faithfully saved for the dream of someday being able to buy a horse and wagon.

Ishi believed that a horse and wagon would give him status, convenience, and place him on an equal footing with whites. Every pay period he would take some of his pay in half-dollars and store them in empty film canisters. The canisters were the perfect size for the silver coins. On a regular basis, he would count the canisters to see how much money he had accumulated toward a horse and wagon.

The man who turned out to be his best friend was Dr. Saxton Pope, a medical doctor who was a surgeon at the University Hospital, right next door to where Ishi lived and worked. Both men shared a mutual love of archery, and Dr. Pope was fascinated by Ishi's skills at making bows and arrows. It was common for the two friends to spend many hours together crafting bows and practicing archery.

From time to time Ishi would sometimes visit Dr. Pope's patients at the hospital and sing to them. After singing, Ishi would smile, wave and go on to the next patient.

So close was their bond of friendship, it is believed that Ishi confided in the very last moments of his life his true Yahi name to Dr. Pope. Pope never divulged the name, and the secret died with him.

Ishi called Dr. Pope either "Popey" or to show his deep respect for Popey's   surgical skills, *K'uwi*, which is Yahi for Medicine Man.

From the day of his capture to the day of his death, donuts and ice cream would remain Ishi's favorite snack foods.

To the day he died, no one, with the possible exception of Dr. Pope, ever knew Ishi's true Indian name.

As always he would ask, "You go?" when friends left and when told, "Yes," he would say, "I stay."

TWO DAYS AFTER CHANCE'S CAPTURE

PRESENT TIME

A drowsy Chance, nearly buried under a pile of animal skin blankets, awoke by a smoldering campfire. Several of the elderly tribal members were sitting there, staring at him. Several others tried hard not to look, but this was the first time in more than a hundred years that many had ever seen a white man up close and personal. They simply did not know what to make of Chance. They couldn't help but stare. Their stares for the most part were hard and menacing or fearful. Many wondered if Chance would try to kill them in their sleep and then make good his escape. It seemed the only exceptions were the young girl and one of Chance's captors who it turned out was the girl's father.

Whenever any of the other tribal members saw Chance looking at them, they quickly turned their heads away. Giving a known enemy free rein in their lodge was something that most found very uncomfortable.

The tribal members were deeply conflicted about the presence of Chance. Something would have to be done, and they kept pressing the Chief to call for a tribal council. They knew searchers would be out looking for the boy as soon as the snow stopped and, upon finding him, the next inevitable step would be the Guards attacking their camp.

The young Indian girl brought over a bowl of steaming stew and several pieces of hot fry bread. Handing it to Chance, she asked, "How do you feel?" She knelt close to him on the edges of his blanket and encouraged him to eat.

"What is this?" asked Chance, thinking it delicious and nearly inhaling the bowl of thick pieces of meat mixed with Indian fry bread and preserved greens. The fry bread was made of acorns ground into a fine powder and rinsed with boiling hot water to remove the toxic tannins from the acorns. The bread was then cooked on a thin layer of bear grease on flat stones placed over a wood fire.

"The meat is from the wolf you killed," she said, suddenly growing concerned as Chance started gagging. She quickly handed him a small bowl of hot dandelion tea, motioning for him to drink.

"No . . ." he said, only to be interrupted by more coughing and gagging.

The tea helped Chance from losing his meal. Once he got over his squeamishness, he actually found the stew to be tasty, and with one last gulp he swallowed the rest down. Her smiling at him certainly helped. He couldn't help but stare at her near-perfect white teeth and liquid black eyes. He seemed almost mesmerized by her beauty, a point not unnoticed by the other members of the tribe—including the only other young tribal member.

"If she were at Summit High," Chance thought, "Everyone would want to date her."

After Chance recovered his voice, she asked more questions.

For the past several days, she had brought food to Chance and insisted he rest by the fire. She told him it was still snowing outside, and even the oldest of the tribal elders were saying they had never seen so much snow in their entire lives.

No one had seen any searchers.

Chance asked her how old she was. Initially, she seemed slightly puzzled by his question but, after further explanation from Chance she said, "I was born as the leaves were falling, sixteen winters ago. That's all I know."

Chance was barely one year older. If she were at Summit, they would be in some of the same classes.

Chance soon found himself looking forward to having her visit. During the day, she managed to come by a half dozen times or more, constantly smiling. She always brought some food and would ask Chance many questions about his life as an Englishman. She had a soft lilting voice sometimes followed by a slight giggle, which Chance found very attractive.

Each time she gave Chance something to eat or drink, she managed to spend just a little more time with him. Her one- or two-minute visits were now stretching out to a half hour or more. She was constantly asking him questions about how the whites lived. He found her idioms from the Nineteenth Century enchanting. Several times she asked if her English was correct. He said yes and shared with her that "iron wagons" were called "cars." After that, she quickly incorporated whatever the new word was into her vocabulary. She would repeat the word several times, always smiling, with both eyebrows slightly raised, wanting him to correct any mispronunciations. Then the new word would become part of her conversation.

In explaining high school to her, he found that she did not have any point of reference. She told him, "Everything I know I learned from my parents and tribal elders." When asked why she carried a bow, she responded, somewhat surprised, "To defend the people for when we are attacked."

In response to his questions about her life, she told Chance that she and Kicking Horse might someday be married, as they were the only two young people left in the tribe. Their parents, with the approval of the Chief and Elders, had promised them to each other. The final decision was theirs. It would then be up to them to carry on all tribal traditions and to care for the elderly. She worried that when she and Kicking Horse were themselves elderly and if they did not have any children, who would prepare them for their journey to the Land of the Dead? Then, answering her own question, she said they would have to make contact with other tribes for help. She asked Chance which tribes were to the north, wanting to make sure none were ancient tribal enemies.

Drawing a map on the dirt floor, Chance answered, "Warm Springs, Wascos and Northern Paiutes live north on the reservation. To the west you have Chinooks, Siletz, Coos Bay and Coquilles. To the east you have Umatilla, Nez Perce, Shoshone, Bannocks and more Paiutes. Southwest are the Rogue River and the Illinois people. Southeast are the Klamaths and some Modoc."

Pleased with his map, Chance added, "Pretty much, you are surrounded by Oregon tribes."

She smiled at the mention of the Modoc. Chance had only a small circle drawn on his dirt map for the Modoc. Thinking of the original Nineteenth Century Modoc territory, she placed one hand on Chance's shoulder and leaned forward to draw a much bigger circle.

The intimacy did not sit well with Kicking Horse.

Glancing to one side, she saw Kicking Horse angrily glowering at them. She abruptly left Chance and went over to Kicking Horse and began quietly talking to him in Yahi. She handed him a piece of fry bread smothered with honey. Kicking Horse threw the bread on the ground and stormed off. Several tribal members happened to be watching. It was the tribal equivalent of a soap opera and the tribal members were riveted by the drama.

They watched as she began pleading with Kicking Horse but to no avail. He refused to acknowledge her.

That night when she returned with more food and water, Chance avoided asking her about Kicking Horse. Instead, he asked her about his father. He wanted to know if anyone had seen him.

She shrugged her shoulders and said no one had seen him because of all the snow. She said it almost like she knew him, which surprised Chance. He asked her how she knew him.

Lowering her eyes, not looking directly at Chance, she responded by saying, "We see a tall cowboy wearing a gun and riding his iron wagon—car—through the woods. Several times he almost came upon us when he was out searching. We thought he was looking for us, but once we saw him tie a man up with metal and put him in his car."

She emphasized the word car with a sense of finality. Smiling, she coyly added, "Plus you look just like him."

Every time she smiled at him, Chance could feel himself starting to melt. He was trying to figure out if it was the eyes or the smile and came to the conclusion, no surprise here, that it was the total package.

When asked about her people and why they remained in hiding, she matter-of-factly replied that they were Yahi, hiding from the whites that were always wanting to kill them. Only later did Chance come to understand that in Indian culture, some of the events that happened over one hundred fifty years ago felt to the people that those events had occurred just that very morning. It was that real.

She told him that the California whites often called them, "Mill Creeks."

She was surprised when Chance told her that he knew a little of the history of the Mill Creeks, especially the story of a warrior named Ishi. Her surprise grew to astonishment as Chance told her what he knew of Ishi and his guess as to how her tribe came to be hiding out in Oregon. She quickly gathered several people around and translated what Chance told her about Ishi.

The Hiders knew Ishi as, "Bones," and all believed that he had been killed by the whites at the Bear's Hiding Place along Deer Creek, well over a hundred years ago. Though even the oldest of the Hiders had never known Ishi, the young girl pointed out several of centenarian elders who were his nieces and nephews, the children of Ishi's sister.

As Chance told the story and as the story was translated into Yahi, the small group seemed almost evenly divided. Half did not believe the story at all. Ishi's family descendants became angry and said it was more lies from the Englishman. Why would a warrior, a man pledged as a defender of the tribe, give up his people to live among the whites. There was no way Ishi or any Yahi would ever do that. That was not the way of the warrior.

The other half did believe Chance and were relieved to hear that Ishi was not a ghost doomed to walk the earth for all eternity, trying to hunt down surviving tribal members. They were pleased to hear that his white friends had in fact cremated Ishi's body so that his spirit could journey to the Land of the Dead.

Between interruptions, the smiling young girl managed to tell Chance about how the hiding Yahi families met and fled Northern California for the Central Oregon wilderness.

All the tribal members were now excitedly talking about the fate of "Bones" and how he came to live amongst the whites. As she interpreted for him, Chance found himself bombarded with question after question about "Bones" living with the whites and actually riding around in an iron wagon.

Chance was now center-stage and answered as best as he could.

In the midst of all the questioning, Chance suddenly turned to the young girl and said, "I don't even know your name."

Then, holding out his hand to her, he said, "My name is Chance. What's yours?"

Lowering her head, she said, "Shasta." Then, softly smiling, she added, "I won't tell you my Indian name because you probably won't be able to pronounce it, but to the people I am called Shasta."

She paused for a few seconds, shrugged her shoulders and said, "All right. It's "Wahkanupa." That means "Little Mount Shasta."

She reached out for Chance's hand but, at best, it was an awkward moment. They shook hands, and for several seconds Chance just held onto her hand until she pulled away

"I should not be doing this because tonight I have been chosen to speak for you before the tribal council. It is not our way to shake hands, and I do not want anyone to misunderstand this, especially Kicking Horse."

"There's no need for you to speak for me tonight," said Chance. "I did what anyone would have done. I knew the water was only waist deep, and I could see where you would be coming up from the ice. It was just a question of jumping in and grabbing you."

"I'm sorry," said Shasta, again lowering her eyes downward, "but you misunderstand. This is not about me. Some of the people feel you are a danger to us. They are saying you are a Guardsman."

Now very nervous and with her face clouding over, Shasta added, "When the Guardsmen last killed our people, it was decided in a long ago Council to kill any white captives. In keeping with our ways, tonight the tribal council meets to decide on whether you live or die."

CHANCE'S TRIAL

Barely several weeks had gone by since the wolves attacked the people in their lodge. The attack had been devastating, especially the loss of the elderly warrior—a voice of wisdom and comfort to all. Now the tribal members had to gather in Council to decide the fate of the young Englishman. None of the Hiders had ever personally experienced this before and seemed evenly divided as to what to do. In just a very short period of time, their entire world had been turned upside down. Many were fearful that if the young warrior, whom they all believed Chance to be, was freed, he would bring Guardsmen to the forest, and all the people would then be killed. A few felt that Chance had risked his life by saving Shasta from drowning and that he proved his bravery by single-handedly killing a wolf. In addition to his demonstrated bravery, Chance had a winning smile and a way about him that made several of the elders think that he was very different from the brutal young Englishmen who hunted down and killed their grandparents.

If Chance were to be set free, the tribe would have to move and find another hiding place. That was a given. They were going to do that in the spring anyway because they were fearful of the flying iron wagon constantly overhead and carrying Guardsmen searching for them.

If the people had to flee, they had already decided to move east to the deep canyons and forests of the land once occupied by the Nez Perce. They believed few people lived there now and that the tribe would be safe for at least another hundred years or so.

In the far distant past, it was the Yahi custom to occasionally spare an exceptionally brave captured warrior and adopt him into the tribe. A tribal council could only make such a decision. This had not happened, however, for nearly the past two centuries. Adoption was not really an option for Chance because all the tribal members knew there would be a big search for him once the snows stopped.

His people would want him back.

Secretly, they all knew that if the vote were to acquit or adopt Chance, then the tribe would have to move immediately to avoid discovery. That would be nearly impossible—a group of mostly elders traveling hundreds of miles carrying everything on their backs through the deep snow would be difficult for all and deadly for some.

They were really left with only one option.

The tribe began silently gathering around the campfire to decide Chance's fate. The solemnity of the moment was not lost upon them. This would be one of the hardest challenges that the people ever faced. Many had fasted and prayed to the Great Spirit for guidance. Two of the women had made ritualistic small cuts on their arms and legs over the impending decision. All were greatly concerned and deeply worried about what was to happen. The safety and security of the tiny tribe depended upon the vote of all.

The time had come. Sitting close to the fire, several of the tribal members pulled warm furs over their shoulders. Outside, the winter storm raged on with strong gusts of wind coming through the brushy entrance. The Guardian moved to one side, trying to escape the numbing chill.

Shasta and Chance sat by themselves, close to the fire but separated from the rest of the tribe. Shasta would be his voice and speak for him. Everyone would be given a chance to speak and to vote. Everyone knew that if the vote were for death, it would be only to protect the tribe.

The Council ruling from long ago had finally come full circle. It was now time for a decision and perhaps even for atonement.

Several of the men felt very strongly that to save the tribe the young man must be forever silenced. Some of the wives, however, were opposed to killing Chance, arguing that attacks by the Englishmen were long over and that the world today was different from that of their grandparents. Several of their husbands asked, "How do you know?" The wives could not respond, as the way of the tribe was proof, not feelings, though in most cases the feelings would later prove to be true.

Several of the wives would always vote as their husbands did. To vote any other way could be viewed as a sign of disrespect.

The arguing and discussion would go on for several hours. Each tribal member would be allowed time to reason with the others, and then a vote would be called for. If the vote went against Chance, then a tribal member would be allowed a one-time plea for adoption, mercy or an alternative sentence acceptable to the majority of the people. If Council selected one of the proposed options, then another vote would be taken. After that, the sentence—whatever it might be—would be carried out.

There would be no further appeals after the second vote was taken. Nor would there be any delay if he were to be put to death. If he were to receive the death sentence, he would be allowed a ritual cleansing, food, quiet time for prayer, and then he would be put to death.

Shasta sat by Chance and continued to pepper him with questions. She wanted to know as much as possible about him, and then she would decide what parts to best present to the Council. She started out by asking him about his family. Chance told her about the recent death of his mother but in a very hesitant way.

Shasta put her hand on Chance's arm. She had also lost her mother and was still grieving even though her mother had died several years earlier. She sensed that Chance had yet to come to terms with his loss.

While describing his mother to Shasta, Chance could feel an asthma attack coming on. The reality of being put on trial was hitting home. He reached for his inhalator and pressed down twice, drawing the spray deep into his lungs. Shasta held her hand out for the inhalator and examined it, returning it to Chance with the observation, "Medicine?" Chance nodded.

Shasta said, "I have to ask. Are you or your father members of the Guards?"

She especially wanted to know about his father because every time he was seen, he was always carrying a gun and appeared to be searching the wilderness.

Chance explained his father's job as a game warden as best he could. Shasta nodded in agreement. All of the tribal hunters, whenever possible, took only adult male deer or elk, sparing the very young. But most of all, she felt a sense of relief that Chance's father was not searching for the Hiders.

"I'm in high school," said Chance, "Over seventeen winters and, no, no one I know is in the Guards—especially not my father or I. The Guards went away when all those old-time settlers died off, and that was more than a hundred years ago. They don't exist anymore. They are forever gone."

Shasta was surprised, now wondering if Chance were telling the truth to save his life. For her whole life, Shasta had heard nothing but how dangerous the Guards were and how everyone must be careful because the Guards were always out there hunting for them. To hear that they were in fact long gone was something the people had never really considered because they always believed new ones would take the place of those who died.

Every time Shasta asked Chance about his life, where his lodge was, did he have any brothers or sisters, what was high school like, what was his life like, it gave Chance equal opportunity to ask her questions about her life. She willingly shared, mainly to please him. She rightly sensed that he was becoming very fearful about his trial.

As a distraction from the tribal members gathering around, Chance asked her if she had ever run into any white people in the woods.

"Only two times," she replied. "One time I was walking around a bend on a narrow trail, and there were two elderly white ladies resting on a log. They were both just sitting there holding their walking sticks. It was too late for me to back away because both had seen me, so I just kept walking toward them. They said 'Hello' as I approached. I said 'Hello' back and started to walk past them. I was very much afraid, but then one lady said, 'That is a beautiful dress. Did you make that?' "I said, 'Thank you' and told her that my mother had taught me how to make traditional dresses and then told them that my family was waiting for me, and I had to go. They said 'Good-bye' and I quickly left."

Shasta added, "I know that they wanted to talk more, but this was the first time I had ever talked with any whites, and I wanted to get away because I very nervous. They seemed nice enough, but I was afraid of what they might tell others."

"What was the other time?" asked Chance, aware of the stares of several of the nearby elders. "You mentioned two times."

For just a fleeting moment, Shasta started to giggle at the memory. "I didn't really talk to any whites the second time. I scared them, instead."

"How?" asked Chance.

"Two men came in their car to the end of the trail and then carried their tent into the woods and made a campsite. They were only a short walk from our lodge, and the people were afraid because the young men were both carrying long guns. Many thought that they were Guardsmen searching to kill us. The men set up their camp, and Council decided to attack them before they could attack us. We kept watch on them until it got very dark. Then Chief Tuliyani sent me to listen in on them. It turns out they were deer hunting. I listened for a long time and deer hunting was all they talked about. Well, that and all their bad talk about women.

"After listening to them for a while, I decided that these men did not respect their women. I came back and told the Chief and Council everything that I heard. I knew that if the deer hunters were killed, then many others would come searching for them and, in the end, our people would be killed.

"So while the Chief and several of the warriors made ready to attack them, I went back to their tent. It was very late at night, and I could hear them sleeping by all their sleep noise. I started screaming and growling like an animal and began throwing big rocks at their tent. They became very frightened. I stood behind some trees and continued to scream and throw more rocks. I moved closer and threw even bigger rocks. Both men were now yelling. The rocks were breaking their tent. They sounded very scared and ran with their guns all the way to their car."

Every time Shasta said the word "car," she smiled.

Every time she smiled, it gave Chance some hope and encouragement.

"She must have some insight into this vote," thought Chance, "Maybe the whole thing is just some type of formality they have to go through. How else could she be so cheerful?"

"They went away very fast. I came back and told the Chief and Council that the men had run away. The next morning we heard them return. It was the same car, but now there were five men, and they were all carrying long guns and pistols. They walked back to their camp and quickly carried the tent and everything else and put it into the back lid of their car. Then they spread out and started looking for tracks.

"Kicking Horse and I were hiding in some brush when they started walking toward us. We threw several big stones at them. They never saw us, but one of the rocks broke their car so they quickly ran back and rode off, and we have never seen them again. They were all scared, but one in particular was screaming the whole way. Another was very fat, and his friends were in such a hurry to get away that they almost left him because he was too slow."

Shasta's mood suddenly changed. Looking around, she quietly said, "It is beginning." Then reaching under the blanket, she grabbed Chance's hand and held it tightly as the last of the Elders took their place by the fire.

JESSE SEARCHES FOR THE HIDERS

SEVERAL DAYS EARLIER

Jesse reined his best saddle horse, Toby, over to the tree line. Toby was a mixed breed of quarter horse and American saddle stock. A large, roan gelding, Jesse picked him up at the Madras horse auction and worked him every day until the two could think as one.

It was one-sided thinking because what Jesse did not know was that the horse was a whole lot smarter than Jesse.

Toby pushed through the deep snow and biting cold. This was the fifth time in as many days that Jesse had returned to where he had watched the Indian lady throw a deer haunch down amongst some rocks. Day after day went by without any more sightings of the lady.

The deep snow, however, changed the landscape somewhat, making it difficult to pinpoint the exact site. Several times Jesse had tried to get Toby closer to a nearby snow-covered embankment, but each time Toby had whirled around and quickly moved away. The horse would not leave the trees. He pawed the ground and refused to budge. No amount of reining or spurs could get Toby over to where Jesse wanted to go.

The snow was waist high—way too deep for Jesse to try to explore on foot. He wasn't even sure he was at the right spot because the snow covered the scattered bones he once saw.

Soon it would be dark, and Jesse would be faced with a long, cold ride back to a line cabin.

Jesse sat astride Toby just inside the tree line. He turned his coffee cup over to drain out the last bit of cold coffee at the same moment that Toby nickered. Then he flared his nostrils. Jesse could almost feel a nervous shiver run up and down the horse's spine. Toby tried to turn, but Jesse managed to hold him in place with the reins.

There, popping up through the snow a mere quarter-mile away, Jesse counted a total of four wolves wiggling their way one by one out of a snow-covered cave. The wolves waited until the fifth one, an immense black wolf, managed to squeeze out from the den. Fortunately for Jesse, they took off on a loping run away from Jesse in search of prey. All the wolves had their noses to the ground, sniffing intently, searching for the scent of a meal. The large black wolf was leading the pack.

It dawned on Jesse that had he walked over to the concealed wolf den, he might well have been dinner. As it was, the wind was blowing toward Jesse and not the other way around. It was Jesse who picked up the scent of the wolves. The smell was overpowering. Jesse decided to wait awhile before riding off to make sure all the wolves were gone.

"I'll be able to smell them a mile off," he thought, "Should they suddenly return."

Several minutes later the elderly Indian lady appeared, gliding on snowshoes to the wolf den. She carried a deer leg over one shoulder. Jesse figured she must have been watching as the wolves left their den. She didn't know Jesse was there, hiding behind some nearby Ponderosas.

Jesse was not a deep or profound thinker but, as he watched her, it suddenly occurred to him what she was doing. "She's feeding them," he thought, "Her scent is all over that deer meat, and she's protecting herself by feeding them."

For one of the few times in his life, Jesse was on the right track. If a dog never bites the hand that feeds it, and if all dogs are descendants of the wolves, then the old lady was buying protection. All Jesse had to do was stay out of the way of the wolves and just follow her back to where her people were hiding. He no longer felt the cold as his excitement level rose. Seeing her was a guarantee of more money than Jesse had ever seen in his entire life. He was mentally counting his bonus as she threw the deer leg down by the mouth of the wolf cave. She turned and quickly retraced her steps.

Jesse gave her five minutes and started to follow her tracks back to her lodge. He knew she had to be somewhere close by. It just made sense, especially as she was traveling on snowshoes through the deep snow.

Jesse started mentally spending his bonus. Fifteen thousand dollars total for one week of work was far more than anyone in his family had ever earned for months of backbreaking, numbing labor. What made it even better was that he would be paid in cash. Jesse didn't like the IRS, and any cash he earned was never declared. It was, Jesse figured, his way of keeping things simple, both for himself and for the Government. The Government had enough to worry about, and Jesse did not want to add to its woes.

Deep down, Jesse also knew that fifteen thousand was a lot of money for pointing out where the Indians lived. If anything happened to them, well, they brought *that* upon themselves. They should have stayed down in California. They had no business being up here and hiding out on Federal land. This was not on him. He had nothing to do with any of that. They were responsible for the consequences of what they did. Their time of obstruction was now over, and whatever came down on them was their problem—not Jesse's.

Her tracks ended at the base of a lava-rock butte. This was the location of her people. Jesse would map out the location for Assistant Vice-President Eldon. He had earned his bonus.

Life was indeed, good!

THE PEOPLE GATHER IN COUNCIL

Chief Tuliyani stood before the small tribe and held aloft the carved talking stick in his hand. To insure everyone's voice would be heard, he reminded the people that whoever had the talking stick had the right to speak without interruption from others. The talking stick would be passed in a circle, and each tribal member would be given a turn to speak—but only if they wanted. Chance, too, would be able to speak in his defense, but he would not be allowed to vote. After the speakers were done, the tribal members would vote. A simple majority would decide Chance's fate. As there were only a total of eleven Hiders left, a one-vote majority could decide the final outcome. According to custom, the Chief would speak first but would cast the last vote.

"I vote last so as not to bend your votes," said the Chief, "And pray that all our votes will bring honor to our customs and laws."

The Chief began: "Our people tell the story of a hot summer day when our band walked to Mill creek and began swimming. My grandparents and great-grandparents lived in this band. Everyone was enjoying the cool waters until one-man suddenly fell forward dead, followed by a loud crack. Then all around were the Guardsmen shooting at the people from behind the trees. Several of the warriors ran to the shore to get their weapons, but they were quickly cut down. Pretty soon the men were all killed, along with some boys about the same age as this young man.

"The Guardsmen had elected as their war chief a man known to us as Anderson. He was a very young man then, but he carried a lot of hate and anger in his heart. His actions always spoke more than his empty words, and he always killed our people at every chance, sparing no one, not even the babies. Soon, after all the warriors were killed, this man Anderson and others began to shoot the fleeing women and children.

"By day's end, most members of our band were dead. Only a few tribal members managed to run off into the woods and survived. One of the Guardsmen shot a young mother fighting her way across the deep stream with her two children. The mother's body was swept away, and the two struggling children tried to stay afloat but to no avail. As the children were crying out for help, the man who shot their mother began laughing and pointing the children out to others. Several of the men then stood by the water's edge and had a contest to see who could shoot the children before they drowned. The shooting was over in moments, and the babies sank. They were never found, and to this day their spirits remain in torment, forever tied to the earth. My grandmother and great-grandmother were two of the only four survivors, and this is the story they have passed down to us."

Chance and Shasta were kneeling side by side as Shasta quietly translated the Chief's words to a stunned Chance. When Shasta initially told him that the trial was for his life, he at first could not believe her. It simply didn't register. The whole experience was incomprehensible, starting with the fact that a tribe of Stone-Age Indians could even be hiding out in the Oregon wilderness. He actually thought, for a few minutes anyway, that they might be rescuing him when they initially took him to their lodge and, not in a million years, did he ever think or believe that he would be on trial for something that other people did centuries ago. It was not fair. He felt as if the Chief was personally blaming him for the acts of others. Even if he was alive during the frontier days, shooting people—especially women and children—was something he never would have done. Now, to be personally blamed for all this was unjust. Chance slumped forward, a sickening knot forming in his belly. He reached for his inhalator and pulled deeply on his medicine. This was not starting well, at all.

Chief Tuliyani passed the talking stick to the tribal Shaman, a small, wizened man who had seen nearly ninety winters. Holding the stick, Night Fire began talking and surprised many with what he had to say. "Our Chief is right to talk about what has happened to us at the hands of the whites, but we have to temper this with what we did to their children. Some warriors from my father's band shot two young white girls because this man, Anderson, and others attacked one of our camps, killing many of our people. So grief-stricken and angry were the surviving warriors that they stained our tribal honor by seizing a small boy and having the child tortured to death by *our* young children. Never before had the Yahi Nation made war upon women and children. As warriors, we fought warriors, never women or the elderly and never, ever, children. On the day we put that child to death, we were no better than the whites and for that killing, many of our people suffered terribly. That was the day that evil found its way into our camps. Now we have this one chance to make right ancient wrongs and to forever bury all the hatred and fear. That is all I have to say."

Whisper next held the talking stick aloft and said, "Night Fire is right in what he says, but this is not about making war on children. We are under attack from everywhere. The wild animals of the forest are trying to kill us, a white hunter shot my husband, and each year we are seeing more and more of the Englishmen in the woods. Every day it seems whites are being dropped from the sky to their nearby lodge. We do not know what they are doing but, whatever it is, it is a threat to our very lives. It is just a question of time until we are found, and then we will be killed. This is the history of our people; this is what has always happened to us. To save our tribe, we must have the strength and the will to do what is right. If that means one enemy life has to be taken to save the people, so be it."

The next speaker was Jumping Bull, father of Kicking Horse, who stood to speak before the tribe. "We took this young man with us, so we might hear the wisdom of the tribe as to what we should do. When we captured him, he had a dead wolf at his feet, and he was carrying a bloodstained lance. These are the actions of a man of honor; a brave warrior whose life should be spared."

Jumping Bull abruptly sat down, without looking once at his son, Kicking Horse. Shasta quickly translated what he said and then whispered to Chance, "That's probably two votes for you and two against."

Left Hand was next given the talking stick. "You know I am a man of peace," he said. "Even though one of my long-ago cousins was made to stand against a barn wall while she and her aunt and uncle were shot by the whites. They had no enmity toward the whites and did nothing to anger them, aside from the fact that they were Indian. The whites killed them because they wanted to kill all the Indian people simply because we were not like them. My heart cries out for vengeance, but to what end? All vengeance does is cause more killing. Sometimes a wise warrior must choose peace over war to protect the lives of the people. That is all I have to say."

Nopanny stood and sided with her sister, Whisper, simply stating, "If we let him live, then he will bring outsiders to our camp, and we will all be killed."

Kicking Horse rose and said, "I agree with Whisper and Nopanny. This Guardsman is a danger to our way of life, and we must respect the wisdom of our ancestors. Their voice to us is clear. We are to kill the enemy before he kills us."

After Shasta translated what the people were saying, Chance whispered, "Kicking Horse's vote just cancelled out the vote of Jumping Bull."

"What counts is not the talking," Shasta said, "But the voting."

He Who Stands rose to his feet. "My great-grandfather was killed at the Kingsley Cave Massacre. That last act drove us into hiding, and we have suffered ever since. The whites wanted to kill all our people—but we have survived. And there may even be more of our people in hiding that we do not know about. Lately I have come to believe that the whites are no longer after us. Whisper, Nopanny and their cousin once came across Indian women out picking berries many years ago, and those Indian women did not seem at all worried about the whites. It appears many people from all tribes have survived the Indian Wars. We see Indians from time to time coming down from the North, hunting in the forest. Hear this: I have an obligation to this young man. He saved my daughter from an icy death. He jumped into a fast-flowing river, not knowing if he would be swept away or if he would freeze to death. He single-handedly killed the wolf that we feasted upon for several nights. I see this young man smiling and eagerly looking around as if to understand how we live our lives. He does not seem a threat. I have been praying to the Great Spirit for guidance, and I will vote to spare him. I am done speaking."

Soon the talking stick came full circle to Chief Tuliyani. He passed the talking stick over to Little Bear while Shasta finished translating for Chance. Chance quietly said, "I am not a Guardsman, and I did not kill that wolf."

Surprised, Shasta said, "Yes, you did! Why are you now saying that? I saw the wolf dead by your feet when you were walking toward us holding the bloody lance."

"No, no," said Chance, emphatically shaking his head, "The black wolf killed him the night before. I tried to push him away from where I was by using the lance, and the blood froze to the lance. But I did not kill him."

As an afterthought Chance added, "I also don't like the way this is going, and I would appreciate you reminding your tribal council that I am not, nor have I ever been, a Guardsman."

Shasta, now rapidly breathing, said, "I need time to think this through because it changes things. Right now, all the people think you killed that wolf. The people respect that act for its bravery. After Little Bear and his wife speak, then it is my turn. After that it is your turn."

Forcing a smile, Shasta again squeezed Chance's hand. "When your turn comes, do not say anything about the wolf. We will see how the people vote and, if the vote is against you, our custom is that any tribal member be given one last chance to change hearts. Let us first see how the vote is. Then we can talk about what to do next, though I fear the voting may be close."

As a sign of respect for the solemnity of the occasion, both Little Bear and his wife stood to address the Council. Little Bear began, "After our people went into hiding, they held a council meeting as to what to do with any prisoners. To protect the tribe, the people voted to kill all captives. That vote is binding upon us. Our ancestors, in sacred council, wisely decided that all white captives would be put to death so that we as a people could survive. I bear no anger toward this young man but, like Kicking Horse, I must honor the decisions of our forefathers and that is how I will vote."

Little Bear's wife, Raven, accepted the talking stick and said, "We have been in hiding since the Kingsley Cave Massacre. So good are we at hiding that we have survived all these years. From time to time, I see unarmed English men and women and children walking through the woods. With so much time gone by, I have never seen any Guardsmen or others out hunting for us. We had only one run-in with a white man here, and he is no longer a threat to us. I don't know why he shot our Chief, but I believe in my heart that it was either an accident or the fact that he stank of whisky. In any event, he is gone. For me, I want to live out my life here with my family and my tribe, and I want to be able to do this without ever taking the life of another. I do not believe the vote of our ancestors to be still binding because I believe the war brought to our camps to be long over. While I respect my husband's decision, I shall vote to spare this young man's life."

The two sat down and Chance watched Little Bear turn and feverishly speak to Raven. He emphasized his point while grasping her wrist. Raven at first appeared flushed—then tried to pull away. Little Bear held tightly to her wrist. Raven stopped struggling and meekly turned her eyes downward.

Shasta caught the encounter and turned to Chance, silently shaking her head.

Shasta rose and simply said, "I believe we are living in a new world, and that those who hunted us down and killed us are long gone. They are dust. This warrior tells me he is not a member of the Guards, and I believe him. He also tells me that the Guards no longer exist. I believe that as well. I, too, shall vote to save his life as he so bravely saved mine."

Bending slightly, Shasta motioned Chance to his feet, whispering, "Speak your words, and I shall translate them to the people. I think the vote is very close, so choose carefully. You only have a minute or two to tell them what you want them to hear."

Kicking Horse glared as Shasta again touched the Englishman in an affectionate way, placing her hand to his back, helping to steady him. Though Shasta denied any feelings toward the captive, Kicking Horse now believed otherwise.

If the vote went against Chance, Kicking Horse would insist on the right to kill this Guardsman.

A LAW ENFORCEMENT STRATEGY MEETING

PRESENT TIME

T he four men met at the downtown Bend Starbucks. It was still snowing heavily and, in spite of the best efforts of the retail storeowners, all they could do was make narrow trails through the deep snow. It didn't really matter, as most shoppers were staying at home anyway.

Special Agent Walton of the Bureau of Indian Affairs and Special Agent Adams of the Federal Bureau of Investigation had worked several homicide cases together with successful convictions. Their mission now was to solve the missing hunter case.

Mason Many Crows and Agent Adams had also worked several homicides at the Reservation. The FBI was always involved anytime there was a homicide on Federal lands. That made three of the four to be experienced homicide investigators.

For Deputy Johansen, the missing elk hunter was his first possible homicide, although the case was still officially classified as a "missing person." Johansen wanted to team up with Walton who had the most experience and a well-earned reputation as a bulldog, following up and tracking down every lead. While Johansen did not have prior homicide experience, out of the four men, he had the most exposure to dead bodies.

"In my two Mideast tours," he said, "I have seen several hundred or more dead people killed in every way possible."

Walton simply said, "You're with me."

Walton was near retirement, and it was very important to him to close out his career and not have any unsolved cases. Out of respect for his knowledge and experience, his peer group recognized him as the lead investigator.

One of the first things he did prior to the meeting was to e-mail everyone a copy of his Bureau of Indian Affairs Yahi file, along with copies of McKenna's Oregon State Police report about the missing hunter.

Warden McKenna was still in the hospital, but he wanted to represent the Oregon State Police upon recovery. What he wanted most of all now was to be out searching for Chance.

The snow was still coming down, and Search and Rescue were out in full force.

McKenna somehow knew in his heart that Chance was all right. It was something he felt, and it helped to comfort him. Chance might be cold, wet, miserable and hungry, but if he stayed in a snow cave, as he had been taught, he would survive.

Mason shared the daily report about Ryan's recovery. "He must be getting better," said Mason. "A nurse caught him heading toward the exit, dragging his IV behind him. She had to force him back to his bed."

The other men all smiled. McKenna was again proving himself to be a thickheaded Irishman.

Thumbing through the Yahi file, Walton observed, "This makes for some very interesting reading. I did not know that *every* time the Yahi came across the whites, somebody died. In most cases it was the Yahi. Whether to protect themselves or out of revenge, the Yahi then did their best to take the fight back to the whites. It seems to me to be just a continuous circle of attack and counterattack until all the participants were either dead or in hiding."

"Just like the Mideast," said Johansen. "It's all about guerilla fighting: swoop, shoot and disappear."

Lowering his voice, Walton outlined his plan.

"We have two guys who were with this Tom Conway on the day he went missing—Bridger Holmes and David Peters. Their story to Warden McKenna was that they left camp with Conway and that a mile or so later, they decided to split up as Holmes and Peters spotted some elk tracks in the snow.

"Conway was to head to the left and Holmes and Peters to the right. The thinking was that if they could push some elk up toward Conway, he would get a shot off. If the elk went downhill, then they would get a shot.

"According to the original statements of Holmes and Peters, they hunted all day. Near the end of their hunt, they started looking for Conway.

They never found him. Turns out the elk tracks were old, and they never spotted any elk.

"Their sworn statement is that they were out in the field all day, had spent hours looking for Conway, and had never heard so much as one shot.

"That story conflicts with their other hunting partners who say they did hear a shot. Plus, the other two gave a deposition swearing that Holmes and Peters appeared to have spent a portion of the day just holed up in their tent. They also appeared very stressed and nervous but couldn't or wouldn't tell the other guys what they were so worried about.

"The decision was made to quickly break camp and leave. Holmes and Peters could barely say good-bye. They just warned the other guys to not stick around and threw their gear in a truck and left. The other two followed them out of the woods.

"Here's where it gets a little dicey. I think there was some kind of an incident up there, and Holmes and Peters are covering it up. Their story about being away from camp and hunting all day never happened. When they found out that the other two guys had seen them in their tent, they changed their story to where they just came back for a quick lunch and to get warm. They claim to have gone right out hunting again, as it was the last day of the season. That also never happened. They were too busy packing."

Mason added, "Ryan told me that he did gunshot-residue tests on all four guys, and the GSR turned up negative. None of them had fired a weapon. So what puzzles me is how could they be involved in, say, a shooting accident and no GSR? I don't get it."

Walton added, "Holmes and Peters are the only two who know what happened, and for some reason, they don't want to share, which leads me to believe they are involved. The State Police offered a lie-detector test to clear them, and next thing you know they both lawyered up. I know they have the right to a lawyer, but it seems suspicious to me to go to the expense of a lawyer if you are truly innocent and you don't really need a lawyer. But maybe that's just me."

The others all nodded in agreement.

"Here's what we do," said Walton. "We set up a meeting with Holmes and Peters at the County Courthouse. Johansen, you get us a couple of interview rooms, preferably with a window in the door and right across the hall from each other. I want them to see each other being interrogated. We tell them some new facts have come up about the case, and it would be very helpful for all concerned to have a little discussion."

"Pow-wow," said Mason, enthusiastically. "We'll have a little pow-wow with them—a meeting of the minds."

"That works," said Walton. "We hold back info about the existence of the Hiders and press these guys about their alibi inconsistencies.

"We advise them of their rights and see if we can't scare the crap out of them.

"We tell them that this is quickly turning into a homicide investigation.

"You know the drill: whoever talks first gets the best deal. Maybe one or both will flip. They *don't* strike me as criminals, especially as neither one has a record but, for sure, they are not being truthful with us."

"Personally," Walton concluded, "I don't think they killed their hunting partner *on purpose,* but right now they should understand that they are persons of interest. That may change; we'll just have to see how all this plays out."

Johansen asked, "How do we discuss this without bringing up the Hiders? I'm assuming that all this tie together."

"It does, and we don't," said Walton, "We're still bound by the Governor's executive order. For now, whatever they might bring up, we'll just have to play it by ear."

They finished their coffees as Johansen finalized the interview arrangements.

Mason, looking down at the empty cups and sighing deeply, remarked, "I thought all Englishmen on expense accounts would be drinking expensive lattes. You're letting the taxpayer off easy. You guys just had regular coffees. I'm so disappointed."

"Let's go get this solved," said Walton, "And dinners on me. I may not even stiff the taxpayer for the bill."

"Really?" asked Johansen.

"No," said Walton, "I'm just kidding. Let's get busy."

CHANCE SPEAKS

C hance stood before the Council and began speaking. All eyes were upon him. For each point he made, Shasta would nod in agreement and then translate to the tribe. Some of the people seemed deeply conflicted about what to do, but several were outwardly hostile. Chance would look and talk directly to each person, pleading his case as if one-on-one. He would speak softly and allow Shasta plenty of time to translate. Taking his cue from those around him, he would speak only to the most important points as to why he should be spared.

He began, "Few people today even know of the existence of the Yahi Hiders. My father has some pictures of four tribal members hunting before the snow fell," he said, indicating Shasta and the other hunters.

"They were taken by a hidden camera in the woods. He showed them to me."

Chance briefly explained the hidden cameras to Shasta who translated his words to the assembled group.

Whisper, shaking her head, yelled out, "Cameras are white man's magic to capture our spirit." Several of the other tribal members nodded in agreement.

Chance took a deep breath and continued, "Without those pictures, I would have just thought that my father was kidding me about a lost tribe in hiding. If he were here today, he would tell you the same thing that Shasta has said, which is that we live in a totally different world from that of the frontier times. I know that whites stopped fighting Native Americans well over a hundred years ago. If one person kills another person today, regardless of their color or tribe, they are brought to trial and judged by their actions, much as I stand in trial before you now. What I am hearing is that you fear exposure because that will lead to whites killing you. I can tell you this: I have never killed anyone, nor has my father, nor my father's father, as far back as we've ever known. We live peaceful lives with all peoples, as do all our friends and neighbors. Life today is *not* at all like the old days."

Chance paused while Shasta continued to translate. Carefully, she presented all his arguments to Council. She nodded to Chance, and he continued, "My father told me the Chief of our State wants to meet you. He wants to know everything about your lives. He wants you to know that you will be protected by him and that you are free to do whatever you want. He is a good man, he knows how difficult it is to remain in hiding, and he wants to help you. He also wants you to know that no one is out looking for you to kill you."

Shasta translated as Chance tried to pull himself together. He did not like public speaking. It made him very nervous—especially considering the outcome. He could feel his voice starting to quiver. He kept his fists clenched tightly together so that no one would see him wringing his hands together. His breathing was much labored.

After Shasta translated, several of the elders voiced their anger.

"More lies from the Englishman," said one. "Lies like sending Indian people off to a reservation where they died from disease and starvation. Every time the white man says he has the best interests of the Indian at heart, it is only to get rid of the Indian. The only promise the whites ever kept was their promise to kill the Indians."

"In the old days," said another, "Your Army chased us all over our homeland and couldn't catch us, and so they turned us over to the Guards, who killed us. And now you tell us that your Chief wants to help us? Where was this help when the Guards were killing us? Why did none of the white chiefs step forward then to stop all the killing? It was the whites that started this war! And why did the white chiefs not send their Army out to capture the Guards for killing our women and children?"

The pent-up anger over past wrongs was at a near-breaking point.

"Enough," said a third, "This storm will soon be over, and then searchers will be out looking for this young man. We need to vote and do what is best for the people. That is all I have to say."

Shasta signaled Chance that the time for discussion was over. Chance felt shortchanged. He had more to say—a lot more. His very life depended upon it. Turning to Shasta, he indicated that he wanted to continue speaking. She shook her head no, saying that the Chief was now asking for the vote.

Chance surprised her. Speaking over the Chief, he asked her to translate while he forcibly stressed his innocence. He punched his open hand with his closed fist telling the people that he was not a Guardsman, no one in his family had ever been a Guardsman and that he should not be judged by what a small group of angry, frightened Guardsmen did hundreds of years ago.

He knew that if the vote went against him, a tribal member would have one last chance to change hearts. Looking around the dimly lit cave, Chance resolved that if the vote went against him, he would make a run for it and escape to the wilderness. It was probably the last thing anyone would expect. He would rather die fighting than meekly submitting to his execution.

"More than likely," he thought, "I would probably die from freezing than fighting."

Given the solemnity of the moment, Chief Tuliyani motioned for Chance to sit down and then quietly asked the people, "Are we ready to vote?"

The tribal members all nodded in agreement. Then the Chief said, "We are voting on whether this young man should live or die. From beyond the grave our ancestors have directed us to kill all enemy captives to protect our people. This young man is the first captive we have ever had, and I am torn between his character and his courage against the wishes of our ancestors. The decision is yours. I shall hold my vote until last."

The Chief then polled all the tribal members one by one. When it was her turn, Raven stood and said that out of respect for her ancestors and for all the tribal members who had suffered so much at the hands of the Guards, that she had changed her mind. Her vote now was to protect the tribe. She realized what this might mean for Chance, but it was the right thing to do. Sadly, she was voting against him.

As the voting continued, Shasta slid her hand over to Chance. She again placed her hand over his and gave him a gentle squeeze of support.

When the votes were all counted, the Council was evenly divided. Five tribal members voted to spare Chance; five voted he be put to death. The Chief's vote would now determine whether Chance lived or died.

Shasta was squeezing Chance's hand so hard that her nails were digging in, causing Chance to pull away and fumble around for his inhalator. He removed the inhalator from his pocket only to drop it and have it roll away from him.

Looking at Chance, Chief Tuliyani solemnly said, "It is with a heavy heart that I vote against you. I believe you when you say that the Guardsmen are all dead and that no one is looking for us. That gives my people hope. You strike me as a young man of bravery and courage, which makes my task all the more difficult. However, when the people appointed me Chief, I solemnly pledged to protect the tribe to the best of my ability. I was also sworn to uphold past decisions of tribal councils. I gave my promise to the Great Spirit to do all these things as best I could. I feel as if my hands are tied now, but I have no choice except to follow our law and ways. To that end, our vote is now six against you and five for you. I wish it were the other way around, but that is not so."

Before Shasta even translated, Chance had a sinking feeling in his heart that the vote had gone against him.

The Chief continued, "Now, as is our custom, one tribal member may speak for you and address the Council. Any tribal member may then change or keep their vote, as they see correct. We will take another vote to see if anyone has changed. That will be the last vote, and it is binding upon us all."

Shasta stood and addressed the Council. "I speak for this man." She then translated to Chance what Chief Tuliyani had said. Several of the tribal members kept averting their eyes. Even Kicking Horse could not look at him, although Kicking Horse was one of the first votes against him.

Chance was taller than all his captors and by far one of the strongest. He felt every cell in his body filling with testosterone. If they were determined to kill him, he was equally determined to go down fighting.

"If Shasta can't pull this off," thought Chance, "I'm going for the cave entrance. Fight or flee—and running is my best option. I can easily get past the Guardian and with the possible exception of Kicking Horse, I can outrun all the others. If Kicking Horse can even catch me, he had better be ready for the fight of his life."

Shasta and Chance both stood before the Council. Shasta turned and looked up at Chance, searching for the words. This time she was not smiling. She was instead very apprehensive.

"You may not understand my Yahi words, but I am asking you to trust me in this. My people are a stiff-backed people, but they all respect courage. By my words I will be putting you in a dangerous situation where your courage is all that may save you. As of right now, the vote has gone against you, and it is now up to me to convince the people to give you this one chance to save yourself and *our* people. If they agree to what I propose, and if you are able to win out over the enemy, then your life will be spared. That is what I want. I know it is what you want."

She told Chance her idea. He was momentarily stunned.

"How could I possibly do that?" he asked. "That's impossible. You're setting me up for failure."

She looked down at the ground for a moment. "It won't be easy. It is very dangerous. Because it is so dangerous, that is something the people will respect. It is our only hope to change their minds and, for now, hope is all we have."

"There's no way I can do this," Chance said."

"By your very words you are inviting defeat. Where is the warrior who faced down the wolves? Where is the man who risked his life to save mine? I am talking to that man, but some stranger is talking back to me. Make your words be 'I can' and you will. All I ask is for you to be the warrior I know you to be. Believe that you can do it, and you can. Then you will succeed and have earned your freedom. That alone is worth the risk. It is up to you."

As an afterthought she quietly added, "Do not try to run. Kicking Horse saw you looking to the entrance and has set an arrow in his bow."

RYAN'S RECOVERY

"You must be getting better," said Mason, "This is the third annoying call from you in just the past hour."

"You've got to get me out of here," said Ryan, "I'm worried sick about Chance. Three days later and there's no trace of him? I can't eat. I can't sleep. All I do is worry about him. I'm checking myself out. They moved me yesterday to a regular room, so I know I'm better. I'll feel even better once I find Chance. My lung is up, I don't have a concussion, and my arm is stitched up and in a sling. I feel almost good except for the ribs, and they just heal on their own. Can you pick me up?"

"Ryan, I don't know how to tell you this, buddy, but I think you need more time to heal. It is still snowing heavily. KZ21 says it should stop by tonight and that we should get some decent weather tomorrow. We can revisit this whole thing then. You watch. Chance will pop up out of a snow cave somewhere, and we'll have to take him to Jakes to re-fuel."

Jakes Restaurant is well known for very large servings.

"Last time I took him to Jakes, he almost bankrupted the owner with all the food he put away," said Ryan. "But I'm really worried about him being out there in this snow and cold. I'm even more worried about him being out there with those wolves."

"Search and Rescue has combed the Paulina Trail several times over," said Mason, "So far—nothing. I thought for sure they would have found his snowmobile by now."

"They haven't even found the snowmobile? What if he slid over the edge? What if he has hypothermia? The wolves attacked *me*. What if they attack him? I just don't feel good about this at all."

"Of course you're worried," said Mason. "You wouldn't be a normal parent if you weren't concerned. We've got our best out there searching for him plus a number of dogs. We'll find him. His snowmobile is probably buried under six feet of snow by now. He's got to be somewhere near that snowmobile. Yesterday Buster and I managed to find some of that police tape you left up there. If we can find that, then Search and Rescue can definitely find a big old snowmobile."

"I didn't know you and Buster were out there. I appreciate that," said Ryan.

"Good," said Mason, "Because I froze my plus-size Indian ass off up there. I think half the State Police are out hiking up and down Paulina, and I know all your warden buddies are here from as far away as Joseph on one side to Astoria on the other. With all this manpower, we will find him. And we will find him sooner rather than later, and he will be fine."

Ryan was silent for a moment, deeply touched by all the support and help. Now more than ever, he wanted to be where the action was.

"I'll be waiting in the lobby," said Ryan, his voice slightly cracking. "The Doc said that all things considered, I was healing nicely. I'll make you a deal. Search and Rescue must have the Sno-Cat up there."

"They do," said Mason.

"Here's my offer," said Ryan. "You, me, Buster and Johansen— we can all squeeze in that Cat. For my part, I promise to leave all the heavy lifting to you guys. I just have to be there. We can cover that trail until we find him. Not being able to do anything is driving me nuts."

Before Mason could even respond, Ryan quickly added, "Just bring me some real food and warm clothing, and I won't do anything to pop my stitches. I promise."

Mason sighed deeply. "All right," he said, "One hour and I'll be out front." Almost as an afterthought Mason added, "But you're not driving the Cat."

SHASTA'S PLEA

Addressing the Council, Shasta began, "This is a brave young man. He is a warrior. He risked his life to save mine. He is also an honest man. It was only just minutes ago he told me that he had not killed the wolf that we feasted on. He did not have to tell me that. I made a mistake thinking that he killed the wolf. He said that, while it may have looked like he had killed the wolf—it was Shadow who killed it, not this young man.

"His honesty and his courage are what I ask you to consider. The vote has gone against him, and he is now under a sentence of death. How would we end his life—with an arrow, with a knife, with stones? Should we hang him as we ourselves have been hanged? What if searchers find his body, and there is an arrow hole in it. Would they not come looking for us now that they know we are here?"

She continued, "Before our last vote is taken, I propose this to you: Let us give him the opportunity to fight as a warrior protecting our people. I propose that we take him to the wolf's cave. We take him there to kill Shadow. If he succeeds, we give him his freedom. If he fails, and the wolves kill him, then when the searchers find his body, they will think it to be an accident. They will think he crawled into the wolf den to escape the snowstorm."

All the tribal members began speaking at once. Several seemed to like the idea except for one who shouted out, "How are we to find the wolf den in this snowstorm? It will be too late for us if we have to wait until the snows end."

Shasta quietly replied, "Whisper can tell us exactly where they live because she has been feeding them."

She said this so softly that it took a moment for the Council to digest. All the tribal members were surprised. Some had wondered and talked amongst themselves why the black wolf leaped over Whisper and instead went for the elderly warrior during the night of the attack. Now they knew.

Whisper lowered her head. She wanted to explain herself but instead started stammering. She was too embarrassed to look at those around her. Several of the women harshly scolded her for taking food from the people and giving it to the black wolf. The widow of the elderly warrior killed by Shadow began sobbing.

Deeply shamed by his wife's actions, the Chief quickly called for the final, binding vote. Many felt that Shasta's idea would be of benefit to the tribe. It was a way to save face, especially for those who voted against Chance. If Chance succeeded, the tribe would not have to live in fear of more wolf attacks, and the young man's life would be spared. The votes were now seven to four. Seven of the eleven had voted to give Chance the opportunity of a warrior's death. Only the Chief, Kicking Horse, Whisper and Nopanny voted against Shasta's proposal.

The Chief spoke directly to Chance, "It has been decided. Tomorrow night, Kicking Horse will take you to the wolf's lair. He will give you weapons. Kicking Horse will watch to see if you kill the black wolf. Once Shadow is gone, the other wolves will run away. Without their leader to protect them, they are powerless. Remember this, though. All the wolves may circle their leader to protect him. To kill the black wolf you may well have to kill all the other wolves. You are not going against just one wolf—you are going against the entire pack. None of our people, as far back as we know, have ever gone against an entire pack."

The Chief paused, "Should Grandfather Creator favor you, you will succeed. If you succeed, your courage and bravery will be always told around our campfire. We will reunite you with your people by taking you to the big lodge on the lake. There you will be released. We would only ask that you not immediately reveal our location to others. We will not put any other burden on you and will pray for your success."

AN UNCOMFORTABLE INTERVIEW

PRESENT TIME

That next morning, the two elk hunters, Holmes and Peters, showed up at the Deschutes County Courthouse with their attorneys. The ground rules for the interrogation had all been worked out. The meeting would be videotaped. The defense attorneys insisted upon bringing their own video cameras. That was agreed upon. The attorneys then lobbied long and hard for a more neutral meeting place but eventually agreed to the Courthouse.

Special Agent Walton and Deputy Johansen met with Bridger Holmes and his attorney, a local known casually to Walton by the name of J. Karneski. Special Agent Adams of the FBI and Police Officer Mason Many Crows of the Warm Springs PD met in a separate interview room with Dave Peters and his attorney. The two interrogations would follow an identical script. Walton opened with introductions, covered the agreed-upon taping format and then immediately informed Holmes of his legal rights. Holmes was not expecting that. Somewhat surprised, he turned to his attorney as Walton explained it was merely a legal formality. Karneski indicated, "No problem."

"Some new information has come to light in the disappearance of your hunting partner, Tom Conway," said Walton. "We appreciate you coming in to help us clear up some inconsistencies in your statements to the police."

Holmes's attorney immediately asked, before Walton had even finished, "What is this new information?"

"I'm not ready to discuss that yet," said Walton, "as this is an ongoing investigation, but it is significant enough to change this from a missing person case to a probable homicide case, and right now your client is a person of interest."

Holmes started to sag in his seat.

This being a "person of interest," did not set well with Mr. Karneski, who asked his client if he wanted to go through the questioning or leave. The attorney knew that is was perfectly legal for the police to lie in an interview in hopes of tripping up a suspect. The attorney also knew that by hearing the investigators out, he would learn some of this new information and be in a better position to advise his client. Still, he had to first respect the wishes of his client.

Holmes said he just wanted to get this finished once and for all.

"I'll tell you this," said Special Agent Walton, addressing Karneski, "we believe there was some type of a hunting incident up there. Conway's wife, naturally enough, is hoping against hope that he is still alive somewhere. I don't believe that for a second. I think he is dead, and that your client knows what happened. Your client and Mr. Peters both passed a field GSR test administered by Warden McKenna. The tests were negative. The other two also passed. None had fired their weapons. Still, as you know, fatal accidents can occur in many ways. We need your client to fill in some of the blanks for us. By helping us, we in turn can help your client and also the Conway family. We want to do that."

Removing his glasses and directing his statement to Karneski but looking directly at Holmes, Walton added, "By the way, I'm sure that you have advised your client that it is a very serious crime to lie to a Federal Agent."

Before Walton could even finish his sentence, Holmes downed a full glass of water in just a couple of gulps.

"Here's what we know," said Walton, again addressing Karneski. "Tom Conway, your client, and Mr. Peters all left hunting camp right after breakfast. It was the last day of elk season, and everyone was getting anxious because no one had filled their tags. The three men left camp that morning and only two returned, *allegedly* that evening. Soon afterward, Deschutes County Search and Rescue was called out to search for the missing hunter. More than twenty people left the comfort of their homes on a cold night to search for Tom Conway. He was never found. Your client and Mr. Peters both claimed to have been tired and, instead of assisting the search party, they went home to sleep. I know hunting at high altitudes is exhausting but that was a little surprising—almost makes me think they knew Conway would not be found."

Holmes started to protest, but Karneski put his finger to his lips.

"Conway's hunting hat with some bloodstains on it was found, along with an empty bottle of Jim Beam. The Jim Beam bottle turned out to have his fingerprints on it and also the prints of your client and Mr. Peters. Your client and Mr. Peters both identified the hunting hat as identical to the one worn by Mr. Conway. Lab tests confirm that DNA from the bloodstains is from Mr. Conway."

Pausing for dramatic effect, Walton looked Holmes squarely in the eye and said, "Now Counselor, I hope you have advised your client that, in the State of Oregon, a murder conviction may be obtained even if the body is never recovered."

Holmes sat silently, shaking his head from side to side. His lips were closely pressed together, and he appeared very distressed.

Still staring at Holmes, Walton continued, "You say that Conway had gone up high, while you and Peters headed low. I don't know. Maybe Mr. Conway slipped on some ice or snow. Maybe he fell in a crevice. We know he was a hard drinker. Alcohol lowers body temperature. Maybe he built a snow cave to stay warm, passed out and never regained consciousness. All kinds of things can happen up there. We do think it's very strange, though, that we never found any of his remains—especially in such a small valley."

Walton paused as if in deep thought. "Here's something else I don't understand. You guys were the only ones hunting in that area. According to your sworn deposition, you and Peters claim to have not heard any gunshots, yet your other two hunting partners state that they clearly heard one gunshot not too far from camp. How do you explain that?"

Karneski interjected with, "It was probably Tom Conway shooting at an elk."

"Then how come your client and his crime partner claim to have not heard any shots at all?" asked Walton. "Again, seems kind of strange."

Karneski strongly objected, saying, "My client does not have a 'crime partner' as no crime has been committed."

Underneath the interview table, Holmes was wringing his hands together.

"It's been almost two years since the disappearance of Conway. In addition to not finding his body, we also never found his rifle. Now, a lot of agencies have put considerable time and money into the investigation of this case," said Walton. "To clear this up, we offered the four hunters a polygraph. The other guys immediately accepted and were cleared. Your client and Mr. Peters refused. What's that all about?"

"I would point out," replied Karneski, "that turning down the polygraph was under the advice of legal counsel. That would be me. I insisted that my client not take it because polygraphs are notoriously unreliable. That's why they are not admissible in court. Just one extra coffee or Coke and the caffeine can race the heart, throwing the whole thing off. And as we both know, my client was well within his legal rights to refuse."

"Good point, Counselor," said Walton, "Though I probably would have taken the damn thing just to show I had nothing to hide. And, as we also know, polygraphs *are* admissible in court if both sides agree beforehand."

"Agent Walton," said a now angry Karneski, "if you continue along this line, we're done here."

"Before you go, Mr. Karneski, be advised that whoever talks to us first and is completely truthful, that person gets the best deal. The other one gets the book if there are indictable charges. And from what I can see in the other room, Mr. Peters seems to be doing a lot of talking."

Karneski didn't respond but started stuffing his tablet and paperwork into his briefcase.

Walton again asked Holmes, "What do you want to tell me, truthfully, about that gunshot?"

Holmes reached for a cigarette.

"This is a nonsmoking public facility," interjected Deputy Johansen. "No smoking allowed."

"What about that gunshot, Mr. Holmes?"

"Don't answer that," said Karneski, now standing, getting ready to leave.

Fidgeting about, Holmes answered, "There were a number of gunshots going off that entire week. I can't remember what I heard or didn't hear on any one day."

"I don't care about any one day," said Walton, "This is a very simple question. Did you or did you not hear a gunshot on the last day of elk season?"

Holmes lowered his head. His job, his reputation, his standing in the community would immediately change if he were ever charged with murder. Legal fees alone would bankrupt the struggling family. He and his wife had worked so hard to move to Bend, and now their lifestyle was at complete risk.

It didn't help that his attorney was telling him to be quiet.

"All right," Holmes said, "I'll tell you what happened, but you'll never believe it. If you want, I'll even take your damn lie detector test to show I'm telling the truth."

At this point, Karneski was loudly shouting, "No!"

"Relax, Mr. Karneski," said Walton, reaching down into a desk drawer and pulling out an old ashtray. "We respect your client's legal rights and will give you plenty of time to visit."

Sliding the ashtray over to Holmes, Walton said, "Just knock on the door when you're ready to continue."

SHASTA AND CHANCE

S hasta was breathing heavily. For the first time in her young life, she had gone up against the tribe. It would take time to sort through everything that had happened, but at least Chance could now fight for his life.

To her surprise, he appeared very upset with her. She had given her all and was completely drained by the experience. In spite of their cultural differences, his anger was very clear.

"Thanks for throwing me under the bus," he said, "Putting me up against a wolf pack with nothing but a bow and arrow."

Stammering, Shasta replied, "I do not know what a 'bus' is, but I can see that you are angry."

"When that first vote was going against me, you could have given me some sort of signal or something, and I could have made it through the cave."

"Then you would have been dead," said Shasta. "I told you that Kicking Horse had set an arrow in his bow, and he would have welcomed the chance to shoot you—especially after the people had voted for your death."

"No," said Chance. "I would have made it down the mountain by the time he realized I was even gone."

"No," she said, snapping at Chance as she was seemingly at wit's end, "because by then you would have frozen to death."

Shasta slowly dropped to the ground and put her hands over her eyes. Did he already forget the words she had given him? She knew that Chance was under a great strain. What he may not have noticed is that she was also under a great deal of stress. With one vote he had been sentenced to death and, when given the opportunity to fight for his life, he instead viewed the second sentence in the same light as the first.

"I have saved your life as surely as you have saved mine," she said. "Yet you do not see that. From this point on, you must believe and act as if you have already killed the black wolf. Think like a hunting warrior. A tribal member on an elk hunt does not say, 'I don't think I can do this because it is so difficult.' Instead the hunter says, 'I can do this and bring home an elk to feed the people.' The right words *will* make it happen."

She did not know if he had ever fired a bow in his life. But at least now he could fight as a warrior and survive. He had a chance. Shasta knew that if he were able to kill Shadow, then the other wolves would run away. She did not believe he was going up against the entire pack. He was going against the pack leader.

"I'll get you some soup and . . ."

"Forget it," said Chance. "I don't want your soup. If you really want to help me, go distract your boyfriend, and I'll take my chances with the weather."

Chance looked over and saw a smirking Kicking Horse staring at him. Chance brushed past Shasta and walked over to Kicking Horse, who started to rise as Chance approached. Chance put one hand on Kicking Horse's shoulder and pushed him back to his blanket. At the same time, Chance grabbed the arrow from the bow and snapped it over his knee. He leaned over and put his face only inches from Kicking Horse as he threw the broken arrow to the ground. He whispered from an old movie line, "You can put that right where the sun don't shine."

A deep blush colored Kicking Horse's face. He did not understand the words, but he recognized the challenge. He immediately rose, while nocking another arrow and drawing back on his bow, pointing it directly at Chance's chest. Shasta yelled out, "No," followed by a flurry of Yahi. She moved and stood directly in front of Chance, forcing Kicking Horse to ultimately lower his bow.

Both argued fiercely—then Kicking Horse stormed away. A shaking Shasta turned to Chance and said, "I do not know what your war words mean, but you have greatly embarrassed Kicking Horse in front of all the people. I have never seen him so upset. He has been angry with you since you first came to our camp."

"The only reason I came to your camp," said Chance, "was because you guys captured me and forced me here. Incidentally, along the way, I jumped into an icy river and saved you from drowning."

"You don't understand," said Shasta, stunned by his rebuke. "I don't know if you ever will."

As Shasta walked over to Kicking Horse, she turned and added, "Stand against the black wolf as you have against Kicking Horse, and you will win."

Then, placing one hand against the back of Kicking Horse, she began softly talking to him.

Kicking Horse shook his head, "No," and sat by the fire, staring into the flames, angrily turning his bow over and over.

THE TRUTH COMES OUT

O ne hour later J. Karneski, Esq., knocked on the interview room door. Agent Walton and Deputy Johansen entered.

"Agent Walton," said Karneski, "my client is prepared to tell you what happened. He is also prepared to take a lie-detector test to verify the truthfulness of his statement. I also know that everything he tells you will be corroborated by his hunting partner, Mr. Peters. My client and Mr. Peters have also agreed to take you and a search team to the exact site of where they last saw Mr. Conway."

Karneski took a moment to catch his breath. Walton wisely guessed he was going for the close. "What I need is agreement from you to not press charges for his somewhat erroneous prior statements, and we especially want immunity from the D.A.'s office to not charge either party with murder."

In police work, that last comment could be construed as a clue.

"Did he murder or assist in any way in the death of Tom Conway?" asked Walton.

"Absolutely not," said Karneski, "Furthermore, while Mr. Conway may or may not have been murdered, it does appear that he was tragically killed. My client and Mr. Peters took great risk in returning to the scene in search of Mr. Conway to help him. They never found him. As a matter of fact, during the commission of this incident, my client and Mr. Peters were themselves almost killed."

Walton said, "I won't file for lying to a Federal officer, but I can't promise immunity from a murder charge. That's up to the D.A. However, I will go to the D.A. and tell him how your client assisted us in solving this case. Agreed?"

Karneski paused for a moment and said, "Agreed."

While the four men resumed their positions around the interview table, Karneski turned to Walton and in a low voice said, "This is the most unusual witness statement that I've ever heard in my thirty years of practicing law. I believe that once you hear my client's story and find the evidence he swears is on site, it becomes very convincing."

Holmes was stubbing out his third cigarette in the ashtray. Karneski, looking at Deputy Johansen, quickly added, "We apologize for smoking in this facility and certainly hope that no citations will be issued."

Johansen nodded in agreement while Holmes hesitantly began his statement.

"Conway, Peters and me left camp to go hunting. It was early morning, and Conway had already made a dent in his whisky bottle. He offered some to Peters and me. We never drink while out hunting, but we each took a couple of small swigs, figuring that was less for Conway. About an hour later, we were walking single-file up a narrow game trail when all of a sudden Conway stops and brings his rifle up. I was behind him and couldn't see what he was aiming at. Then I see some buckskin, but it just doesn't look right. I'm trying to process what I'm seeing. Conway's a big guy, and he's blocking my line of sight. My first thought is it was a doe. Turns out it was an Indian man just standing there in the middle of the trail holding some kind of a spear. The man seemed confused and startled—like he didn't expect anybody to be around."

Wiping his eyes Holmes continued, "I see Conway's getting ready to shoot, and I yell out, 'No!' Peters is right behind me, and he's also yelling. By now Conway has fired, and I could see where the bullet smacked the man right in the upper chest—maybe his shoulder. He whirlwinds backwards a few feet and then collapses to the ground. Conway is weaving around, reloading and pointing his rifle at the man on the ground when all of a sudden two other Indians jump out of the brush and start shooting arrows at Conway. My impression was that they were firing at Conway to stop him from shooting at their friend. I don't know how many arrows they fired, but Conway was hit at least several times. He goes to the ground almost in slow motion. The only sound I hear him make was a muffled 'unnhh.' Then he doesn't move. He just lies there; eyes wide open, not making any more noise. A couple of other Indians are now pulling the old man off the trail. I don't know where they all came from, but I could tell the man was still alive because I could see him crawling away while the others supported him under each arm."

Holmes looked down while trying to reconstruct what happened. "Peters and I just stood there. We were dumbfounded. Conway had just shot somebody. Not a deer. He actually shot another human being. Then he was filled with arrows. Next thing I know, the guys who shot Conway are now shooting at Peters and me. We just turned and ran. I bet they shot at us a good dozen times or more. Their arrows were bouncing off the trees and rocks all around us. One of the arrows struck a tree right next to Peters and splintered. That's how close they got. The Indians shooting were running after us, still firing, but they seemed a lot older and couldn't catch us. We were so scared that we were running as fast as we've ever run."

Sipping some water Holmes added, "Peters and I didn't stop until we got all the way back to camp. We hopped in my truck and locked the doors and turned the engine on. We started to leave several times but couldn't decide whether to keep going or to stay around so our other hunting partners wouldn't get hurt. Then we see nobody's behind us. The Indians either couldn't keep up, or they went back to help their friend."

Holmes shook his head from side to side. "This was playing out like a bad nightmare. The whole time we kept saying, 'what happened? What happened?' We couldn't believe our eyes. None of it made sense. Whoever would have expected Indians to be out there so far from the reservation and all dressed in buckskin during hunting season? I just couldn't figure it out. It didn't make sense. None of it did."

Holmes continued, "I stood guard while Peters ran to the tent for some water and a first-aid kit. He couldn't find any water, so he just grabbed a short case. We were both totally dehydrated. We kept trying to decide what to do and kept drinking the beer. We were worried about Conway and about the man he shot. I thought Conway might be dead, but what do I know? I've never seen a dead person before."

Holmes sat quietly, shaking his head at what had happened. "There are no cell towers up there so we couldn't call for help. The only thing we did, which we know was real stupid, was drink more beer. I don't know what we would have 'blown,' but by now I'm pretty sure we are both way over the legal limit. We kept talking about what we should do—drive out of the mountains and call the police, try and warn the other guys who were nowhere to be seen, or go back and help Conway. We were hoping that maybe Conway was still alive and that we could get him to the hospital. We were even thinking that we would take the Indian man with us unless his friends had already driven him there."

Sipping more water, Holmes added, "I know Conway has a real reputation as a jerk, mainly because of the alcohol, but I'll tell you this. If your truck broke down somewhere at two in the morning, Conway would come out there and help you, even if he had to drive as far as Millican. He wouldn't let you forget it, but he was always there to help people. When the first big storm hit, I couldn't even get through to him because he was out shoveling a neighbor's walkway, and then he took her to her doctor's appointment. He does have a good heart—it's just that damn alcohol screws him up."

With a note of finality, Holmes directly addressed Walton and simply said, "Conway was drunk, and I think he thought the Indian was a deer, and he fired figuring that he was just getting some camp meat. I know shooting a deer during elk season is illegal, but it is the only thing that makes any sense to me, and it is something that he has done before. I know *that* for a fact."

Law enforcement was still bound by the Governor's gag order and for now had to avoid talking about a lost tribe of Indians. Both lawmen knew it was also common practice for some hunters to bag a doe for camp meat, even on the last day of the season. It wasn't right—it just was. Aside from jotting down a few notes, Walton and Johansen remained silent.

Holmes regained some composure and continued, "Peters and I stayed in the truck, but nobody showed up. We thought for sure we would be followed. We were not thinking clearly—not at all. I think part of it was the shock at what had happened, and the other part is that we were buzzed. Our thinking was, if we called the police, who would even believe us? Then we had that issue of being the last ones to see him and how that automatically makes us suspects, especially if we were both over the legal limit."

Tearing up, Holmes added, "We felt terrible about not standing up for our friend. Instead, we turned tail and ran for our very lives. Peters said that if that happened to him or me that Conway would have been there for us. So, we decided to go back and get him, even if he was dead. I know the police want you to leave a dead body where you find it, but we were just not thinking right. We wanted to get him to the hospital. I knew in my heart that he was dead, but Peters kept saying, 'No, no, he was hit with arrows, not bullets. He's alive, he's gotta be.' So, we headed back. We couldn't wait any longer for the other guys and figured they would never believe us anyhow. We were so blitzed they would probably think one of us shot him and were trying to cover it up."

Holmes looked around at the other men. "As we got close to where the shooting occurred, we left the trail and went straight through the woods. We recognized the site right away, but Conway was gone. He was not there. We couldn't find Conway or any Indians. There were no footprints there nor did we find any arrows. Due to the snow we couldn't find any blood on the ground. The whole area had been like sanitized. It was as if nothing had happened."

Holmes added, "We spent maybe another twenty minutes searching, then we left. I had this scary feeling that we were being watched, but I couldn't see anybody. As we headed down the trail, I passed that one tree where an arrow splintered when it hit. I can find that tree again. It has a big twist to it, and I know there's got to be an arrowhead in there somewhere."

Now Walton was faced with a dilemma. The story was falling into place, especially after his reading of the Yahi file. However, his hands were tied by the Governor's order. Walton always kept something back in a criminal investigation, something known only to the investigators. Walton would hold back the existence of the Hiders until released from the executive gag order. Then, hopefully, the puzzle would all tie together.

Walton especially liked the idea of finding the Hiders and solving the disappearance of the missing elk hunter all in one fell swoop. If he could bring both cases to fruition, he would put in his retirement papers that very day. He would even celebrate with an oversized martini.

Now what he needed was some forensic evidence and the cold and wet was simply not going to deter him—not when he was so close.

While he didn't hold out much hope for finding a body, he thought a line search might turn up some type of clues, at least enough to clear or charge Holmes and Peters. From that point on, he would focus on the Hiders, especially as they had to be living close to where they were hunting.

"The snow's tapering off," said Walton. "Mr. Karneski, I assume you want to join us to protect your client's legal rights. I suggest you bring some warm clothing because it will be a little chilly up there. We will meet here at 7 a.m. tomorrow with a search party ready to go."

Turning to Johansen, Walton said, "Contact the Academy, and tell them that this is an emergency, and that we need some boots on the ground tomorrow for a cadaver and evidence search. Make sure they bring snowshoes, warm clothing and metal detectors."

Walton added, "If there are no further objections, we can do that polygraph now."

Both men passed.

MERCENARIES

Ten minutes after Jesse had given his report, Assistant Vice-President Eldon was on the phone to Oregon Arms.

"Good news," said Eldon, "Jesse found an area where the Indians live. It's time to send in the Rangers. We bought a little time with this snow, but we want all negotiations finished before plant construction starts."

The conversation was short and stilted. When asked how Jesse found the lost tribe, Eldon said, "Jesse knows the high country, and he followed one of the Indians to some brush piled up in front of a small butte. He followed the tracks right to the brush and then they disappeared. Most buttes around here have lava caves. That's where they live. All I need now is for your guys to meet and persuade," added Eldon.

"So what I'm hearing is that this Jesse will direct my Rangers to the secret Indian cave. Correct?"

"Correct," said Eldon.

"Then we visit with them, right?"

"That's right."

"We need to discuss the rules of engagement. My guys are seasoned combat veterans and they need proper Intel in order to make the right decisions. What are your expectations from this? What limitations, if any, are we putting upon our meeting?"

Eldon said, "All I want from your guys is to convince these Indians to move back to California. I don't want anybody harmed. I don't want them threatened. I don't even want anybody yelled at. I just want the Indians out of here and relocated down there or someplace else, wherever."

"Agreed," said his contact. "What else?"

"There is no nothing else," said Eldon. "Just meet with them and get them to go. I need them out of here so the media doesn't make a case of the big bad corporation pushing some lost tribe of Indians off the land. That kind of publicity would shut us down in a heartbeat."

"Agreed," said the Oregon Arms Director, "But now we have a few process questions. What if they refuse to go? What are the limitations on our negotiations? Will the presence of this lost tribe stop or delay the project? How do your superiors feel? What if somehow the media should get wind of this? How far are you willing to go to keep this completely confidential? What if they start shooting at my guys? How are we to transport them to wherever they want to go? Many, many questions here and we need to get them resolved."

"You're the experts in all this. I don't know how your guys can successfully communicate with them when I'm told that these people don't even speak English," asked Eldon.

"My guys don't speak Arabic but they were always able to get their point across whenever meeting with village elders, "said the Director.

"Yeah," thought Eldon, "you point a gun in somebody's face, and they will comply with you. That's nothing but a temporary fix where people will agree to almost anything."

Still, Assistant Vice-President Eldon had no choice. He was instructed to use Oregon Arms to resolve certain problems, and that's what he was doing. It wasn't his call—it was senior management's.

The two men spent the next twenty minutes hammering out the process.

Two Rangers were to arrive the next morning. Jesse would point out the cave. The Rangers would open negotiations with the Hiders. The Rangers would then deal with the problem under the agreed-upon rules of engagement. Their rules of engagement were very simple—negotiate with the people to get them to move.

All field operatives of Oregon Arms were independent contractors, not OA employees. When the contractors signed their employment agreement, there was a little clause in there stating that contractors would use only " . . . that amount of reasonable force necessary to defend themselves or to accomplish their mission."

That clause allowed contractors to use deadly force if they deemed it necessary, especially if they were fired upon. The contract clause was the only way Oregon Arms could get specialized operatives to work for them.

The Rangers knew about the little clause, so did the Oregon Arms Director. The only one not in on that body of knowledge was Assistant Vice-President Eldon.

A HIGH MOUNTAIN SEARCH

PRESENT TIME

Ten cadets from the Sheriff's Academy surrounded Walton, Johansen and Mason. The five men and five women gathered around as Johansen explained the parameters of the search and what they were looking for: at least one—and possibly two—bodies, a hunting rifle and anything that appeared to be of Native American origin.

Each of the searchers carried a long metal probe for poking through the snow. Every third person in line carried a metal detector. All had state-of-the-art snow gear. Several Crime Scene Investigators would assist in the search and process all evidence found—if any.

Mason stepped forward and added, "A Native American man was shot up here. That's a fact. We don't know if he was killed or just wounded. An elk hunter who is also missing shot him. That's also a fact. So we are looking for one, possibly two bodies. If you find something or if the detectors pick up on something, call us over. Do not touch or move anything you find. That's for CSI. You find it, put out the markers, and give me a wave. CSI will take it from there."

Pointing out the four men who were standing at the very edge of the group, Mason continued, "We have two attorneys and two persons of interest here to show us what they saw and in what location. To protect the legal rights of the parties involved, keep anything you find confidential, and do not strike up a conversation with the persons of interest or their attorneys."

The large group started out single-file through the deep snow until Holmes and Peters signaled Walton that they had arrived at the site. Johansen then had the recruits form a straight line, shoulder to shoulder and slowly begin their search. Every third recruit was slowly panning back and forth with metal detectors.

For the first hour, the only sound was the deep crunch of snowshoes through the snow. The metal detectors did not beep.

Leaving the Cadets to do the search, the lawmen followed Holmes and Peters as they kept walking back along the snow-covered game trail. For every little curve, they had to adjust. It was a narrow trail with old growth Ponderosas on either side. Peters soon spotted the twisted tree where the arrow splintered next to his head while he and Holmes were running for their lives.

"This is it," Peters said, pointing to a thick sap mark at about the six-foot level of the tree. Walton handed Johansen his knife and asked him to cut around the sap and bark. Ten minutes later, Johansen had a one-inch circumference cut around the oblong hole and then started digging in another several inches.

"I got something," Johansen said, "There's something here but I can't quite get it.

Walton called CSI over and they went to work with long, needle-nosed pliers. Several minutes later, they placed an obsidian arrowhead into an evidence bag.

Holmes and Peters were ecstatic. "I told you," said Holmes, "You can even see a little bit of wood on the end where the arrow broke off."

The search continued.   All that morning the search party meticulously went over the site, inch by inch, looking for human remains. They found nothing.

As the Cadets were stamping around the deep snow searching, Walton called for a lunch break. Cadet Yolanda Betinez grabbed a sack lunch and walked over to a nearby stream. The fast-rushing stream was choking up with ice. She brushed the dry snow off a fallen pine and started to eat a cold roast-beef sandwich—her back resting against another tree.

"If it's this beautiful in a snowstorm," thought Yolanda, with thick flakes falling all through the pines, "I should bring the kids up here in the summer. We can have a picnic lunch and make a fun day of it."

Tired from the high altitude and continuous hours of searching, Yolanda closed her eyes for a few minutes of rest. She started to nod off, then jolted awake. Something didn't feel right. She opened her eyes and looked around. She had a distinct feeling that somebody was watching her. Somebody very close by.

One of the things she had been taught at the Sheriff's Academy was the importance of following her gut instincts.

"It's not paranoia if somebody really is sneaking up on you," said her instructor. "It's just you correctly interpreting your environment."

Yolanda looked all around. No one was there—at least no one outside the search party and company. Most of the group was but a few hundred feet away, finishing up their lunches. It seemed as if everyone was accounted for.

Yolanda gathered the last little bit of her lunch and walked over to the stream bank. She scattered some crumbs in the open water to see if any fish were around. She watched the crumbs get caught up in the current and swept under some ice.

Then Yolanda looked down into the water and saw three pieces of white bark sticking up from beneath the sand and gravel. She started to reach down into the stream, thinking that if it were a polished branch, it would look good on her fireplace mantle.

As she got closer, she thought she could see blackened joints between the bark segments. Then it suddenly dawned on her. This was not a tree branch.

At that moment, several large rocks narrowly missed Yolanda, striking the snow and water around her. At first, Yolanda thought one of the Cadets had started a snowball fight. Then the next rock hit her arm. It had been thrown with force—and it hurt. Yolanda screamed, grabbed her arm, dropped her markers and began running to where the rocks were coming from. Through the falling snow she saw a fleeing shadow.

Walton, Johansen and Mason were immediately right behind her.

Yolanda continued running through the deep snow toward the nearby trees where she the rocks came from. Mason was running behind her. He found some fresh snowshoe tracks that circled around to the water's edge—then disappeared.

Mason split up the Cadets, sending some to the left and some to the right, looking for the tracks. Several minutes later, snowshoe tracks were found but were soon lost among the lava rocks and mountain brush. He had the Cadets continue searching while he returned to the riverbank.

Johansen came over and looked down to where Yolanda was now pointing. He went to the water's edge, knelt by the bank, and plunged his hand into the icy water, pushing several large rocks and some gravel and sand aside. Within seconds, more bony fingers came to the surface. Then Johansen uncovered the tip of a rusty hunting rifle.

While Johansen was on the radio calling for the Crime Scene Investigators, both Walton and Mason congratulated Yolanda on the find.

"Good eyes," said Walton, "It appears you may have found our missing elk hunter. I'm also pretty sure that whoever was throwing rocks wanted to discourage us from finding this."

Yolanda had mixed feelings about her find. She rubbed her arm where she had been hit, thinking that somewhere someone who loved this person would be crushed. On the other hand, she was happy that she had made the find and in some small way would help the victim's family find closure. That was almost enough to make the pain go away.

One hour later, the skeletal remains were exhumed and bagged. The senior CSI waved Mason and Walton over.

"First time in my life I've ever seen this," said the CSI, pointing to an obsidian arrowhead deeply imbedded in the left hipbone. The investigators finished their search of the crime scene and then Walton, as a courtesy, allowed the two attorneys to view the remains.

"It appears your clients were telling the truth," said Walton, "And for now, I'll need both you and your clients to sign a confidentiality statement agreeing to keep today's finds quiet. I can't go into too much detail, but if everybody signs, your client's legal problems go away."

After a brief discussion, both attorneys assured Walton that they and their clients would sign.

Johansen was pumped. Rock throwing and snowshoe tracks leading to nowhere meant that the Hiders had to be somewhere close by. This narrowed the search parameters down from an entire mountain range to a postage stamp patch of forest.

Johansen had a germ of an idea he wanted to follow up on. It was something he had been mulling over, born of his experience. He did not know any place in the U.S. where this had been tried, but it was every-day technology in the Middle East, and now it was time to bring that same technology to Paulina.

He even knew the right person to go to.

NEW SEARCH TECHNOLOGIES

PRESENT TIME

That night, the two men met in the bar section of the Deschutes Brewery. When Johansen walked in, the other man was already hunched over his computer with a small control box balanced on the edge of the table.

"Hell," said Johansen, "I was going to buy you a pitcher, but you haven't even left me room for a draft."

"I'm just getting everything set up for you," said his friend, a technophobe geek from their high school days.

Hitting the keyboard, he showed Johansen an aerial view of the Deschutes Brewery with Johansen walking through the door.

"*FLIR*—forward looking infrared technology," said his friend, "Latest version on the market. I bet you didn't even know you were being filmed. This resolution is so good; it can pick up a moving blade of grass from a mouse fart at an altitude of fifteen hundred feet. It doesn't get any better than that. And all this from what's basically a flying camera the size of a football."

"I'd hope to shout," said Johansen, in enthusiastic agreement.

The two men high-fived each other.

Johansen continued watching as the drone flew eastward toward Costco. The roadway was choked with snow. Two plows were pushing the snow off to one side of the road. All the cars, trucks and people on the roadway were clearly identifiable. Several minutes later, a crystal-clear, black and white image of rangeland and junipers came on the screen.

"Everything it sees, it records—with absolutely no noise. Mostly, I use color for aerial views of property. Clients really like that because it gives them a 360 of all the terrain. That way, no neighborhood surprises such as a broken down truck parked on somebody's front lawn. At nighttime, though, it's all-infrared. This even measures heat signatures to separate, say, deer from people."

His friend was the managing principal broker of a local real-estate company. Knowing his friend well, Johansen said, "You would have bought all this even if you weren't in real estate."

"You got that right, but now I get to play and write the whole thing off my taxes," said his friend.

Drone technology had arrived in Central Oregon.

"Here's where we need the fly-over," said Johansen, spreading out a large forest service map of the Ochocos. Taking a red pen, Johansen made a small rectangular box on the map. At the center of the small rectangle was the recovery site of the missing elk hunter.

Being careful to not give away too much info, Johansen lowered his voice to a mere whisper and said, "We're looking for both a lost teenager and a group of people holed up somewhere in this area. It is very important that we find them. We believe the people only come out at night and we believe they live," he said, tapping the rectangle, "in a lava cave. We need the location of that cave."

"Vampires?" asked his friend.

"No, not vampires," said a laughing Johansen, "But definitely people we want to talk to."

"They are up there in this kind of weather?" asked the broker.

"Yes," said Johansen, "We know they live up there year-round. Not the teenager. He and his Dad were snowmobiling and became separated.

"So it's either some type of crazy cult or a bunch of meth-heads making product!"

Johansen shrugged his shoulders and said, "We're especially interested in anybody wearing Indian clothing, if that helps." Then he asked, "How long before you find them?"

"If they are up there, I will find them," said his friend, "probably within a few days if they even show themselves during this storm. I can program the drone to do nighttime fly-overs and then return to base— which is actually my garage—to recharge the batteries. The software will record any movement, and we can see if it is your guys or just a bunch of deer. Give me a little time, and I'll have this whole area covered."

Then his friend quietly asked, "So, why are vampires wearing Indian clothing?"

"They are not vampires. Just so you know, there's no such thing as vampires." To distract him from the question, Johansen quickly added, "I'm on a task force, and we can compensate you for your search."

"Compensate me for my search? Correct me if I'm wrong, but I don't go out in the woods for anything. I'm the brain trust here. You're not paying me to search—you're paying me for my equipment and knowledge. All I do is set the search parameters, pull the covers up over my head and review the tapes the next morning. It doesn't get any easier than that."

"You do realize you're a realtor who just turned down an opportunity for some easy money," said Johansen.

"Who turned down easy money?" asked his friend. "I'll bill you guys a nice, fat fee, which I will promptly turn around and spend on even more software. I also know that when I find your *vampires* or the kid, you will spring for that pitcher *plus* an entire meal. How's that for turning down 'easy' money?"

Johansen could feel the pieces now coming together.

THE HIDER'S LODGE

PRESENT TIME

C hance slept fitfully. He would just start to drift off, then jolt awake with the anxiety of the challenge before him. He guessed that at most he had maybe four hours of interrupted sleep.

Several times during the night, he awoke and looked to the cave entrance. A Guardian filled the entryway, staring at Chance.

"Thanks, Shasta, you have really done me in," he angrily thought. At least they had not tied him up as Whisper and Nopanny wanted to do.

Just as he was drifting off, he was rudely poked, only to find Kicking Horse standing over him, holding a bow and arrows in one hand and a hot bowl of soup in the other.

Kicking Horse brusquely handed the soup to Chance and said, "Eat." Chance looked him over and asked, "You speak English now?"

Kicking Horse did not respond. Instead he looked over his shoulder to where Shasta was kneeling on her blankets. Wearily, Shasta pulled herself up and walked over to Chance. Her eyes were red, and her long black hair was all tousled. She appeared exhausted.

"He does not speak English," she said. "I told him to say that to you when he gave you the soup. I didn't know what else to do,"

"You look like you have hat hair," said Chance, still angry but starting to melt at her appearance. Even with hat hair, there was just something about her. Then it dawned on Chance. He had been so preoccupied with Shasta and his trial that he had not even thought of Ashley for two days.

"Mom would say, 'I'm smitten'," he thought, smiling in spite of himself.

Instinctively she touched and straightened out her hair.

"I see you are still stubborn and irritable," said Shasta. "Good. That will help you tonight when you go up against Shadow."

"Look, I'm . . ."

"Stop," said Shasta. "You may not appreciate this, but my life *has* changed. Several of the people refuse to even speak to me. One of them is my Aunt who practically raised me after my mother died. This is my tribe. These are the only people I know. These are the only people I have ever known. Now my own Aunt won't even talk to me because I spoke for you. As for this one," she said, indicating Kicking Horse, "He said that when I voted for you, I voted against him. I tried to explain, but he wouldn't hear of it. I think he has too much anger in his head."

Shasta struggled with her next words. "It is important that you remember what I say because the Chief has directed him to take you to the wolf's cave tonight. You and he will go alone. Be careful. Something has come over him since you were captured. He is not the same. I am seeing a side of him that I have never seen before, and he and I grew up together."

Chance just nodded, "Okay."

Shasta continued, "The Chief has asked my father to teach you how to use the bow."

"I know how to use a bow," said Chance, "I have my own hunting bow at home."

"Good," said Shasta, "But tonight you will have an Indian bow. I'm guessing they are not the same. My father will practice with you this afternoon. Whether you do or don't is up to you, but I would tell you that my father is one of the best bowmen we have. I would say one more thing. All warriors keep several arrows in their bow hand for quick use. You are going up against a pack of wolves and will want to do the same."

Kicking Horse interrupted her conversation. He did not know what she was saying to the Englishman, but again she was taking way too long to say it.

Shasta looked over at Kicking Horse than back at Chance, and for just a fleeting moment thought, "He is definitely so much taller than Kicking Horse."

"If it were possible," she said, with a nervous strain to her words, "I would hold you and wish you success. I cannot do this because the people are watching. It is not our way. I will tell you one thing: I believe you are a strong warrior with a heart of courage and that you will either succeed tonight or you will die trying. That is the path for all warriors. That is how I see you and, like our Chief, I will pray to our Grandfather Creator for your success."

"That's not one thing—that's like three or four things," said Chance, giving her a slight smile.

Shasta slipped her obsidian knife discreetly to Chance. "This belonged to my great-grandfather from a long time ago. Protect yourself, and then come back to me. Promise me that."

With that Shasta held her hand out and solemnly shook Chance's hand. Chance noticed that she was tearing up in spite of herself. She continued to hold his hand for several more seconds then softly pulled away.

"Good-bye my English friend," she whispered, "While you must go, I must stay."

"Good-bye Wahkanupa," he said, emphatically adding, "I *will* return your knife to you."

Looking up at Chance she now smiled and said, "You remembered. You even said my name correctly. And best of all, you *will* see me again because you said you will return my knife to me. That means you will. You speak now like a true Yahi warrior. I no longer hear defeat or fear. Now I hear success."

Kicking Horse interrupted, yelling at her in Yahi, forcibly escorting her back to the fire. He may not have understood her words, but he definitely picked up on Shasta's softness and tone toward the Englishman.

Turning to Chance, he began angrily shaking his bow in the air.

RANGERS ARRIVAL

PRESENT TIME

The two Rangers, both somewhere in their mid- to late-thirties, stepped off the private Oregon Arms jet carrying their gear. Both men had shaved heads covered with thick, black watch caps to ward off the cold. One was short—the other tall.

Greeting them was the Project Oregon helicopter pilot, himself ex-military. The men shook hands all around and quickly boarded the helicopter.

The Rangers had just barely enough room to change from travel gear to fatigues and boots. Then they began loading their weapons. Long, banana-shaped clips curved out from each assault weapon, both of which were fully automatic Kalashnikovs. Each man stuffed extra clips into their pouches, strapped Glocks to their hips and attached percussion grenades to their fatigues. The men hooked small round snowshoes to their belts.

They were now ready to meet with Jesse. After Jesse pointed out where the Indians were hiding, all he had to do was collect his bonus and disappear. The Rangers did not want any untrained personnel on site. Untrained personnel were a liability. They could also be an adverse witness in case things got dicey.

After being dropped off at the forest trailer, Assistant Vice-President Eldon shook hands with the shorter Ranger. The taller one kept both hands wrapped around his gun. Neither Ranger offered to shake hands with Jesse. Eldon unfurled a forest service map, and Jesse pointed to a brush-covered butte.

"They are in there," he said. "I don't know how many or if they are armed or not."

After studying the map, the Rangers put on their snowshoes and left.

Jesse received a thick envelope from Eldon.

"There's your thirty pieces of silver," thought Eldon, as a beaming Jesse pushed Toby through the snow down to his truck.

ARCHERY 101

He Who Stands picked up his bow, quiver and several wooden hoops. He motioned for Chance to follow. The two went to the back of the cave, and He Who Stands demonstrated how to shoot the bow. Chance watched closely as the bowman pulled back on the bow, muscles slightly straining and his face set in harsh lines. The arrow was released and passed through the small hoop set into a dirt bank.

He Who Stands repeated the process several times. Each time his arrow went dead center through the hoop.

Chance noticed that his technique was unlike that of most archers. The difference was that He Who Stands pulled back on the arrow while holding the arrow nock with both his thumb and pointer finger. Chance had been taught to place one finger above and two below to hold the arrow in place. When Shasta's father released his arrow, the bow was allowed to spin in his hand as follow-through. Chance could actually hear the taut bowstring vibrate. Chance also observed that the bow was held at an angle to the body—not perpendicular, as Chance had been taught.

The Indian passed the bow to Chance. He watched as Chance nocked an arrow and pulled the bowstring clear back to his chin. Sighting down the arrow, Chance released and completely missed the hoop. He was so far off it wasn't even close.

Chance thought he missed due to the heavy pull weight of the bow. It took a lot of strength to pull back the arrow and aim. He Who Stands made it look easy. Chance was given another arrow and missed again. The third time he came close and, several arrows later, he was finally able to get one through the hoop.

The two practiced together for the next two hours until Chance could barely pull the bow back. He Who Stands was a patient teacher and from time to time would show Chance how to improve getting the arrow through the hoop.

A break was called, and the two men rested. When it was time to resume, a fellow tribal member stood near the dirt embankment while He Who Stands aimed and signaled. The tribal member rolled the hoop forward in a fast throwing motion. Instantly, He Who Stands pulled back, gave a small lead to the rolling hoop and released the arrow. The arrow flew through the hoop center and imbedded itself into the dirt. The whole process was repeated over and over, almost in slow motion, so that Chance could visualize how to do it.

Out of twelve arrows fired, He Who Stands missed only once. He grimaced at the miss, rubbed his shoulder muscles and gave the bow to Chance.

Chance missed the first six hoop rolls and connected on the seventh. Then he missed another six and again connected again on the seventh.

With each miss, He Who Stands corrected Chance's lead.

The tips of his fingers were raw and bleeding from pulling and holding the arrows. He held them up to his instructor who merely shook his head and gave another arrow to Chance. Then he upped the challenge by having Chance run and shoot at the same time.

Within the hour, Chance was consistently both running and shooting the arrows through the hoop while He Who Stands nodded in encouragement.

He Who Stands had patiently taught Chance Indian bow techniques until he felt that Chance could go against the wolves. The one thing he could not change was how Chance pulled back and held the arrow before release. Chance followed every other instruction but that one. Several times he tried to hold the Indian way, but the arrow always went far off course. When he used the three-finger hold, he consistently hit the hoop and was able to lead and shoot even while the hoop was rolling, and Chance was running.

Chance was now ready to take on the wolves.

BRINGING THE FIGHT TO THE WOLVES

That night Kicking Horse walked over to the cave entrance and looked out. A full minute went by before he motioned Chance to come over. The snow had finally stopped, and a bright moon was forcing its way through the black clouds. The wind came up and blew most of the clouds away. The forest trees were groaning under the heavy weight of the snow. As Chance looked up, the whole sky appeared filled with blinking stars. Chance had never seen so many stars in the heavens.

Kicking Horse was holding his bow and a quiver of arrows. Chief Tuliyani pulled an elk coat off a wall peg and handed it to Chance. Another tribal member stepped forward and gave him a pair of snowshoes.

The two young men were ready to go. Shasta waved to Chance and signed that she would see him again.

Whisper told Kicking Horse the location of the den and to look for a small den opening at the base of a large rock wall. The plan was that when the wolves picked up the scent of a human, they would come out to investigate. That was their instinct. It was something they had to do to protect the pack.

If Chance was close enough, he could probably pick off the wolves one at a time as they came out of their lair. The people felt that Shadow would be the last one out. He would send the other wolves out first to investigate. Then he would emerge.

The widow of the elderly warrior killed by Shadow stood near the cave entrance. As Chance and Kicking Horse approached, she began singing. Her song was one of the old songs. It was a song of strength and courage to warriors going off to fight for the tribe. Several others quickly joined her in the singing. Then all the people stood in a small circle singing to Chance. The singing went on for a full minute. Several were now patting him on the arms. Raven came up and, standing on tiptoes, embraced Chance with a hug, two small tears flowing down her cheeks.

A sullen Kicking Horse waited and then motioned for Chance to follow. They exited the lodge. Behind them they could still hear the tribal members singing. Now it was a new song. Though Chance did not know it, it was a death song being offered up for his bravery.

Kicking Horse stopped when barely out of the lodge. He had Chance hold his hands out and bound them with a milkweed rope. Grabbing one end of the rope he pulled Chance along behind him.

"So much for escaping," thought Chance. "Now I'll really have to go through with this." Chance decided against using Shasta's knife to cut the rope to flee. He didn't want to risk losing the knife to Kicking Horse should he prevail. He also knew he was facing one of the greatest challenges in his life. Strangely enough, he was looking forward to it. He would make his Dad proud.

The forest was lit up by the full moon. Both looked up at a falling star blazing across the sky. In seconds it was gone, leaving them standing in the white forest carpeted with stands of thick pine. The wind had died down, and all was quiet.

Chance followed Kicking Horse as he made his way to the wolf den. About a mile later, Chance could pick up the scent of the wolves. A slight wind began to stir as he and Kicking Horse moved downwind of the lair entrance. Surrounding the small opening was a large wall of lava rock against the back of a hill. A small ledge and another cave opening were about halfway up the wall. All around was the deep forest.

Several deer bones were scattered about on the snow. Chance guessed that the hungry wolves had been gnawing on the bones, cracking them open to get at the nutritious marrow.

Kicking Horse held his hand up and they stopped. He cut the rope from Chance's hands while at the same time looking around for a tree to climb. Finding an old growth pine with plenty of low hanging branches, Kicking Horse handed his bow and quiver to Chance, bent over and removed his snowshoes, motioning for Chance to do the same.

Reluctantly, Chance removed the snowshoes, wondering why. Maybe Kicking Horse meant for him to go up a tree or to climb the rocks and shoot downhill as the wolves left the den. Maybe it was more important to Kicking Horse to have Chance kill Shadow than to have Kicking Horse kill Chance.

Kicking Horse held his hand out for Chance's snowshoes. Then it dawned on Chance—without snowshoes, he could not run away.

Kicking Horse signed that he was going to climb the tree. Chance started to remove some arrows from the quiver when Kicking Horse shook his head no, not wanting Chance to make any noise, signing for Chance to wait. Soon the wolves would pick up his scent and come out to investigate.

Noise would force the wolves to attack.

Safely up the tree, Kicking Horse motioned for Chance to go to the den. Chance gingerly made his way through the deep snow. When he was almost there, Chance removed three arrows from his quiver and set one to his bow while holding the other two.

Not a sound could be heard. Chance wondered if the wolves were in their cave or if they were out hunting. It was eerily quiet. For a moment, Chance thought about removing the bulky elk coat. He didn't want any restrictions when pulling back on the bow. The cold won out. He managed to slide his arms out from the sleeves but kept the warm fur around his shoulders.

The arrows didn't feel quite right. They seemed out of balance, lighter. Maybe it was just nerves. Looking down Chance saw all three arrowheads were missing. All he had was the blunt end of the arrow where the arrowhead had once been. His surprise quickly turned to anger.

Out of nowhere Chance heard a loud gourd being shaken from high up a tree.

Then the wolves began to howl.

CONFRONTATIONS

The first gray wolf was squeezing out of the den. With his head barely out, he was sniffing around for a scent. He cocked his ears forward as he listened to the gourd being rattled. Still sniffing, he kept crawling up and out through the snow-covered cave opening.

For just a moment, Chance wondered how Shadow could ever get out of the den if the other wolves had such a tight fit. Then for several seconds, he felt a numbing paralysis overcome him. Reality was setting in. He had been set up to fail. This was deliberate. No one was around to help, and it was up to him to do whatever was necessary to survive. He remembered overhearing what his mother had once told his father, "Courage is not the absence of fear—courage is action in spite of the fear." His fear was now driving him to action. It was either that or just accepting his fate, but Chance knew he would go down fighting before ever quitting. Managing his fear as best he could, he removed Shasta's knife from under his coat. He used the obsidian blade to quickly shave the blunt arrow to a long, narrow point.

Hearing the wood being chipped, the wolf turned and spotted Chance. The wolf now had his two front paws out and pulled himself completely out of the den. Chance was only a few yards away. He drew the bow back full length and fired at point blank range. So powerful was the shot that the arrow passed completely through the wolf's neck. For several seconds the stunned wolf just stood there then his legs began shaking. He tried to move forward as Chance sent another sharpened arrow through his side. Almost soundlessly, with just the slightest whimper, the wolf ran for a few feet, collapsed and died.

Now the second wolf was emerging. Chance was frantically pulling other arrows out but all the arrowheads were lying in the bottom of the quiver. Some still had long strands of sinew from where they had been attached to their arrows. Someone had pulled all the arrowheads off and he knew who did it. Chance was frantically shaping two more arrows.

Two or three shaves with the obsidian knife, and he was ready. In the space of a few seconds, he had two more sharpened arrows.

The second wolf was smaller and faster. He practically leaped from the cave and began running toward Chance. The deep snow slowed him down. Struggling, he had to porpoise his way through. As he got closer, Chance held the bowstring completely pulled back. He gave the wolf the slightest of leads and released. The arrow hit him directly in the chest. The wolf instantly stood rock still. He tried to move toward Chance, but his trembling legs could no longer support him. Whimpering once, as did the wolf before him, he collapsed into the snow surrounded by a growing pool of blood. Lying on his side, he tried to paw through the deep snow toward Chance. Then he died.

For but a brief moment, Chance felt terrible about shooting such magnificent creatures. This was different from shooting a deer. Shooting a deer was acceptable because he knew it was part of the hunting process. A deer he would always take home and eat. The wolves he had to shoot. He had no choice. If he did not kill them, they would kill him. They had the strength and power to literally tear him apart. This was to be a fight to the finish.

Chance truly felt some primeval instincts were at play. He was in combat, and he was now fighting for his very life. He felt a tremendous surge of adrenalin as he waited for Shadow. Every muscle and cell in his body was preparing for the final showdown.

Hearing muffled sounds and a pained cry from outside the den, the remaining wolves anxiously gathered around Shadow, awaiting his next move. Shadow looked at each wolf, and pressed his nose against a large gray. The selected gray started to climb out from the underground cave.

Chance at the same time was frantically re-tying one of the arrowheads to an arrow. He saw the wolf coming out and screamed, "No!" The startled wolf slipped on the icy edge and slid back to the cave floor.

Shadow immediately pounced on him. He grabbed the wolf behind the neck and began shaking him. Shadow threw the grey against the den wall. The wolf recovered and came at Shadow. The two wolves, snapping and snarling, were fighting in an ever-tightening circle. The gray lunged at Shadow's throat. His fangs tore into Shadow, piercing an artery, now drawing blood. Shadow slashed at the gray, biting his muzzle, forcing him back. The gray knew he must kill Shadow to survive. Mercy was an unknown in the wolf world. Fighting the alpha leader always came down to kill or be killed. It was that simple.

The two wolves kept circling. Both were lunging and biting at each other. Shadow's neck wound began pumping frothy blood. Sensing a weakened Shadow, the gray charged in, exposing his neck. There was a terrible crunching sound as Shadow grabbed the gray around the throat. He clamped down and held firm until the grey stopped moving.

He held the gray for a full two minutes before dropping him to the ground.

The remaining wolf wisely went for the cave entrance and began to climb out as fast as he could. Shadow was behind him biting and snapping at his legs.

Chance had retied one arrowhead to an arrow. Not perfect but enough to hold and penetrate.

As the gray wolf pulled himself out from the cave, he neither looked to the left or right. He ignored the loud gourd rattling from a nearby tree. He ignored the scent of the human. He ignored the two dead wolves in the snow. He faced east and, with his paws crunching through the snow, he ran for all he was worth. He fled into the surrounding forest and vanished.

Chance put the knife down. He needed both hands to better tie the arrowhead in place. The loud gourd was still rattling. Chance heard a scraping sound and risked a quick look around, wondering if the wolf that had just run off might be circling back. He nocked the one good arrow to his bow.

The scraping sound he heard was Shadow's claws against the overhead ledge as he made a long leap toward Chance.

ALPHA COMBAT

Chance was bowled over. He felt the heavy muscular weight knocking him to the ground. The snarling wolf was trying for the back of his neck. Chance found himself face down in the snow, surrounded by dripping blood. Panic and instinct were setting in. His bow and arrow was out of reach. The knife was somewhere in the snow. He threw himself against the black wolf in a failed effort to get up. The wolf had all the advantages if he could keep Chance pinned in the deep snow. The wolf was getting tangled up in the elk robe, giving Chance just enough time to spin around and, with his feet beneath him, to give a mighty push.

Shadow spun around from the push trying to keep his balance. He tottered between standing and falling. He was hurting and appeared disoriented. Chance reached over for his weapons and scrambled to his feet.

The weakened wolf pulled back, making ready for another charge. Chance could see that Shadow's neck and chest were dripping large amounts of blood into the snow. Shadow just stood there as Chance grabbed the bow and arrow. As Chance pulled back on the bow, all he could see was a large, snarling form now coming toward him. Chance momentarily held the shot and then released the arrow at point-blank range.

He almost missed.

When Chance fired, Shadow was just starting his leap. He managed a split-second twist trying to avoid the oncoming arrow. The arrow skimmed along Shadow's side and imbedded itself deeply in his left rear leg. Shadow felt instant, excruciating pain. He crashed to the snow while Chance was scrambling away, trying to distance himself from his attacker.

The enraged alpha snapped at the arrow sticking out from his leg. Pulling on the arrow with his teeth, the arrow separated from the arrowhead now deep in the wolf's leg. Shadow broke the arrow with just one bite. Then he curled around trying to pull the painful arrowhead out. The more he pulled and rolled, the deeper the arrowhead went. His blood continued to pump onto the white snow.

Shadow could not get the serrated arrowhead out from his leg muscle. His wounds slowed him down, but he continued the attack. He would kill his attacker and heal while putting together another pack. This is what alpha males did. This is what they had always done. Instinct and experience drove him forward. Attack was the only way to protect the pack. Meeting and killing the enemy head-on was the way of the wolf. It was what they had always done. Instinct and strength would allow Shadow to prevail.

While Shadow was biting at the arrowhead, Chance quickly stooped down and picked up Shasta's knife. Holding the twelve-inch blade in front of him, Chance slowly backed away. He simply had no time to shape another arrow. With a great deal of effort, Chance managed to put a few more yards between himself and the black wolf.

Shadow stopped biting at his leg. He now stood facing Chance, bleeding heavily from his wounds. Viciously snarling, long fangs completely over his lips, Shadow began inching toward the human who had caused him so much pain. He was not running fast. It was a slow, deliberate move forward, narrowing the gap between him and Chance.

The deep snow and blood loss were slowing him down.

Momentarily distracted by the sound of the gourd, Shadow dropped his head. He was having trouble focusing. It was as if some unseen force was pushing his head down. Several drops of blood now fell from his nose. He moved forward again with his large paws breaking through the snow. Blood began leaking from his mouth. Preparing himself for a long leap, Shadow dropped his hindquarters down. He rose for just one second with his front paws completely out of the deep snow. Instantly the paws went down as he pushed with all the strength of his hindquarters, lifting himself completely out of the snow. His front paws came up as

Shadow started his leap. They were curled under his chest and then, almost in slow motion, stretched outward.

It was a long leap for Shadow to reach Chance. Watching Shadow gather himself for the jump, Chance squared his shoulders and braced himself, raising the razor-sharp knife before him. He waited until Shadow was completely airborne.

Instantly dropping to one knee Chance stretched both arms out as Shadow was almost upon him. It was too late for the wolf to spin or turn. He was committed to the leap. He opened his mouth wide to grab Chance by the throat.

As the black wolf was flying toward him, Chance made a slight feint to his right. Shadow tried to compensate, slightly moving his head to adjust for Chance's move. The move was just enough to expose his chest. His huge paws slammed into Chance, bowling him over in the deep snow.

In spite of the powerful blow, Chance managed to hold the knife out before him. As Shadow landed on Chance, the outstretched knife plunged deeply into Shadow's chest. Shadow had impaled himself.

His huge, heavy weight had pushed Chance completely backward into the deep snow. Chance struggled to pull the knife from Shadow just as Shadow lifted his head, trying for Chance's throat. Shadow ended up with nothing but a mouthful of coat fur. The knife was imbedded solidly in muscle and bone. Yanking with all his strength, Chance pulled the knife out. As he pulled the knife back, the fight seemed to go out of Shadow. Quickly standing, Chance made ready to strike again but instead watched as the fire went out of Shadow's eyes. Chance held the knife high; ready to strike, when the yellow eyes flamed out. Shadow slowly lowered his head down. He did not whimper or make a sound. He did not move. He slowly collapsed as his head dropped down to the deep snow.

In that very moment Shadow died.

All the surrounding churned-up snow was now bright red.

Noise from the gourd had stopped.

ACCUSATIONS

C hance could not move. He was beyond exhaustion. Trembling, he collapsed to the ground. He had killed three wolves all in the space of a few minutes. He had killed Shadow. He had overcome the wolf pack in their natural environment.

The immense black wolf lay stretched out before him in the snow with both paws pressing against Chance's chest. Chance heard another scraping noise from the ledge where Shadow attacked him. There was to be no rest for Chance. Pushing Shadow away, Chance struggled to his feet. He froze as he watched a large white wolf run from the den. Behind her were five small pups. They were struggling to keep up with their mother.

The five pups were all white.

The last wolf from the den was a black pup, almost twice again as big as his littermates. The black pup looked down at Chance, then to Shadow. He stopped, raised his head to the bright moon and, with lips curled back against his tiny milk teeth; he gave a long, mournful howl. Then he ran back into the cave. The alpha female and the rest of her litter ran off into the forest.

Inhaling and exhaling deeply, it was several minutes before Chance heard Kicking Horse making his way over the snow. Out of habit Chance started to reach for his inhalator but found he didn't need it. His breathing was naturally restoring.

As Kicking Horse approached, there was a look of absolute disbelief on his face. Kicking Horse was shaking his head as he looked at each of the dead wolves. He bent down to examine Shadow when Chance grabbed him by his coat. Fueled by adrenalin, Chance threw a punch at Kicking Horse. He connected solidly. Chance was beyond angry that Kicking Horse set him up to be killed.

Kicking Horse bounced back and managed to tackle Chance. The two began furiously pummeling each other. Each landed several blows to the other. Most of their blows were ineffective—harmlessly bouncing off shoulders and arms. The fighting came to an end minutes later when the two men simply could not fight any more. They were exhausted. They were both absolutely drained. The fighting was at a stalemate. Each was red and raw from being hit.

Chance pulled the quiver off and threw several of the arrowheads at Kicking Horse. He grabbed a blunt arrow and waved it into Kicking Horse's face.

The expression of surprise on Kicking Horse's face was seemingly genuine. He appeared perplexed. He shook his head, no, to sign that he had nothing to do with the removal of the arrowheads. This was not his doing. The two just stood there, glaring at each other. Then Kicking Horse held an arm out to help Chance to his feet.

Putting the fight behind him, Kicking Horse walked from wolf to wolf and stood over Shadow. He held out both hands and again shook his head, no. He appeared as mystified as Chance. He gave another look to Chance and again signed that this was not his doing. Then he motioned for Chance to help him turn Shadow over.

At first Chance just stood there, trying to figure out if Kicking Horse was telling the truth or not. His gut feeling was that Kicking Horse appeared to be telling the truth. Still, he felt anxious and went on guard as Kicking Horse withdrew his knife.

Kicking Horse made long slits through the pelt and legs of Shadow. Then he signed for Chance to help pull the pelt off. Carefully, Kicking Horse peeled around the skull. The two struggled with the pelt and, when the wolf skin was almost off, Kicking Horse looked up to the overhead ledge of the wolf lair. He signed that he would be right back. He started to climb up the rock wall. As he began climbing, Chance continued cutting around and pulling on Shadow's pelt.

Five minutes later, Kicking Horse returned. He had a squealing pup bagged up in a deerskin parfleche. Holding the bag open, Kicking Horse showed the angry bundle to Chance.

It was the black pup.

A MOST JOYOUS WELCOME

Theh two sat in silence as they put on their snowshoes. The snow had completely stopped, and the storm clouds were gone, blowing to the east. The forest was filled with brilliant moonlight. Some trees were still cracking with the weight of the snow. Both men again looked up to the stars. They appeared so close they could almost be touched.

Chance now believed that Kicking Horse was not responsible for the removal of the arrowheads from the arrows. Still, a small part of him knew that Kicking Horse was the only one with motive. He had to follow the evidence. Who else could it be? He was one of four who had voted against giving him the right to a warrior's death. Shasta had also warned him about Kicking Horse. It could not have been the Chief as the Chief said he would pray for his success. No way was it the widow of the man killed by Shadow. It could not have been Kicking Horse's father, Jumping Bull, as he had voted to spare Chance. It was definitely not Shasta, as she seemed to have some deep feelings for Chance, which brought it right back to Kicking Horse. He was the only one with the means, opportunity and motive.

Chance was determined to get to the bottom of this. He would give the removed arrowheads to Shasta to see what she could find out. Whoever did this wanted Chance dead and to have his body conveniently disappear. What better way for the tribe than for Chance to be recycled through a pack of wild wolves.

Kicking Horse held the squirming bag in one hand and offered Shadow's pelt to Chance. He considered the pelt to be a badge of honor, and that honor rightfully belonged to Chance. Kicking Horse would not deny that to Chance. Chance grasped the heavy pelt, wrapping it around his shoulders. He picked up the empty quiver and placed both the arrows and arrowheads in it. He handed the bow to Kicking Horse.

Taking the lead, Kicking Horse led the way back to the hidden lodge. He started pulling the brush back. Not a sound could be heard.

There was no singing, talking or even whispering. It was deathly quiet. Warm air from the lodge fires quickly enveloped both men. Kicking Horse entered the lodge first, holding the parfleche bag in one hand. He held out his other hand, signing for Chance to wait.

Kicking Horse removed the squealing pup from the bag by the scruff of the neck. All of the small tribe stood near the cave entrance. All stared at the pup, while in a flurry of Yahi, Kicking Horse told everyone how Chance had killed Shadow and two other wolves. He described how the white wolf and her pups ran off in the same direction as the one escaping gray.

Chance was waiting outside the brushy entrance. The pelt was wrapped around him, fur side down. In the nearby forest he could hear the soft crunching of deer making their way through the snow, heading towards the hidden cave. Initially that surprised Chance. He thought the scent of the wolf would scare them off.

Chance next heard a loud cheer and shouts of joy from the tribal members. Then the people began to sing. It was a joyful uplifting song that Chance guessed to be from the old days. Shasta seemed to be singing the loudest. Now Kicking Horse motioned for Chance to enter. The first thing the tribal members could see was the black wolf pelt—then a grinning Chance. Looking to Shasta, Chance waved a wolf paw at her.

She was smiling from ear to ear while all around her the others were enthusiastically shouting, singing and even dancing.

All the tribal members rushed to Chance, patting him affectionately while reaching out at the same time to touch the wolf pelt. One of the men gingerly reached over to pet the baby wolf. He pulled his hand back when the pup growled. Several of the women were in tears, alternating between hugging Chance and singing the old songs.

Chief Tuliyani was smiling. He Who Stands was beaming. Shasta stood before Chance singing with the most beautiful voice that Chance had ever heard. One of the elders began beating on a drum. Several warriors began a small dance circling the large communal fire in the middle of the cave.

The Chief pulled an old ceremonial war bonnet overflowing with eagle feathers from a nearby wall peg and joined the men in their dancing. Everyone was so happy that even the Guardian left his post and joined the dancers.

As in the old days, several held lances or hatchets as they danced.

Kicking Horse stood off to one side, dancing in place while cradling the baby wolf.

All were happy. This was one of the most joyous days of their lives. The black wolf had been killed, and Chance had earned his freedom. His life would be spared. So happy were the people that several were ready to approach the Chief about adopting Chance. They would give him his freedom—that had been promised to him—but by adoption, he would always be a part of the tribe. His bravery would be celebrated over and over.

While the others were singing and the men dancing to the loud beating of a rawhide drum, Shasta whispered, "You brought my knife back to me, and you have killed Shadow. You are truly a great warrior. You have found your way as I knew you would."

Chance started to hand the knife to her, but Shasta refused it, saying, "It is yours. You have earned this. It once belonged to a great warrior, and you are now that warrior."

With that she reached out and placed both her arms around Chance. He heard her softly crying. Embarrassed, not knowing quite what to do, he awkwardly returned the hug, acutely aware of a near-by Kicking Horse. Chance looked over to Kicking Horse who was still smiling, busily scratching the wolf pup behind the ears, and not even looking at Shasta.

"We need to talk," he whispered to Shasta.

Holding in his hand several of the arrowheads, Chance then quickly told Shasta what had happened, adding, "Somebody didn't want me to come back, and, strangely enough, I don't think it was Kicking Horse."

Shasta was surprised. More than surprised. Several times she had to clarify what Chance was telling her. Still holding onto Chance, she looked over to the Chief and said that she would ask him to find out what happened. She had no idea who would have removed the arrowheads.

Chance heard a slight rustling sound coming from behind. Before he could even turn, he found himself being pushed to the ground with a rifle barrel pressed against his head. Somebody had found the cave.

Shasta screamed, "Guardsmen!"

"Hell no," came the angry reply, "Rangers, not Guardsmen."

THE SEARCH

Paulina Lodge had only a few security lights burning as Mason helped Ryan into the Sno-Cat. Power was coming back on, and cell phone service was mostly restored, but the outlying districts were still without electricity. The Lodge was operating solely on back-up generators.

Ryan winced as he slid into the front seat. He was managing the pain as best he could, but broken ribs flat-out hurt. Johansen and Buster were seated in the back, and Mason was getting ready to drive.

Johansen's cell rang, and he had Mason wait while he took the call. Grabbing a notebook, he wrote down some coordinates. He took his tablet and turned it on while giving his e-mail address to the caller. He handed the directional coordinates to Mason mouthing the word "Bushnell."

Mason entered the numbers into his Bushnell. Within seconds, a bright red line appeared on screen from where they were to where they wanted to go.

Looking directly at Ryan while finishing the call, Johansen gave him a "thumbs up." Thanking the caller, Johansen announced his friend had found the cave *and* a lost snowmobiler standing outside the cave. According to his friend, he was sending some pictures to Johansen's tablet that he thought they would find very interesting.

The pictures were barely one hour old.

Ryan was reaching for the tablet when Johansen said, "My buddy had his drone making continuous passes over where we retrieved Conway's body when the camera picked up two guys who crawled out of a cave and through some brush. Both are young guys, and both are wearing some type of fur coats and they're on snowshoes. One of them has real long hair and is holding a bow. He has the hands of the other guy tied. Then my buddy got a picture of them looking up at the sky. One guy is definitely Indian; the other one I think you might recognize."

A series of pictures appeared on Johansen's tablet in a slide show format. The first picture showed one man standing near a thick brush pile. The second picture showed the other man starting to stand.

Ryan quickly enlarged the picture. He gasped, instantly recognizing his son. He was alive. The third picture showed Chance being tied. The fourth picture was of both men looking to the heavens.

An enormous weight was lifted from Ryan's shoulders. Chance was alive, and they knew his location. Then Ryan had to deal with the fact that Chance was tied up and being led off by one of the Hiders, one of the very same men that Buster had caught on his "critter-gitter" camera.

Showing the pictures to Mason, Ryan said, "It's Chance. He looks okay, but he's tied up and being taken somewhere. I don't know what's going on, but we have to get up there as fast as we can."

Looking at his Bushnell Mason said, "We are a good hour or more away, especially with deep snow and trying to get through downed trees to the cave."

Wanting to reassure Ryan, Mason added, "They would not have kept him alive to suddenly take him out in the woods and harm him. They even gave him some fur to keep him warm. They probably found him, sheltered him during the storm, and now they are going to release him. I don't think he is any real danger because he has only that one guy with him. If it was something else they would have more people."

"Just get us there as fast as you can," said Ryan, staring at the tablet, "He's all I have."

TWENTY-FIRST CENTURY GUARDSMEN

T he drumming stopped. The men dancing remained frozen in place. All the people were staring at the cave entrance. Standing before them was their worst fears. Two heavily armed men with rifles and pistols—Guardsmen!

The invaders pointed their rifles at the warriors and signed for them to drop their weapons.

The Ranger standing over Chance was now nudging him with his gun barrel. "Why don't you have everyone come over here and sit," he said. "We're going to have ourselves a little pow-wow."

Chance said, "I don't speak their language."

Shasta spoke up and said, "I will tell them. These are my people."

Chance started to say something when one of the Rangers said, "If you don't speak their language, then just shut your pie hole, and let the little lady talk. Better yet, lead by example. Take a seat next to the old Chief," referring to Chief Tuliyani, the only man wearing a headdress.

Shasta was deeply frightened but told her people to gather around. Fearful of what was about to happen, they reluctantly formed a small half-circle seated before the Rangers. The same thought was on everyone's mind—imminent execution. Chance was pushed over to sit beside the Chief.

One of the Rangers grabbed the black wolf pup, and the pup clamped down on a finger. The Ranger flung the pup across the room, cursing at the bite. The pup landed on some soft fur blankets.

Kicking Horse quickly grabbed the squealing pup before he could escape.

"Hey you," said the taller Ranger to Shasta, "What's your name."

Shasta told him, "Wahkanupa."

"What is it?" said the other. She repeated her name.

"What the hell kind of name is that? Don't you have a real name like Tiffany or Amber or something like that?"

The smaller Ranger turned to his partner and in a disgusted tone said, "These people don't even have American names."

Shasta remained silent.

"Tell you what," said the taller man, "I read that when Lewis and Clark came through here, they had an Indian woman with them they called 'Janey,' so that's your new name—Janey!

"Now, Janey, here's what we want to know. Why are your people living here, taking up space that is not theirs and living on land that rightfully belongs to the United States of America? We can't have that, Janey, not in this day and age. It's against the rules."

Turning to his partner, the tall Ranger added, "I bet these people don't even pay taxes. That means you and I are paying more taxes for a bunch of freeloaders. Don't seem right."

Both men laughed.

Shasta began translating the Guardsmen's comments to Chief Tuliyani.

The Chief told Shasta that if the people were to be killed, they would rather die fighting than meekly waiting for execution. He took off his headdress as if to fight.

The shorter Guardsman said, "Okay Chief, we get it. Big yawn. Nobody cares that you want to fight. Nobody cares what happened to you in ancient times. Right now, we got some good news for you and some bad news. We'll give you the good news first. We may not shoot you. Okay, Janey, translate that to the Chief."

Shasta translated while looking directly at the Chief. The people were trembling, fearful of what was to come next.

"Now here's the bad news, Janey. We *will* shoot all of you if you don't do exactly what we say. It's very simple. You and your people are moving. Consider that more of the good news."

The taller Ranger added, "You are going to pack up your belongings and whatever food and stuff you want to carry. Then we are going to walk you south for a couple of days. When we are far enough south, you continue walking back to your old homeland. Then you are on your own."

He continued, "I know it's cold out. I understand that some of your people might die due to whatever. I simply don't care. If you want everybody to survive, you convince him or her of the need to move. The move starts in one hour."

He went on to say, "If there's any who are tired or angry or suffering from the heartbreak of not wanting to move, just have them so indicate. We'll arrange it so that they don't have to leave. You got that, Janey? If any of these people refuse to go because you didn't do a good job of convincing them, well, that's on you, so you'd better give it your best shot, Janey— their lives depend on you."

The two men again laughed. The people appeared very scared, which was exactly what the Rangers wanted.

Shasta translated the threats. Most of the elderly were terribly upset and very fearful. This was what always happened to the Yahi at the hands of the whites. Nothing had changed. The widow of the man killed by Shadow was shaking so hard she couldn't stop.

The Rangers were getting impatient with Shasta's translations and interrupted her, telling her to hurry up or shut up. Shasta continued speaking, talking over the yelling Guardsmen.

Sneaking a glance at her captors and seeing their now casual attitudes, Shasta yelled out to the people that she was a warrior in the best Yahi tradition and that she was not going to move. The Guardsmen were not going to shoot her or kill any of the tribe. She told Kicking Horse to drop the wolf pup and that when the fighting began; he had only one target—the smaller of the Guardsmen. His only job was to stop the smaller Ranger. She named two other warriors to help Kicking Horse. The Chief and the rest of the people would swarm and overpower the tall one.

Shasta had risen to the forefront. In the old days her actions would have made her a war chief, a common practice in the Yahi culture. Several of the people raised their fists in support. They were animated now and were not going to go down without a fight.

The first fist up belonged to the tribal Shaman, ninety winters of age.

The shorter Ranger again laughed. Not perceiving any real threats that they couldn't handle, both men stood with their rifles seated on their hips. The gun barrels were now pointed straight up in the air. Their fingers were off the triggers, resting alongside the metal magazines. They seemed indifferent to the people—even laughing at them. No way did a bunch of old people and a few teenagers represent a threat. Not with what these Rangers had been through.

Both men felt that everyone would comply. The sooner they got them down towards California, the sooner they could leave and collect their paychecks. Ideally, no one would get hurt, and they would all survive the long march. Although the Rangers were under strict instructions to not shoot anyone, their menacing threats were working, and the people would comply.

The wolf pup was still squirming and whining, trying his best to get away. While looking at the Guardsmen, Kicking Horse reached over to the fire and grabbed some soft fry bread.

The Rangers watched as he tore off a small piece and fed it to the wolf. The tall Ranger nudged the smaller one and said, "Hope he gets bitten."

The Rangers took their eyes off Kicking Horse and were scanning around the cave. Shasta caught Kicking Horse's eye and nodded while looking to the smaller Guardsman.

Kicking Horse managed to wrap some fry bread around a heavy flat lava rock, disguising it. He relaxed his grip on the wolf. The pup would be his diversion. As the wolf ran off, Kicking Horse rose as if to chase after the pup. The smaller Ranger motioned for Kicking Horse to sit down. Smiling in a disarming way, Kicking Horse held the rock covered bread out to the Ranger and said, "Eat."

The Ranger laughed, saying to his partner, "Do you believe this? Do I look hungry to you?"

Kicking Horse tried again. "Eat," he said.

The Ranger told him to sit back down and shut up. Kicking Horse remained standing.

Shasta told the Ranger, "He does not speak English. 'Eat' is the only word of English he knows."

The Ranger moved closer to Kicking Horse and pointed to the ground, wanting Kicking Horse to sit down. Kicking Horse smiled, pointed to the ground with one hand and started to lean back as if he were going to go the ground. With the covered rock in one hand, he instantly swirled around, smashing the rock into the face of the Ranger.

The Ranger collapsed to the ground as if he were a sack of potatoes. Blood was pouring from his nose. He had been sucker-punched so fast that he was unconscious in the space of mere seconds.

The tribal members all started to swarm.

The tall Ranger immediately tried for an assault position. A seated Chance grabbed at one of his boots, momentarily pulling him off balance. Shasta scooped up a fistful of sand from the cave floor and threw it into the Ranger's eyes.

Chief Tuliyani rushed the Ranger, knocking him to the ground. The Ranger felt his rifle being pulled away. He began frantically rubbing his eyes. He rose to his feet with both Chance and the Chief holding him. He shook the Chief off and delivered a punishing blow to Chance.

Chance rebounded and punched him hard in the Adam's apple. That gave the tall Guardsman some pause. He Who Stands and Jumping Bull joined the fray. They each managed to grab an arm. Chance stood before the Ranger and began repeatedly punching him in the head and neck. The weakened Ranger continued fighting, collapsing to the ground, trying to shake his attackers off.

Both Chance and the Ranger were about the same size, and both were in excellent physical condition. The Ranger had experience and muscle. Chance had youth and muscle, which gave him an edge on stamina.

Kicking Horse then jumped on the Ranger's back and caught him in a chokehold. With Kicking Horse squeezing for all he was worth, the Ranger's head was fully exposed. Chance delivered several more punishing blows to the Ranger's head, and he went down, pulling Kicking Horse with him.

The Ranger continued fighting but was now held down by He Who Stands and Jumping Bull. The Ranger was almost unconscious.

Picking up his bloody rock and holding it over his head, Kicking Horse looked down at the Ranger and saw a pinned man before him. He threw the rock to one side. The fight was over.

Both Rangers were down and out. The people were joyous. In the space of mere seconds, they had gone from being prisoners to being captors. Considering their history this was a great moment. Things had finally gone right for the people after centuries of fighting the Guardsmen. A universal shout rose up from the tribe. The two Rangers were quickly tied up with milkweed rope.

Shasta yelled to Chance, "Are you okay?" He said yes though he was bleeding all around his face. She asked the others. All were okay.

Nopanny ran over and pulled out her knife while standing over the unconscious short Ranger. She knelt down and raised her arm just as Chief Tuliyani grabbed her wrist. He appeared visibly angry with her. He would not let her or any of the tribal members kill the two Rangers. All the people in Council according to the tribal customs and traditions would decide the fate of the Guardsmen. Not just one person. The Chief was angry because Nopanny knew that.

All their weapons were taken—guns, knives and grenades—even the Kevlar vests. The two Rangers were completely subdued. Both Chance and Kicking Horse looked as if they had been in a train wreck.

Chance just happened to notice the small, black wolf bolt for the cave entrance and run off into the wilderness. Seconds later the moonlit entrance went black. Chance thought it was again clouding over.

Like Shasta before her, Whisper suddenly pointed to the cave entrance and screamed, "Guardsmen."

"No," said a deep booming voice, "Mason Many Crows, Indian."

RECONCILATION

The cave entrance was filled with the hulking frame of a smiling Mason Many Crows. Several of the people had not yet seen Mason; so busy were they with the Rangers. Chance yelled out, "Mason!"

"I heard some commotion," Mason said, "but it looks like you have everything under control."

All the tribal members visibly pulled back. They had never before seen such a huge Indian, swollen even bigger with his heavy parka and red bandana.

Behind Mason another Guardsman stood. He was dressed in uniform and carried a gun on his hip. In the space of just a few seconds, the people went from abject fear to joy and now back to fear as seemingly another nightmare entered their lodge.

Then two more Englishmen entered. Ryan rushed past the others and ran to a stunned Chance. At first neither one could speak. Ryan embraced Chance, wincing slightly, telling him over and over, "It's okay! It's okay! Thank God you're safe. It's okay."

"How did you find me?" Chance asked, holding tightly to his father, "and what happened to you?"

Ryan pulled back and smiled, "Wolves, but you look a lot worse than me," he said, "Probably from tussling with these guys who look even worse than both of us."

The four rescuers had to park the Sno-Cat and approach the cave on foot. They couldn't get the Cat past some of the downed timber. Even with snowshoes it took some doing. They did not know the Rangers were there. They did not know Chance was there, having safely returned from the wolf lair. Their priority plan was to find and rescue Chance.

As they approached the cave, they heard the screaming and fighting. Mason rushed past the others and started to crawl through. It took some doing to get past the narrow entrance and by the time he entered, everything was over.

Both Ryan and Chance were speaking at once. As father and son were talking, Mason sensed that the surrounding people were visibly scared. He raised his right hand in the universal sign of peace. Smiling, looking around first to the Chief and then to the elders and then to Shasta, Mason said, "Howdy."

Shasta said, "Howdy" back. Several of the people, seeing Mason smiling, also said "Howdy." Mason asked Shasta, "Are you the one who was speaking English?"

She said, "Yes."

He asked, "Do the others speak English?"

Shasta said, "No."

Mason said, "Please tell your Chief and the people that we mean no harm. We come in peace."

Shasta quickly translated.

Patting his large chest, Mason added, "We would have been here a little sooner, but I had a hard time getting through that cave entrance."

Shasta laughed as she made the translation. Several of the elders began to smile.

Pointing to Ryan, he added, "Ryan is his father."

Shasta said, "I know."

She then began translating Mason's comments into Yahi. While she was translating, Buster helped Johansen handcuff the Rangers. The Rangers began stirring, significantly aware that they were no longer in charge. They appeared embarrassed more than anything else. They knew that if this had happened in the Mideast, they both would have been dead. At the same time, if this had been the Middle East they would not have relaxed their guard.

Chance whispered to his Dad, "I don't think you'll have to worry about the wolves anymore."

Buster had his First-Aid Kit out and started applying bandages to the Rangers. "Two broken noses for sure," said Buster.

Mason was re-assuring the tribal members that they had nothing to fear.

He told them, "My name is Mason Many Crows. My tribe is the Warm Springs people, and we live to the north of your lodge. We come in peace."

Shasta translated for him.

For the next hour, Mason and the people spoke. Mason could see he was making inroads as he saw the look of fear start to fall from their faces. Several were now speaking and smiling, beginning with Chief Tuliyani.

As Mason and the Chief were bonding, Ryan and Chance sat by the warming fire. Ryan had one arm over a now heavily bandaged Chance. Shasta stood by them, rapidly translating all around. Chance whispered to Ryan all that had occurred, including his killing of the wolves. Ryan, surprised, relieved, and very proud of all that Chance had done assured him that, together, they would sort it all out, federally protected animals or not.

Several times Ryan noticed how Shasta was looking at Chance. "She seems smitten," he whispered. Chance smiled back, staring intently at Shasta.

Johansen meanwhile advised the two Rangers of their rights, then the charges, starting with breaking and entering, menacing, and attempted kidnapping. He emptied all the guns of their bullets. Then he added, "I'm pretty sure you are not on active duty or that you have a permit from ATF to be in possession of fully automatic weapons—to say nothing about grenades. That's a federal offense. We're talking some serious time here."

The smaller Ranger said, "There's a legal service that we have in Portland. We have nothing to say until we have legal representation. We will also have our attorney file charges against these people for felony assault, battery, poaching, fishing without licenses, not paying taxes, not paying attention, not speaking English, dressing funny and anything else we can think of. Then we'll go after them in Civil Court and own all of their possessions."

"Good luck with that," said Johansen, looking around the lodge, "If you prevail, you might get some smoked fish and firewood."

The two Rangers remained silent and invoked their right to not answer any questions without legal counsel. They had played this game before.

Buster finished patching everybody up. A second Sno-Cat from the ski resort was on the way. Soon the people would be left to themselves. Mason decided to stay with the Hiders until everyone else had been transported safely back to Paulina Lodge. He made arrangements with Johansen to hitch a ride out in the morning.

Mason poked Ryan and said, "I think the Governor is waiting for your call."

Within twenty-four hours, the State had swung into action.

JESSE'S ARREST

TWELVE HOURS LATER

That very next morning, Jesse drove his old Ford pick-up down the narrow logging road heading from Paulina Mountain toward Prineville. Inside the truck canopy, he had two young Angus calves with their feet roped off and tied down to the truck bed. Finding the calves deep in the woods was just more icing on the cake. His plan was to put the calves in a friend's barn, and then to put some of his bonus money into the bank. Maybe, just maybe, the next time he was on Paulina, he might be able to snag that old Indian lady and make even more money.

Hopefully the Rangers didn't screw that up for him.

Life was indeed good.

Threading his way through the lower elevations, negotiating the snow and ice, Jesse was surprised when a Deschutes County Sheriff's truck suddenly appeared behind him, red lights flashing, and the driver signaling for him to pull over. Jesse could see a young deputy behind the wheel, accompanied by a very large Indian with long black hair pulled into a ponytail. He could just make out a badge pinned on the Indian's coat. Jesse pulled over, nervously hoping his story would hold.

A smiling Deputy Johansen walked up to the driver's side of Jesse's truck and politely asked for his driver's license, registration, proof of insurance and either a bill of sale or appropriate paperwork for the transport of cattle. Several times Johansen had to repeat himself over the bawling noise of the calves. Mason came up on the passenger side of the truck and watched closely as Jesse started rummaging around for the paperwork. Mason noticed a thick envelope on the passenger seat. On top of the envelope was a tablet.

"If I can see it, they can't cry 'illegal search and seizure'," thought Mason, watching as Jesse discreetly pushed the envelope down between the seats.

The envelope containing all of Jesse's money would soon be booked into evidence.

The best Jesse could do was an expired driver's license. He did not have any truck registration, proof of insurance or paperwork for the transport of cattle. When pressed by Johansen about the two calves tied off in the back of the truck, Jesse stated that the Circle G Ranch employed him as a ranch hand and that he was bringing the calves to the barn due to bad weather. He apologized for not having proper paperwork but stated that, since the storm, all the cowboys had been very busy trying to round up the cattle so they wouldn't die from the cold and exposure. As for having an expired driver's license, well, that had just slipped his mind as he meant to renew it the next time he was in town.

Mason stood by, looming over the seated Jesse, intently staring at him.

Johansen meanwhile radioed in for wants or warrants on Jesse. He also asked dispatch to call the owner of the Circle G to verify Jesse's story.

A full five minutes went by before Johansen returned to the truck. He asked Jesse to step out. When Jesse was out of the truck, Johansen told him to turn around and place his hands behind him.

"Why?" Jesse asked.

"Because you are going to jail, my friend" said Johansen, advising him of his legal rights. "You have an outstanding warrant for failure to appear on a speeding ticket, plus I'm going to slap some cattle theft charges on you. Your bigger problem is the owner of the Circle G says you were fired and that he did not ask you to pick up any of his calves due to the bad weather. Helping yourself to his calves is apparently what got you fired in the first place. Then when he questioned you about the missing stock, you couldn't even man up to it. That's very disappointing."

Jesse denied everything—especially the alleged cattle theft. "I was returning these calves to the Circle G. I figured the owner would appreciate that and give me another shot at my old job. He and I had a little misunderstanding, is all, and I know he would like these calves safe and sound. I found them up in the mountains and figured they were so small that they had to be brought in or they would die."

"Well, according to the owner, the little misunderstanding you had with him is that you were stealing his calves and then lying through your ass about it, so he fired you," said Johansen, as a smiling Mason nodded in agreement. "Therefore, you are not employed by him."

"Did I say that?" asked Jesse. "I'm pretty sure I said that I 'had been' employed by him. You must have misunderstood me, or maybe I didn't say it right. I sometimes do that."

Mason broke in, saying, "Maybe that envelope that accidentally fell between your seats is the proceeds of your cattle thieving. Is that right?"

A cloud came over Jesse's face, but he held his tongue. He had earned that money. It was his.

"Hand me the tablet," said Mason. "This yours?"

"Friend of mine loaned it to me. I'm returning it to him soon as the roads clear."

Smiling, Mason said, "We'll give him a call and he can pick it up from the evidence locker. Maybe we can talk him into pressing charges."

Johansen, still smiling, asked, "What can you tell me about these hog-tied calves?" The bawling calves were struggling against their tie-downs. Jesse remained silent.

"Is it possible that those calves took it upon themselves to climb into the back of your truck and then truss themselves up like that? Maybe they did that so you would feel sorry for them and take them someplace where they could get warm."

"Like his barbeque," said Mason. "Having his stoner buddies over for some veal and beer." Jesse continued to stay quiet.

Mason walked over and stood next to Johansen. Both men towered over Jesse. Reluctantly, Jesse turned, faced the truck and placed his hands behind him. Johansen quickly cuffed him while Mason placed a massive arm across Jesse's back, holding him in place. Mason asked if he had any weapons on him. Jesse said he did not. Mason started to pat him down and found a pistol underneath Jesse's coat. He took the pistol out and held it before Jesse's face. "What's this?" Mason asked.

"Oh that," said Jesse, "I thought you meant something illegal. I have a concealed-carry permit for that. I apologize about the confusion; I thought you were talking about something else."

"Where's your concealed permit?" asked Johansen.

"It's in my wallet," said Jesse.

A quick search of Jesse's wallet revealed no permit.

"It must be in the glove box," said Jesse.

It was not in the glove box.

"Damn," said Jesse, "I was holed up with some cowboys when this storm first hit and I bet one of them stole my permit. Be just like them."

Johansen shook his head in disbelief. Looking at Jesse's expired license, Johansen asked, "Jesse James. How did you come by this name?"

"My family was great admirers of the James family, so they gave me his name. Seems the James family had to overcome a lot of adversity in life, and my folks gave me his name, so I could do the same. One thing for sure, old Jesse would never have been hassled by law enforcement for helping out a neighbor by returning lost stock."

"True enough," said Mason, "But the original Jesse James was a murderer and robber, we just don't know about him being a cattle thief. For sure, he took from the rich but did not give to the poor. He took from the rich to make himself rich so that way he wouldn't have to do any real work which probably would have tired him out. Who needs that?"

As an aside, Mason added," Is this your real name or an alias."

Jesse said that his real name was in fact Jesse James.

"James is your last name?" Mason asked.

Jesse didn't answer. Mason repeated the question. Jesse still didn't reply.

"You know that when we run your prints through the system, we are going to find out if this is your real name or not."

Jesse snorted, "I come from an old respected ranching family down in Northern California."

Mason sighed. "The last name of that old respected ranching family down in Northern California would be?"

Jesse pressed his forehead against the truck door and looking down mumbled, "Carty."

TWENTY-FOUR HOURS LATER

PRESENT TIME

Deschutes County District Attorney Ivar Hamm finished up his witness statements and commented, "If my law professors ever told me that I would be taking down witness statements from an extinct tribe of Indians in a cave in the middle of a forest, I never would have believed them. This is definitely going down as one of the highlights of my life."

Standing by his side, Shasta was interpreting the District Attorney's comments to the assembled Yahi.

District Attorney Hamm looked at the assembled lawmen around him, then at the tribal members and said, "Law enforcement and I believe the people's stories have checked out from all sides. According to statements from tribal eyewitnesses, Tom Conway fired his gun, hitting Chief Tuliyani in the upper shoulder. The other tribesmen then fired at Conway, whom they believed was reloading and lifting his rifle to fire again. To protect their Chief, they shot Conway with arrows. That story jibes with the witness statements of Holmes and Peters who said pretty much the same thing. As such, and after consultation with the State's Attorney General, I am ruling that the Tom Conway case was one of justifiable self-defense. Therefore, no charges will be filed against any of the tribal members who shot and killed Conway."

After Shasta's translation, all smiled—nodding their heads in agreement. The smiles were genuine smiles of relief. The gathered Englishmen did not appear angry or hostile. They all stood around smiling and shaking hands with each other and then with the Yahi. It took an adjustment for the tribal members to shake hands but after watching their Chief and Shasta shake, the rest followed. Initially, while they first feared that they might be taken away and hanged, they now felt a little more at ease.

Their lives had dramatically changed—this time many felt for the better. Even Kicking Horse managed a smile and a few handshakes. It was truly a new day for the Yahi Tribe.

"As a sidebar here," the DA added, "I was notified this morning that Special Agent Walton has submitted his retirement papers to the BIA. He said he is going out on a grand slam, and it doesn't get any better than that."

Looking down at his tablet, the DA further added, "I've also had a flurry of phone calls from officials' way up the food chain in Homeland Security. They want me to drop all charges against the Rangers, both of whom are highly decorated veterans. I refused to do that. What I can do, however, to save the taxpayer some expense is to consider reduced charges. It involves a plea bargain without any jail time. The whole thing may well be a moot point as I'm told that the two Rangers are now on special assignment in the Mideast with one of our alphabet agencies.

As for Mr. Jesse James Carty," he added, "his attorney and I have worked out a plea agreement. He agrees to plead to carrying a concealed weapon and, in exchange, I'm recommending nine months in the county jail plus a fifteen thousand dollar fine for all his cattle thieving, tablet thieving and failure to pay fines for an outstanding warrant."

"What about the Oregon Project Assistant Vice-President," asked Mason?

"Technically, he did not break any laws, so no charges have been filed. However, I'm told that his company is very unhappy over his handling of events. Apparently, they are flying in tomorrow and removing him from office. He is out of a job."

After the meeting, the DA pulled Shasta aside to thank her for her interpretations.

"Should you ever decide to leave the mountains," he said, "I'm pretty sure I can find an intern position for you." The DA smiled and held out his hand.

Shasta sensed he was a nice man. Without hesitation she shook hands with the DA and said, "Thank you."

A few minutes later, standing between Ryan and Chance, Shasta asked, "What is an intern?"

Ryan told her.

Turning to Chance, Shasta said, "I have something to tell you and then something to ask you."

Chance said, "Go for it."

Shasta laughed and with just the slightest giggle said, "I can see I will have to fix up my English so I know what you are saying."

Somberly, she added, "Chief Tuliyani found out who removed the arrowheads. He asked a number of people. You were right when you said it was not Kicking Horse. Then he asked several of the warriors. It was not they. He asked me, and I told him it was not I. He said he didn't think it was me, but he had to ask.

"Then he started questioning Whisper. She said it was not she but that the Chief should ask Nopanny. He did and when Nopanny lowered her head and refused to look at him, he knew it was she. He asked her why. She didn't answer."

Shasta continued, "Later, Whisper told the Chief that Nopanny was struggling with being the second wife of the Chief, especially as she was the older sister. She felt she had to prove her worth. All her actions were to support their husband. That's why she rushed over and pulled her knife on the Guardsman. Voting against you was not enough. She felt that if the wolves got you then the Chief's standing among all the people would prove him right in his respect for our traditional ways. She felt she had to do something to protect the wishes of the Chief."

Pausing she said, "The Chief told Nopanny that he would have to tell the Tribal Council what she had done. In the old days she could be banished from the tribe and that would be a death sentence."

She added, "The Chief said that would not happen because he will speak up for her. He wants her to stay with both he and Whisper. I don't think anything more will happen, especially as Nopanny wants to apologize to you and to the people."

Chance simply said, "Okay."

Shasta looked down and said, "Please do not think badly of me, but there is one thing I would like you to do for me."

"Which is?" asked Chance.

Shasta said, "I have been thinking about this since you first came to our camp. I want you to take me in your car to the English world. I want to see your lodge and this Summit High School. I want to go inside your trading posts. I want to eat what you eat and see what you see. I want to walk with you in your moccasins. I would like to see an ocean. I want to see what the life of the Englishman is like. Is this possible? Can we do this? Can you do this for me? I know there to be a world out there that I have never seen, and I so want to see it."

Chance assured her that it was all possible. He said he would bring clothing to her and, if she wanted, that no one would ever know that she was from the Hiders. It was up to her. He would take her to all the places she asked—plus to a dance at Summit High School. She would like the dancing although it was unlike any of the tribal dancing. He would teach her.

Ryan added that Shasta could sleep in their lodge and that Chance would show her how to ride a horse.

"I'll even take you to Goody's for some ice cream," Chance added. "After that you may not want to return home."

A slight blush came over her face.

"Maybe," she said, "especially as the people are now thinking about returning to our homeland."

"What about Kicking Horse," asked Chance?

Shasta replied, "We talked about this, and he told me to go. He said he is going to stay here or go with the people. This is all he knows, and he doesn't want to leave. I also think," She added, "that he has some new interests."

Pointing to the back of the cave, Ryan and Chance could see Kicking Horse on the ground, scratching a black pup behind the ears. The pup rolled on his back by the warming fire, and Kicking Horse began rubbing the fat belly.

"If I didn't know better," said Ryan, "I'd almost swear that's a wolf pup."

"Nope," said a smiling Mason, "Couldn't be. I found that little fellow out in the woods. Someone abandoned him, but it looks like now he has a good home."

THE KILLING OF ISHI

In the fall of 1915, Ishi went to see his friend, Popey, the K'uwi. Ishi told Dr. Pope that he was not feeling well, which he attributed to spending too much time in the closed rooms of the University Museum of the white man. Ishi shared with his best friend that he was feeling fatigued and that his breathing had become very difficult. He was also suffering from a constant cough, which he could not shake.

Dr. Pope ran a series of tests and concluded that Ishi was suffering some upper respiratory infection. Medicine was prescribed, and Ishi was advised to get as much bed rest as possible.

Months went by and Ishi again came to the hospital as a patient. He said he could no longer drink the white man's water and requested some 'sweet water.' Dr. Pope found a nearby spring and began bottling water for Ishi's needs. The spring water helped but only for a while.

Then Ishi started to lose weight. The weight loss was not through diet or exercise. Ishi was now pushing food away from the table, telling Dr. Pope that he was not hungry. Concerned, his friend kept a close medical eye on him, trying different medicines and more tests. The tests did not show anything positive, such as blood in the sputum, but Dr. Pope soon suspected that Ishi was in the early stages of tuberculosis.

His suspicions increased when Ishi could not keep any food or even the spring water down.

Soon after, Ishi returned to the hospital for more tests.

Dr. Pope wrote *The Medical History of Ishi* in 1920. He stated this about Ishi: "After taking food, he apparently experienced great pain. Even water caused him misery, and I have seen him writhe in agony, with tears running down his cheeks, yet utter no sound of complaint."

Dr. Pope added that Ishi had a ". . . very large pulmonary hemorrhage," soon after re-entering the hospital.

Unfortunately, even with the advanced medical knowledge available in 1916, there was simply no cure for tuberculosis. The best medical advice at the time was for the afflicted to seek out the dry beneficial climate of Arizona.

Ishi did not want to go to Arizona. He wanted to stay at the University facilities where his friends were.

In March of 1916, Dr. Pope re-admitted Ishi to the University Hospital. Ishi alternated between bouts of feverish sweating and coughing to periods of restless sleep. He started spitting up blood.

To Dr. Pope this was proof positive that Ishi had contracted tuberculosis. The only medical thing he could do now was making Ishi as comfortable as possible while the disease ravaged his system. Dr. Pope knew from experience that his best friend would soon die from tuberculosis.

Day and night Ishi was in pain. He could not sleep. He was running a constant fever with deep coughing. He continued spitting up blood and losing weight at a dramatic pace.

Finally, on March 25th, 1916, Ishi dragged himself from his sick bed to pose for one last picture with Dr. Pope. The picture shows a thin, haggard Ishi looking very weak and drawn. His black hair was pulled back into a ponytail, and his overall appearance was that of a cadaverous man on the verge of total collapse.

The photography session was cut short. Ishi fell back into his hospital bed and pulled up the covers. He now had less than one hour to live.

His best friend, the K'uwi, was about to give him a large dose of morphine. It is not known if the two ever discussed the full impact of the shot. The medicine would prove to be a double-edged sword. At the very least it would greatly reduce his pain, but such a large dosage would absolutely kill him.

Dr. Pope knew that. He may well have agonized over the irony of being an Englishman taking the life of the last known Yahi but decided, in the end, to release Ishi from his pain. He proceeded with the shot.

It is believed that during the very last hour of his life, Ishi revealed his true Indian name to the one man he considered his best friend. Dr. Pope never revealed Ishi's real name—taking the secret to his grave.

He also never wrote about or discussed what Ishi may have found after his all-night canyon search of his homeland back in 1914. The thinking was that Ishi was searching for other Yahi Indians, especially his missing sister and her companion. After his search, the returning Ishi told Dr. Pope's son, Saxton, Jr., "It is good. None are lost. They have found their way."

In 1920 when Dr. Pope wrote *The Medical History of Ishi,* he stated that due to Ishi's increasing medical complications, "I was called to his side. He was very weak and faint. I administered a large dose of morphia. He died soon after, at 12:20 p.m., March 25, 1916."

After the shot of morphia, Ishi looked up at Dr. Pope and softly patting his arm whispered:

"I go," he said, "You stay."

ACKNOWLEDGEMENTS

Thanks to my wife, Suzanne, who supported and encouraged me to write about the brutal life and times of Ishi and then formatted the book to publication standards; to Christina Hill, for editing the book; to DeeAnn Glazier, graphic artist, for cover design; and to Laura Starr for her help with the manuscript and patient listening.

This book is a combination of historical facts along with dramatic fiction. It is a melding of two literary genres. I am deeply indebted to those who have gone before me for all their in-depth research and insights into Ishi's years of hiding and ultimate capture--especially Theodora Kroeber, Dr. A. L. Kroeber; Dr. T. T. Waterman, Dr. Saxton Pope, and authors Orin Starn, Richard Burrill, and Bradley Campbell.

Thanks to Ursula Le Guin, sci-fi author and daughter of Dr. A.L. and Theodora Kroeber, for taking time from a busy schedule to write a letter in response to my questions about Ishi.

Many details of the California Indian massacres were obtained from the published books of two frontier Guardsmen: Captain R. A. Anderson and Sim Moak, although I'm not giving them a post-mortem thanks because of all the innocent lives lost in their alleged guise of protecting the pioneer community!

Only one historical name has been changed to protect the family identity. The rest of the pioneer names were found on the Internet, in history books, Guardsmen books, and old newspapers from various Northern California museums.

Thank you to Jessica Follini, University of California Berkeley, for navigating me through the various UCB Departments.

On the fictional side, any resemblance to persons living or dead is purely coincidental. The same is true for the business companies, government agencies and/or politicians mentioned. All errors and mistakes are mine alone.

Jim Callahan, January 2018

ABOUT THE AUTHOR

Jim Callahan has a Bachelor of Arts in American Studies from California State University, Los Angeles, specializing in the study of Ishi and the Northern California Indian Wars. An ex-Deputy Sheriff with the Los Angeles County Sheriff's Department, Jim moved to Oregon where he has several times encountered timber wolves on his property, only ten minutes from the heart of downtown Bend.

He is also the author of several documentary scripts for Dallas McKinnon, "The Voice of Disneyland" plus feature stories for both national and regional magazines. A one-time theatrical stage employee with I.A.T.S.E. Local number 33, Jim worked on a number of popular T.V. shows, such as Laugh In, The Andy Williams Show, and The Dean Martin Show.

After moving to Oregon Jim first worked as a ranch hand on the Circle G Ranch. He then worked a number of years part-time at the Confederated Tribes of the Warm Springs Indian Reservation, where he came to know and hear war stories from some of the grandchildren of the

U.S. Army Indian Scouts, including the descendants of Chief Billy Chinook.

Level-jumping from a free-lance magazine writer to debut novelist, Jim is writing his second novel, this one about the closing days of the Civil War several months after General Lee surrendered at Appomattox.

YOUR PERSONAL REVIEW

I hope that you enjoyed reading this book as much as I enjoyed the research and writing. I would really appreciate it if you would drop me a line via Email and let me know your thoughts about the book.

If you would also like to be on my mailing list and receive information about my future books, let me know that as well.

My email is jcallahan@bendbroadband.com. It may take a while to respond so please bear with me. I will get to your Email as soon as possible. For further information, visit my website at www.amazon/jamesjcallahanjr.

Thank you,

James J. Callahan, Jr.

AMAZON KINDLE BOOK REVIEWS

"Great story! I love the detail about the state." J. Malcom

"Fantastic book." Erica

"Outstanding!" Lora N.

"This book was a surprise in many ways and an absolute page turner. For those unfamiliar with the stories of the settlers and the Indians in the Far West, it is a must read. The author weaves together a compelling narrative that underscores the conflicting cultures and economies that led to brutality on both sides…This book is a rare find; combining adventure, history and great storytelling!" V.A. Beck.

"Great story-telling technique, switching from the past to the present, presenting in graphic detail the conflict between whites and bands of Indians in the 19th century, blending and bridging the historical to a contemporary narrative. This is one of the few books that I had a hard time putting down." Gail

"I wished I could have met the legendary Ishi. This is a well-written account of the history of a tribe I had never heard anything about until now. The narrative definitely grabs you from the start. It begins in present-day Central Oregon with wolves increasing in the area and why. The author writes with gentle humor and sensitivity. He thoroughly knows his subject." C.M.

"Great story. I hope the author writes many more books." Fred Fisher

36649862R00177

Made in the USA
Middletown, DE
16 February 2019